Boon Island Light Station, Maine.  *U. S. Coast Guard official photo.*

# AMERICA'S LIGHTHOUSES

## An Illustrated History

By

FRANCIS ROSS HOLLAND, JR.

DOVER PUBLICATIONS, INC.

NEW YORK

FOR JUNE

There are no words to express the feelings that induce a sailor to offer fervent prayers when he sees this mark of sympathy expressed by his fellow men. Suddenly he sees that he is no longer alone in the midst of the ocean waves: he sees that people are caring for him with paternal solicitude.

*Lt. Lavrentiy Alekseyevich Zagoskin on sighting the lighthouse at Sitka, Alaska, in 1839.*

Nothing indicates the liberality, prosperity or intelligence of a nation more clearly than the facilities which it affords for the safe approach of the mariner to its shores.

*Report of the Lighthouse Board, 1868*

The lighthouse and lightship appeal to the interest and better instinct of man because they are symbolic of never-ceasing watchfulness, of steadfast endurance in every exposure, of widespread helpfulness. The building and the keeping of the lights is a picturesque and humanitarian work of the nation.

*George R. Putnam*

The author gratefully acknowledges the permission granted by the following publishers to quote brief passages from the following works:

*Lt. Zagoskin's Travels in Russian America, 1842–1844,* edited by Henry N. Michael (Copyright, Canada, 1967, by the University of Toronto Press).

*Coasting Captain: Journals of Leonard S. Tawes Relating His Career in Coastwise Sailing Craft from 1868 to 1922,* edited by Robert H. Burgess (Copyright 1967 by The Mariners Museum, Newport News, Virginia).

Published in Canada by General Publishing Company, Ltd., 30 Lesmill Road, Don Mills, Toronto, Ontario.
Published in the United Kingdom by Constable and Company, Ltd.

This Dover edition, first published in 1988, is an unabridged and slightly corrected republication of the third printing (1981) of the work originally published by The Stephen Greene Press, Brattleboro, Vermont in 1972.

Manufactured in the United States of America
Dover Publications, Inc., 31 East 2nd Street, Mineola, N.Y. 11501

**Library of Congress Cataloging-in-Publication Data**

Holland, F. Ross (Francis Ross), 1927–
America's lighthouses.

Reprint. Originally published: Rev. ed. Brattleboro, VT.: S. Greene Press, 1981, c1972.
Bibliography: p.
Includes index.
1. Lighthouses—United States.  I. Title.
[VK1023.H65  1988]    387.1′55        87-27289
ISBN 0-486-25576-X (pbk.)

# Contents

# Contents

# Preface

IF ONE had to indicate the single most important year in the history of this nation's aids to navigation, it would unquestionably have to be 1852, the year the Lighthouse Board came into existence. At that time the United States' lighthouses and other aids to navigation taken as a whole gave this country a third-rate lighthouse service. The lighting system that illuminated the lighthouse towers was not only out of date, but in its best days did not come up to the quality of that of other nations with similar systems. Many towers had been poorly constructed, and many aids to navigation had not been placed so as to be of maximum advantage to the mariner. The nation's coasts were not adequately marked, lights were poorly maintained by poorly trained keepers, many of whom were political hacks. Moreover, the administration of aids to navigation could be termed, at best, inept.

The Lighthouse Board took the nation's aids to navigation and over the years brought order to them, instilled dedication among the service's employees, and added lighthouses, beacons, fog signals, buoys, and lightships so that the country's shores, Great Lakes, and principal navigable rivers were fully illuminated and shoals and other hazards to navigation were marked. Efficiency, reliability, and quality came to have meaning in the lighthouse service. By the time the Lighthouse Board had become outmoded as an administrative organization, it had so firmly set the lighthouse service on the path to being among the world's best that its successors—the Bureau of Lighthouses and, subsequently, the Coast Guard—became imbued with the same spirit of quality so that they, too, retained the same dedication to progress in maintaining a first-class system of aids to navigation in the United States.

Lighthouses are one of the more romanticized subjects in the history of this and other nations. I

hope that I will be forgiven by the lighthouse buff for puncturing a few balloons of romance. I consider aids to navigation a serious subject worthy of critical consideration by the historian.

Although aids to navigation have been written about extensively, there has been no full scale history of this country's lighthouse service nor hardly any effort to analyze the changes and technological advances that occurred. I have tried to present at least an outline of the history of this country's lighthouse service and to give an account of the technological changes made in the lighthouses through the years. There is much yet to be written about lighthouses and other aids to navigation, and it has been my hope that the effort presented here will form a basis for more detailed research by others.

This book cannot claim to mention every United States lighthouse, nor every light familiar to tourists. I have tried instead to discuss the more significant lights in the development of the lighthouse service, as well as those lights whose history gives us some insight into the lives of the people who made our system of navigational aids what it is today.

The dates shown in parentheses in the subheadings and from time to time in the text are, in the absence of indications to the contrary, dates of *first lighting* of the light station in question. This date may or may not coincide with the date of construction of a particular light tower.

I wish to thank Mrs. Hope Holdcamper of the National Archives, who for eight or more years has been of great assistance to me in guiding me through the records of the lighthouse service now residing in the Archives. I am grateful to her colleague, William Sherman, who has been helpful in locating pertinent records. My deep appreciation also goes to my friends and associates in the National Park Service's old Division of History in the Washington Office, particularly to John D. McDermott who read parts of this manuscript and offered valued suggestions, and Erwin N. Thompson, Edwin C. Bearss, Anna C. Toogood, John D. R. Platt, and Charles E. Hatch, Jr., who in the course of their researches took time to note for me information they came across on lighthouses. I wish also to express my deep appreciation to my colleague, the historical architect David Battle, who did the sketches of lighthouse equipment.

I am also grateful to my National Park Service colleagues in the Historic American Buildings Survey (HABS). James C. Massey, John Poppeliers, Denys P. Myers, and Nancy Beinke were most helpful in locating illustrations that would be useful for this book. For more than thirty years the HABS program has been making drawings of and photographing historic buildings in the United States; many of their subjects have been light stations, so that today the HABS collection, which is housed in the Library of Congress, contains a number of photographs and detailed drawings of light towers and related structures.

Chief Warrant Officer Joe Greco and others of the U. S. Coast Guard's Public Relations Division have been unfailing over the years in their cheerful assistance when I used the records and library at Coast Guard Headquarters in Washington. Coast Guard personnel, whether stationed at a light station or assigned to a district headquarters or to a repair facility such as Curtis Bay near Baltimore, have consistently been friendly, courteous, and helpful. When time permitted, their hospitality extended to a cup of coffee in the kitchen of a keeper's home or the mess hall of an all-male station. These visits are moments I remember and cherish both for the camaraderie and for the information I gained about the particular station. These encounters have given me a deep admiration for the dedication of the men of the Coast Guard, from high-ranking officers to the newest seamen.

A deep and special thanks goes to my wife, June, not only for her encouragement, but also for typing this manuscript in its final form.

*Walnut Creek, California*

# I

# The Foundation

AS LONG as primitive man in his equally primitive water craft confined his operations to his home lagoon or to a few relatively nearby ones, and as long as he restricted his activities to daylight hours, all he really needed in the way of aids to guide him safely past hazards, to help him find his destination, or to tell him his location were a few prominent headlands along the shore. And as long as his movements were limited, the body of knowledge he developed through memory about these and other features was quite adequate to serve his own needs.

But as man improved his vessels and he ventured farther from home and into strange harbors and bays, he had to record in some way the features and peculiarities of these places, for he might visit them again. He had no *Coast Pilot* to tell him where the shoals were, nor were there buoys marking the channel into the harbors he visited, or distinctive lighthouses to guide him or tell him where he was along a coast. The early-day mariner had to approach each harbor or bay with a great deal of caution until he added to his personal knowledge, through experience, information about the peculiarities of it. Sometimes, undoubtedly, he talked to fellow seafarers, and in a general swapping of information, gained knowledge of the best means of navigating into unfamiliar ports and along inhospitable shores.

Perhaps the first sailors kept a record of this navigational information on crude nautical charts. The Carthaginians used this technique, and so jealously did these great seafarers guard this information to keep it from falling into a rival's hands that on at least one occasion a Carthaginian skipper, while being pursued by the Romans, ran his ship onto the rocks, drowning all his crew, rather than let this information fall into the enemy's hands. And his countrymen later praised him for the deed.

As the early mariner had little in the way of written directions, so he had little in the way of man-made structures or lights to aid him in navigating an unfamiliar coast or to guide him into a strange harbor. This failure to provide navigational aids was probably deliberate, since most port cities were hesitant to provide a structure that would be useful to an invading enemy squadron. Alexandria, the site of the earliest known lighthouse, had with its aid to navigation a strong fleet guarding its harbor.

## EARLY LIGHTS ABROAD (300 B.C.–A.D. 1811)

The first aid to navigation was most likely a fire set on a hillside to guide some late-arriving fisherman back to his home port. Probably between the time of that light and the building of the Pharos of Alexandria, there were other structures that could be called lighthouses in the truest sense, but history has left scant record of them. Indeed, history has left little information about Alexandria's lighthouse. According to the evidence, the Egyptians began building the tower on Pharos, an island at the entrance to the harbor of Alexandria, around 300 B.C. Finally completing it twenty years later, the Egyptians dedicated it "for the safety of mariners." Accurate pictures of the tower do not survive, but archeologists think the structure rose about 450 feet into the air. Its light was an open fire on the summit of the tower. The lighthouse lasted for about 1,000 years, and the unlighted tower remained for another 500 years before being toppled by an earth-

1

quake. It had been an impressive and magnificent structure, and many contemporary writers listed it as one of the Seven Wonders of the World.

Numerous people have speculated that another one of the Seven Wonders, the Colossus of Rhodes, served also as a lighthouse, which, depending upon the teller, either had lights burning in its eyes or held a fire in its hand. But the evidence is by no means conclusive that this heroic statue of Apollo, in addition to being an outstanding work of art, was also a lighthouse.

The Romans erected a light tower about a half century before the birth of Christ at one of their principal ports of trade, Ostia. A structure with increasingly smaller stories rising over 100 feet into the air, this tower was surmounted by a flame beacon. It was a sturdy building with a number of rooms and windows and was used in the defense of the city.

Ostia was not the only lighthouse erected by the Romans. Historians have been able to identify at least thirty lighthouses in use in the Roman Empire before it began to decline in the fifth century A.D.

Some twenty years before the birth of Christ one traveller reported a lighthouse in Spain near the mouth of the Guadalquivir River. Without question there was a lighthouse at Corunna on the northwest coast of Spain at least as early as the fourth century A.D. Most likely built earlier than that time by either the Phoenicians or the Romans, probably the latter, this lighthouse was known as the Tower of Hercules. The tower was a square stone structure some 130 feet tall, which, according to legend, had been erected by Hercules, who placed a fire on it that burned continually for 300 years. Reputedly useful to ships bound for England, the tower in time went out of service. Years later the Spanish government restored the pillar and encased it in a light tower made of granite. Still functioning as a light signal today, it is apparently the world's oldest lighthouse.

The Roman Emperor Caligula on a visit to France in A.D. 40 ordered constructed at Boulogne a tower to hold a fire that would aid sailors who plied those waters. Constructed as an octagonal shaft of red bricks and gray and yellow stone, the tower rose 124 feet into the air. It was twelve stories tall with increasingly smaller stories placed on top of each other, like the one at Ostia. In time the tower fell into disuse, but around A.D. 800 Charlemagne decided to put it back into service and ordered its

relighting. Also known as Tour d'Ordre, and to English seamen as the Old Man of Bullen, this structure served off and on as an aid to navigation until July 29, 1644, when it collapsed in a heap of stone and dust. Over the years, materials had been removed from the tower for other buildings in the neighborhood and erosion had undermined the cliff on which it stood; it was inevitable that disaster should someday overtake it.

As the nations of Europe emerged from the Dark Ages, around A.D. 1100, and began trading among themselves more, they constructed lighthouses to facilitate the increased shipping. During the Middle Ages, Italy, Turkey, France, England, Ireland, and Germany erected lighthouses. The Italians were the first in this period when they raised a tower at Meloria in 1157, and a light remained there until 1304 when the Pisans replaced it with a tower at Leghorn. In time the Italians erected other towers at Venice and Tino and one near the Straits of Messina.

The Italian's most famous lighthouse, however, was the one at Genoa. Built at least as early as 1161, this tower in 1449 had as its keeper Antonio Colombo, uncle of Christopher Columbus. Perhaps it had been Uncle Antonio who had first stirred Christopher's interest in the sea; it is doubtful that his other relatives did, since they were all weavers. Damaged by several wars, the Genoa tower had to be replaced in 1544 with another structure consisting of two square towers, one a little smaller than the other. The smaller one was placed on the larger, so that the completed tower rose 200 feet into the air. With such great height the tower was subject to damage from lightning. For centuries the local inhabitants attempted to avert this danger by erecting nearby a statue of St. Christopher and by cutting pious inscriptions in the walls, but the lightning continued to descend. Perhaps the recent declassification of Christopher as a saint helps explain the failure of this technique of preventing storm damage. In 1778 the Genoans finally took the more practical step of installing a lightning rod on the tower. No longer used as a lighthouse, the tower serves today as a daymark for vessels sailing these waters.

In the sixteenth century, travellers to Turkey noted an octagonally shaped lighthouse at the Bosphorus. Little else is known of this tower.

A number of French ports had navigational lights, some of which were exhibited from castle towers.

## Early lights abroad

A few of these lights were on display as early as the twelfth century. Dieppe, Havre, and Boulogne were some of the ports having such lights. In addition, there was a particularly well known one on the island of Cordouan at the mouth of the Gironde. This latter lighthouse's fame derives chiefly from the structure subsequently erected there in the seventeenth century. According to tradition, Charlemagne erected a chapel on the island and stipulated that trumpets be sounded as a warning to vessels. In the late fourteenth century, evidence indicates that an English prince built a tower on Cordouan that was topped by a huge fire designed to serve as a navigational aid. This structure, a chapel and plain tower, survived for about 200 years, when it was replaced by the famous Louis de Foix tower. Under contract with the French government, de Foix began building his tower in 1584. His building was an elaborate structure reflecting the architectural tastes of the period, which leaned strongly toward the ornate. De Foix erected a huge circular structure that contained a lower hall fifty-two feet in diameter. The next floor was a large chapel. A huge lantern and chimney surmounted the edifice; the lantern was designed for a wood fire. Pillars, parapets, windows, and ornaments, such as statues, decorated the exterior of the tower. The builder originally thought the tower could be completed within two years, but work went slowly, and twenty-six years later the tower was ready to display its light. All sorts of problems had beset the builder, but the most serious was the erosion of the island, an unhappy condition that was ameliorated only by surrounding the tower with a wall and parapet. In time the island disappeared, leaving only the tower and its protective wall. An interesting feature of the completed structure was a spiral stairway off to the side so that the main part of the building would not be sullied by the keepers transporting wood and equipment to the lantern.

For many years the keepers kept an oak wood fire burning brightly in the tower, but with the increased consumption of wood caused by the enlarging of the fire, the French government turned to coal as a fuel. Coal was used but a few years, for the French began experimenting with lamps and reflectors, both stationary and revolving, as an illuminant for lighthouses. Meanwhile, engineers recognized that the tower needed repairs badly, and in 1788 the French government commissioned Jo-

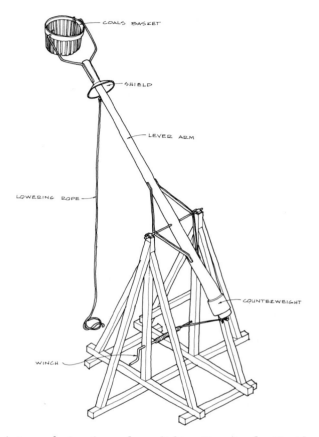

A type of *vippefyr* or lever light. *Drawing by David Battle.*

seph Teulere to undertake the work. Teulere removed the upper portion of the building and set on the structure a circular stone tower sixty feet tall, achieving a far less ornamental effect. It is this structure that survives to the present.

Of the number of lighthouses France built during this period, two of the more interesting ones architecturally were those at Frehel and Stiff. Designed by the same man, each consisted of two towers, side by side, joined on several floors. One tower contained the keeper's quarters and supplies and the other held the light, or fire, thus permitting the keepers to tend the light without dirtying their quarters with coal dust and cinders.

During the seventeenth and eighteenth centuries the number of lighthouses increased in the maritime nations of Europe. The British lighthouse historian D. Alan Stevenson estimates that coastal lighthouses grew in number from 34 in 1600 to 175 in 1800.

Generally speaking, the other maritime nations of Europe did not erect as architecturally elaborate lighthouses as did France, but they were, nevertheless, just as effective. The ultimate in simplicity and ease of maintenance was achieved by Denmark when Jens Pedersen Groves designed a structure that utilized the lever principle. He planted one end of a huge pole in the ground and balanced a cross-member, or lever, on its upper end. One end of the cross-member held a large fire basket, while the other end was weighted to facilitate raising the fire basket into the air. The whole thing resembled a gigantic ducking stool—a device Puritans used to punish their wayward brethren. The fire basket could be lowered when the keepers needed to fill it with coal, thus saving the back-breaking work of hauling the coal to the summit of a tower. Denmark introduced this lighthouse, called a *vippefyr*, in 1624. Despite its simplicity, the structure apparently did not achieve popularity. It was brought, however, to the New World. A picture of the town of Christiansted in the Virgin Islands in the eighteenth century shows a *vippefyr* on the quay near the harbor.

*Eddystone Light (1698)*

Unquestionably the best-known lighthouse erected in the seventeenth century was the one placed at the Eddystone Rocks. It is one of the few—indeed, if not the only—lighthouse that became the subject of a popular folk song—a song that begins:

My father was the keeper of the Eddystone light,
And he slept with a mermaid one fine night.
From this union there came three,
A porpoise, a porgy, and the other was me.
Yo ho ho, the wind blows free;
Oh, for a life on the rolling sea.

The Eddystone Rocks constitute one of the world's great hazards to navigation, and before man succeeded in putting a light there, many ships came to grief on its rocks and shoals. The fame of the lighthouse lies partly in this fact and partly in the achievement represented by the fact that a lighthouse could be placed there at all. The rocks offered precious little base on which engineers could anchor a lighthouse. Moreover, this wave-swept reef required a structure that could stand up under strong winds and severe pounding from the surf.

The first to build a tower on Eddystone was Henry Winstanley, who obtained a contract from the British government to erect the lighthouse. Beginning work in 1696, Winstanley anchored the structure to the rock with iron rods twelve feet long, enclosing them in a stone base twelve feet tall. In 1697 a French privateer delayed work when it captured the work crew and hauled them to France where they remained in custody until exchanged as prisoners of war. The returning prisoners resumed their work, and in 1698 Winstanley and his men completed the lighthouse which rose eighty feet into the air. As it neared completion, the tower underwent successful structural testing when a severe storm rocked that section of the coast. Lighting the tower in November of that year, Winstanley closely watched it in operation and observed that too often waves swept over the top of the lighthouse. He realized that the tower needed to be raised, and in 1699 he closed down the light. He doubled the size of the stone base, enlarged the structure above, and raised the light forty feet. He must have really driven his crew, because he displayed the light again before the end of the year. The light consisted of a large lamp and sixty candles.

By November, 1703, the lighthouse needed repairs. Winstanley collected some workmen and went out to the structure, in the face of the threat of a storm. The men reached the lighthouse, and the storm struck. It was of memorable severity, one of the worst storms to ravage that coast. Days later, when the blow eased and visibility increased, the landspeople saw that the lighthouse had disappeared. No trace was found of Winstanley, the workmen, or the keepers; only a few iron rods protruding from the rock testified to the fact that a lighthouse had once even been there.

The value of Winstanley's structure had been recognized, however, and the need for a lighthouse on Eddystone was apparent; soon maritime interests began agitation to secure another one there. In 1706 John Lovett and John Rudyerd applied to build a lighthouse at Eddystone. Lovett had the money and Rudyerd the know-how. An act of Parliament authorized them to erect the structure and to collect light dues for ninety-nine years.

Rudyerd secured the foundation of the tower to the rock with iron bolts. He then laid a base of stone and wood, and constructed the remainder of

4

Composite drawing of the Eddystone lighthouses. From E. Price Edwards, *The Eddystone Lighthouses.*

*Reproduced from the collection of the Library of Congress.*

the tower—shaped like a cone—also of stone and wood, sheathing it all with wood planks. He surmounted the tower with a lantern made of wood.

Rudyerd lighted the tower on July 28, 1708, and for the next forty-seven years it served humankind. Then disaster struck, not from the sea this time, but from within. On December 2, 1755, the wooden lantern caught fire. The keepers attempted to put it out, but the fire crept slowly down the wood-clad tower, forcing the keepers eventually to seek safety on the rocks at the base. While helplessly standing there, one of the keepers—an elderly gentleman—looked up at the burning structure with his lips parted and a glob of hot lead fell into his open mouth and down his gullet. He said he felt no pain. Later, after being rescued, the keepers were examined by a physician. The old man reported the incident of the hot lead, but the doctor examined closely his mouth and throat, found no evidence of either having any burns, and dismissed the man's complaint. Several days later the old man died; afterwards an autopsy revealed a piece of lead weighing nearly half a pound in his stomach.

The corporation that by now owned the lease for the Eddystone light decided to erect another tower on the spot, since it had fifty years to run on the lease. The directors contacted John Smeaton, a civil engineer, and asked him to undertake the task. Smeaton settled upon a modified cone design; that is, the bottom of the tower flared out more to give a broader foundation. Smeaton decided to make the tower completely of stone, and those responsible for such things in England went along with him, despite the fact many felt that any lighthouse to survive on Eddystone would have to be made of wood, because of the give that material possessed.

Smeaton began work in 1756. In the meantime, his employers fitted out a vessel as a lightship and stationed it at Eddystone so that the corporation could continue to collect light dues. The lightship remained on station until Smeaton completed the tower and exhibited the light on October 9, 1759. The light consisted of twenty-four candles.

For 123 years this tower and its light warned ships away from the rocks and shoals of the Eddystone. In 1882, the Trinity House (a corporation chartered in 1514 by Henry VIII, charged with furthering British commerce and navigation, and with establishing and maintaining lighthouses), realizing the foundation was not as secure as it originally had

been and that the lantern was not as high above the waves as it should be, ordered a taller lighthouse constructed to replace the older one. Smeaton's tower was taken down piece by piece and reconstructed at nearby Plymouth when the new one was built.

## Inchcape (Bell Rock) Light (1811)

Encouraged by Smeaton's successful tower on Eddystone, the Scottish lighthouse service, which was to develop into one of the world's best, decided to erect a lighthouse on a submerged rock, or reef, on the east coast of Scotland. Known as the Inchcape, or Bell Rock, the reef lay near shipping lanes on the northern side of the Firth of Forth. As shipping to that coast increased in the eighteenth century, and as shipwrecks on the rock increased in frequency and number, agitation for a lighthouse there grew in volume. The first efforts centered around building beacons, but each of these had been unable to withstand the forces of nature, and each had succumbed.

In the early 1800's, Robert Stevenson, engineer of the Northern Lighthouse Board, began gathering information for such a lighthouse and concluded that a stone tower with a flared base similar to Smeaton's on Eddystone would be feasible for Bell Rock. The board and a consulting engineer from London agreed with him, and in 1806 he began work on the structure. First of all Stevenson erected a beacon on the rocks and stationed a lightship nearby. He then started work on the tower. He excavated the rock to obtain a pit forty-two feet in diameter. To keep water from rushing into the pit Stevenson raised a concrete wall around it. When the pit was completed, he bolted the first course of stones to the bottom. The second course overtopped the water level and work became easier—the builders did not have to fight the problem of keeping the pit clear of water. The workers laid the first course of stone in August 1808, and they continued work on the tower through 1809 and 1810. Even with their primitive equipment, the builders often laid the stone faster than it could be quarried and delivered. Some of the laborers lived aboard the service ship and some lived in the beacon, which stood adjacent to the tower, connected by a suspended walkway. Storms lashing the Inchcape rattled the nerves of the workmen in the beacon at times, and

The Bell Rock lighthouse in 1824, by Turner. From Robert Stevenson, *An Account of the Bell Rock Light-house.* *Reproduced from the collection of the Library of Congress.*

these men possessed little faith that their abode was substantial enough to withstand nature's onslaught. But they worried, fortunately, in vain, for no major calamity occurred, and the beacon survived.

While workmen continued the laying of the stone at the rock, artisans ashore constructed the lantern for the tower. In the fall of 1810, the service vessel transported parts of the lantern to the tower. Workers reassembled the lantern—heart of the lighthouse —on the tower and fitted it with Argand lamps and reflectors positioned on a rotating, four-sided chandelier. Stevenson covered two sides of the chandelier with red glass to give the light a distinctiveness that other lights in the area did not possess. The manufacturer was slow in delivering the red glass, and Stevenson had to delay displaying the light. During this period Stevenson used the workmen ashore to erect four quarters for the keepers and their families. The glass finally arrived and the keepers lighted the lamps on February 1, 1811, thus permitting the lightship to put out its light and steer a course for port. A light has continued to shine from Bell Rock through the years to the present.

The significance of the Eddystone and Bell Rock light towers lies in their construction. The fact that man could successfully erect towers on these two inhospitable spots illustrates that engineering skill and technology had progressed to a stage where man could place his lighthouses anywhere to warn sailors of dangerous areas.

European countries generally had gained much experience in the building, lighting, and maintaining of lighthouses, and the efficacy of these aids to navigation had been demonstrated to the point that it was an accepted truth. By the time Europeans settled the New World and maritime commerce had grown to the point that merchants saw the need for lighthouses, there was a large body of information for builders to draw upon.

## COLONIAL LIGHTS

The first lighthouse in the New World was probably a lantern dangling from a stick stuck in the ground near some harbor entrance. Just when the first permanent structure designed specifically as a lighthouse was built cannot be stated with any degree of certainty. It is generally believed that the tower erected on Little Brewster Island in Boston Harbor was the first lighthouse in North America. However, there is vague evidence that a lighthouse may have existed in Havana, Cuba, in 1671. In regard to the Boston light, though, there is the positive evidence of its existence, and it was the first lighthouse built in the United States.

### Boston Light (1716)

The growth of lighthouses in the United States followed the same pattern as it had in Europe; that is, the first ones came into service near important ports of trade. It was not until many years later, when the central government received control of aids to navigation, that lighthouses were established where serious dangers to navigation existed but where few people lived, such as at Cape Hatteras or at the Keys off Florida. There were, of course, many reasons for the failure to erect lighthouses or other types of aids to navigation at dangerous points, but the basic reason was localism. Local people erected and maintained lighthouses; no one had a desire to spend money in another colony or territory for a lighthouse that did not benefit him directly.

Local people, usually merchants, agitated for lights, and generally they appealed to the local colonial government for such an aid to navigation. The country's first lighthouse—the Boston light—followed this pattern. In 1713, local merchants petitioned the General Court of Massachusetts for a "Light Hous and Lanthorn on some Head Land at the Entrance of the Harbor of Boston for the Direction of Ships and Vessels in the Night Time bound into the said Harbor." In this statement lies a concern that is little appreciated today in the age of machine-driven vessels. A ship with an engine has a reliable and consistent source of power and as a result can arrange to be at a port at a specific time; it can, if it so desires, arrive at a port in daylight hours. But in the days of sail, ships had only the wind to rely upon for motive power, and ship masters could not precisely predict, or control, when they would arrive at a harbor. Consequently, if the ship arrived at night, rather than run the risk of going aground, it would cruise off the coast until daylight, with the dangers that action entailed.

There are references to lighthouses in Boston Harbor in the seventeenth century, but these were mistaken identifications. In the seventeenth and

The original Boston light tower, the first lighthouse in the United States (lighted 1716). Fire damaged the tower in 1751, and in 1776 the British blew it up. It was replaced in 1783. *U. S. Coast Guard photo 26-LG-5-55 in the National Archives.*

eighteenth centuries, local people, fearful of enemy attack, placed beacon fires about the harbor entrance. Men on guard had instructions to light the fires if they saw three or four ships approaching in a group. The warning would give the authorities time to gather the militia and prepare defenses to meet the enemy. Such beacons were not uncommon in the colonies. Down the coast in New Jersey, local people placed beacons on the Highlands of Navesink to warn of pirates or foreign privateers.

Upon receiving the petition of the merchants, the General Court appointed a committee to look into the need for a lighthouse. The committee quickly recognized the need and recommended erecting a light on Beacon Island—a small island (now called Little Brewster) connected to Great Brewster Island by a bar—at the entrance to Boston Harbor. The Court concurred, and in June, 1715, appropriated the necessary funds for the structure. Construction apparently began shortly thereafter, for little over a year later, on September 14, 1716, the keepers displayed the light for the first time. The lighthouse,

built of stone, was a tall, graceful tower, and its light consisted of either candles or lamps.

To defray the cost of the lighthouse and its maintenance, the court instituted light dues consisting of "one Penney per Ton Inwards, and another Penney Outwards, except Coasters, who are to pay Two Shillings each, at their clearance Out, and all Fishing Vessels, Wood Sloops, etc. Five Shillings each by the Year."

The Court hired George Worthylake as the first keeper and agreed to pay him 50 pounds a year, admonishing him that if he should be derelict in his duties, he would be fined 100 pounds. In addition to keeping the light burning from sunset to sunrise, this country's first lighthouse keeper also undertook piloting jobs.

Worthylake had served as keeper for two years when he fell victim to tragedy. On November 3, 1718, he, his wife and daughter, and two men drowned when the boat in which they were returning to the lighthouse capsized. Benjamin Franklin, then a young lad, memorialized the event in a poem

9

entitled "Lighthouse Tragedy," which his brother printed and young Ben hawked on the streets of Boston. Copies of the poem have not survived, and probably just as well, since Franklin later said the poem consisted of "wretched verses in point of style, mere blindmen's ditties."

In 1718, the General Court raised the salary of the keeper to seventy pounds, and a year later placed a cannon at the lighthouse to serve as a fog signal, the country's first. In 1734, the General Court designated the keeper as a principal pilot of the port so that he could supplement his income by getting preference on piloting jobs.

In 1751, a fire burned all the wooden portion of the lighthouse, including the stairs and several floors. A ship's lantern on a stake forty feet high served as a temporary light until workmen could effect repairs. On several occasions through the years lightning struck the tall tower. The people of Boston who oversaw the light refused to put up a lightning rod, thinking "it vanity and irreligion for the arm of flesh to presume to avert the stroke of Heaven." But in time they reconsidered and installed a lightning arrester. In 1775, American troops removed the lamps from the tower and set fire to it so that the Boston light would be of no benefit to the British. A week later, though, the British, protected by a marine guard, began repairing the tower. On hearing of this activity General George Washington dispatched 300 troops under the command of Major Benjamin Tupper to halt the work. Landing on the island from whaleboats, the Americans defeated the guard and destroyed the repair work. The British sent reinforcements to drive Tupper and his men from the island, but the Americans would not be deprived of their objective, and Tupper and his men held their ground and defeated this force also. Later, Washington commended Tupper and his troops for their good work.

The final blow to the country's first lighthouse came a year later, on June 13, 1776, when the British fleet, before leaving Boston, blew up the tower. It was not replaced until after the war.

### Brant Point Light (1746)

The second lighthouse built in this country came thirty years after the erection of the first and barely deserves the title of lighthouse. At the behest of sea captains in the vicinity, the town of Nantucket established a lighthouse in 1746 on Brant Point on the south side of Nantucket Harbor. Cheaply built, it was little more than a beacon. Fire destroyed it twelve years later, and the town rebuilt the light in 1759. This structure remained until 1774 when "a most violent Gust of Wind that perhaps was ever known there" destroyed it. The town again replaced the light, and this time it lasted just nine years until fire consumed it. Another, and even smaller, beacon came into existence there in 1783, but it proved so unsatisfactory, because of its dim light, that another beacon was erected three years later. This time a storm took the light, and in only two years.

### Tybee Island Light (1748?)

The Tybee light station has a history that can be traced back to the earliest days of the Colony of Georgia. When General James Oglethorpe founded the colony in 1732, he felt that a coastal landmark was needed to guide ships into the waterways leading to Savannah, some twenty miles inland. The coast was low-lying with a certain sameness to it that presented nothing distinctive. Shortly after he arrived in Savannah in 1732, he assigned carpenters to the task of prefabricating an octagonal wooden tower, something mariners could take a bearing on. Oglethorpe had hoped to have the tower in place on Tybee Island, the outermost of the coastal islands, by 1734. But various problems arose and the workmen did not complete the tower and erect it until 1736. The tower, ninety feet tall, was twenty-five feet across at the base and tapered to twelve and a half feet wide at the top. Oglethorpe had siding placed on it to twenty-six feet above the ground and left the remainder open. Resting on a brick foundation, the lightless, roofless tower had two floors above ground. It served until 1741 when a storm toppled it. Apparently the tower had served a useful purpose, for the Trustees, who governed the colony under charter from the king, had another one fabricated and floated to Tybee where workmen put it in place in March 1742. Similar to its predecessor, this tower was four feet taller and had a roof and a staircase that ran all the way to the top. Although the first tower had had no light, the second tower, at least in its later years, apparently did have one, possibly qualifying it as the country's third lighthouse;[1] it was tended by a pilot stationed

---

[1] There is some doubt about this. See pp. 105 and 107.

at Tybee. The second tower served until the eve of the Revolution when sea erosion threatened it, and the colonial government decided to erect a brick tower, which it did in 1771–73.

### Beavertail Light (1749)

Although authorized by Rhode Island in 1738, the Beavertail lighthouse on the southern tip of Conanicut Island in Narragansett Bay was not built until 1749. This rubble stone tower, sixty-four feet tall, principally served traffic to Newport. The original tower lasted until 1856 when a granite tower replaced it. Later in the nineteenth century the Lighthouse Board used this light station to test fog horns.

### New London Light (1760)

The country's fifth lighthouse went up on the west side of the entrance to New London Harbor in 1760. Probably a masonry structure, the lighthouse barely survived into the nineteenth century, being replaced in 1801 by a stone tower.

### Sandy Hook Light (1764)

Only one of the colonial lighthouses survived into recent years, and that is the one at Sandy Hook, New Jersey. Built in 1764 at the behest of New York merchants and financed through two lotteries, it was known for a long time as the New York lighthouse, since it served primarily traffic bound for that port. As with the other lighthouses built at this time, light dues supported it. A newspaper account of 1764 described the masonry structure as being

"of an Octagonal Figure, having eight equal Sides; the Diameter at the Base 29 Feet; and at the top of the Wall, 15 Feet. The Lanthorn is 7 feet high; the Circumference 33 feet. The whole Construction of the Lanthorn is Iron; the Top covered with Copper. There are 48 Oil Blazes. The Building from the Surface is Nine Stories; the whole from Bottom to Top 103 Feet."[2] The builder, Isaac Conro, could take considerable satisfaction in his work. In 1852, the Lighthouse Board reported that it was one of the three best masonry light towers in the United States.

The fact that the building has survived to the present is further testimony of the builder's fine work. Even calculated attempts at destruction failed. Fearful that the light would be useful to the British, American forces tried to damage or destroy the light tower during the Revolution. But the tower was too well built and resisted the Americans' efforts. The tower has survived to the present, and today is the country's oldest lighthouse.

### Cape Henlopen Light (1767)

About the same time as the building of the Sandy Hook lighthouse, workers began construction of the Cape Henlopen lighthouse at the entrance to Delaware Bay—the seaway to Philadelphia. Although in Delaware, the lighthouse was built at the behest of Pennsylvania businessmen. It was a stone structure similar to the Sandy Hook light tower, and it had been built upon the most precarious of foundations: sand. Throughout the history of this country, sand has been the cause of the destruction of many lighthouses, usually within a few years of construction.

---

[2] One has difficulty reconciling the height of the Sandy Hook lighthouse as given in the 1764 newspaper account with the height as given in the current *Light List,* which states that the height of the tower from the base to the top of the lantern is eighty-five feet. Indeed, the 1838 *Light List,* the country's first, gives the tower as being seventy-seven feet tall from the base to the lantern. If the tower has been shortened, it happened prior to 1790, for a drawing of that year depicts the tower as being the same height as it is today.

In view of the fact that military activity swirled around the lighthouse during the Revolution and the fact that it was the desire of the Americans and the British to deny each other the benefit of aids to navigation, the thought crosses one's mind that perhaps, in an effort to eliminate effectively the lighthouse as an aid, one or the other side

damaged the top of the structure and after the war the Americans removed the injured portion, thus lowering the tower.

Although this thought is plausible, there is no evidence to support it. The most recent research indicates that the Americans only dismantled the lighting apparatus and did not damage the tower. Similarly, there is no evidence that the British did anything to the tower.

If the tower was reduced in height at some period in its life, nothing has yet turned up that says when and how it was done, or even that it was done. Therefore, one could justifiably assume that the reporter in 1764 simply was in error about the height of the tower. I am inclined to think this was the case. But whatever the event, the fact remains that the Sandy Hook tower stands today as the oldest lighthouse tower in the United States.

But the Cape Henlopen light tower was able to postpone its date with tragedy for 159 years. In 1926, after the lighthouse service had spent years battling the sand and the wind, a violent northeast storm washed the sand from under the tower, and the lighthouse toppled over.

During the Revolution, British troops burned the Cape Henlopen tower, and the state government did not have it repaired and put back into operation until after the war.

### Charleston (Morris Island) Light (1767)

The South Carolina colonial government established a lighthouse in 1767 on Morris Island at the entrance to Charleston Harbor that survived well past the Civil War.

### Plymouth Light (1769)

The Massachusetts legislature provided for a lighthouse on Gurnet Point at the entrance to Plymouth Bay, and erected one there in 1769. Like the Brant Point light, the Plymouth light was hardly more than a beacon. The lighthouse was twenty feet long, fifteen feet wide, and twenty feet high, and at each end the builders placed a lantern containing two lamps. The first keeper was John Thomas who received 200 pounds per year and on whose land the lighthouse had been built. When the state of Massachusetts turned the light station over to the federal government in 1790, Thomas's widow was serving as keeper.

In 1778, a stray cannonball from a battle taking place between a British ship and a nearby militia fort injured the lighthouse. Apparently the shot did not impair the functioning of the lanterns, and the light continued in operation. The battle damage was repaired after the war.

### Portsmouth Light (1771)

A wooden lighthouse was erected in the Ports-mouth, New Hampshire, harbor in 1771. Since Portsmouth was a principal shipbuilding port during the Revolution, this light saw a number of vessels slide down the ways and out of the harbor to do their part for independence. John Paul Jones took command of the *Ranger* here in 1777, and returned here again in 1781 to take command of the *America,* a ship he had the disappointment of seeing taken away from him and given to the French. The original harbor light served until 1804 when another wooden structure replaced it.

### Cape Ann Light (1771)

The eleventh and last of the colonial lighthouses went up on Thatcher's Island at Cape Ann on the northern side of Massachusetts Bay in 1771. To give a distinctiveness to the light, the Massachusetts Bay Council ordered construction of two towers, each forty-five feet high. The keeper was a well-known Tory, and the local patriots forced him out at the beginning of the Revolution. As a result, the lights were out throughout the war. The state government relighted them after the war, and they continued in service until 1861 when two taller towers replaced them.

Most of these early lighthouses survived for many years after the Revolution, and they, along with the few lighthouses built or started between the end of the war and 1790, formed the basis for this country's lighthouse system—a system whose creation was one of the first acts of the federal government in 1789. On this base the United States built a lighthouse system that today ranks with the best in the world, but it was not an easy growth, and ineptness, conservatism, poor management, penury, political patronage, technological backwardness, and waste marked its path before the country began steering the course that led to a great lighthouse system. But before going into that story, it would be well to understand the evolution of the lighthouse's light.

# II

# The Light

WHATEVER its design, shape, material, height or thickness, the light tower has one primary mission: to support the light the mariner needs to see. The tower serves a secondary purpose as a daymark, hence its often distinctive coloration. Nevertheless, the lighthouse is principally a night-time aid and, as a consequence, the most important aspect of the lighthouse is the light.

Over the centuries the light tower has supported a variety of lights, but until the most recent years, when electricity came into use, the light has been a flame in one form or another. The history of the development of the lighthouse light is the story of the refinement and adaptation of the flame. It was so refined through the years that by the time of the introduction of electricity, the flame was virtually no longer a flame—it was a glowing gas ball.

## Early Fuels

As stated previously, the first light that served as a navigational aid was probably a wood fire on a hillside that faced seaward. Later, when man began to build towers as lighthouses, he simply transferred that wood fire from the ground to the top of the tower. For centuries upon centuries wood continued as the principal fuel for the light. But the use of wood had certain inherent problems. Wood burned rapidly, and stoking the fire kept the light keeper on the move. Moreover, there was a tendency to use up forests near light towers.

Around the beginning of the sixteenth century, keepers began using coal in lighthouses and this fuel produced a light that sailors highly favored. A coal fire was bright and could be seen from a considerable distance. Moreover, keepers liked coal because it burned slower and, consequently, the light required less attention. On the other hand, the sailor often found the light was not so bright during inclement weather when he most needed a light; not all keepers wanted to expose themselves to the elements to keep the fire properly stoked. Conscientious keepers, however, in order to keep a bright light showing during bad weather, kept an intense fire burning with the result that the fiery coals melted the grate holding them. Attempts to enclose coal fires resulted in the soot coating the glass. At one point, to increase the intensity of the coast light, early-day lighthouse engineers introduced reflectors; but the reflectors, too, quickly became covered with soot. The light at Isle of May in Scotland and the one at Cordouan in France are but two examples of the many light towers that at one time had coal fires for lights. Many of the lever lights, such as Denmark's *vippefyrs,* used coal.

At the same time, and perhaps even before the use of coal, some lighthouses used candles as their illuminant. Candles certainly were not as messy as coal, and keepers could tend them with relative ease. Lanterns holding them were enclosed, so the light was steady. Many lighthouses, notably Eddystone, at one time used candles. Despite their reliability, candles simply did not give off as bright a light as other illuminants. Nevertheless, they remained in use in some lighthouses until well into the nineteenth century.

## Early Lamps

The next refinement came with the introduction of lamps. Some of these early lamps used solid, circular wicks, and others used flat wicks. Smeaton,

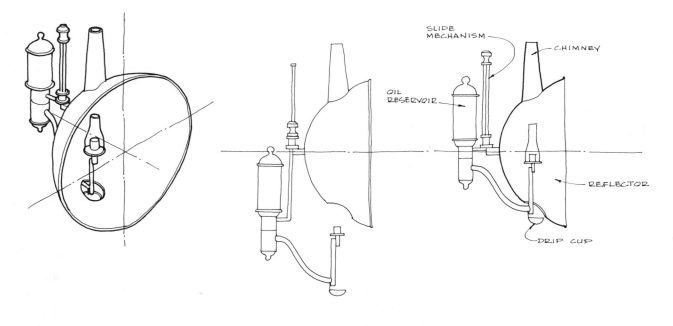

SLIDE MECHANISM

CHIMNEY

OIL RESERVOIR

REFLECTOR

DRIP CUP

LAMP IN LOWERED POSITION

LAMP IN NORMAL POSITION

The Argand lamp, developed in 1781, and the parabolic reflector. Oxygen, flowing through and around the hollow, circular wick, produced an intense, smokeless light equal to the light of seven candles. The superiority of this lighting system over its forerunner, the spider lamp, led to its adoption by the United States lighthouse serv- ice in 1812, and delayed for forty years the adoption of an even better device, the lens developed by Augustin Fresnel of France in 1822. The wick of the Argand lamp was later modified for use with the Fresnel lens. *Drawing by David Battle.*

for example, used flat wick lamps in the Eddystone light in 1759. Generally these lamps gave off a light smoke that hazed over the glass of the interior of the lantern, thus dimming the light. One innovation in lighthouse lamps came with the introduction of a lamp that was a pan of oil with four wicks protruding from it. These lamps were first used in the United States in the Boston light around 1790. Called spider lamps, they proved unsatisfactory, since they gave off acrid fumes that burned the eyes and nostrils of the keeper and thus curtailed sharply the length of time he could remain in the lantern. Yet these lamps continued as the principal illuminant in United States lighthouses until the introduction of Winslow Lewis's lamps and parabolic reflectors in 1812.

The first major revolution in lighting lighthouses came in 1781 when Ami Argand invented a lamp that had a hollow circular wick. Since oxygen passed along the inside and outside of the wick, the flame burned intensely and brightly, and, more important, smokelessly. The brightness of the flame was equivalent to seven candles. The Trinity House

first installed these lamps in English lighthouses in 1789. About the same time England began using reflectors and soon fitted eighteen- to twenty-inch reflectors to the Argand lamps. Europe had been experimenting with the use of reflectors since at least as early as the seventeenth century, and toward the end of the eighteenth century these experiments had refined themselves into the parabolic reflector, with the flame of the lamp being at the center of the reflector. The Argand lamp and parabolic reflector served a long and useful career as the illuminant in lighthouses, achieving its pinnacle of success in England and France. Indeed, Argand's hollow wick was later adopted and modified by Fresnel for the lamps used in his lenses.

*Winslow Lewis and the Parabolic Reflector*

The Argand lamp and parabolic reflector did not reach the United States for some years. In 1810, after several years of testing and experimenting, Captain Winslow Lewis, an unemployed ship captain, persuaded the federal government to adopt

14

## Argand adapted, Fresnel ignored

his Argand lamp and parabolic reflector system as the means of lighting this country's lighthouses. At a public exhibition at the Boston light tower before government representatives, Lewis demonstrated that the lamp and reflector were greatly superior to the old spider lamp system. In addition to giving a brighter light, Lewis's lamps used about half as much oil as the older lamps.

A lucerne, used by nineteenth-century keepers to light the concentric-wicked lamps in Fresnel lenses. *Drawing by David Battle.*

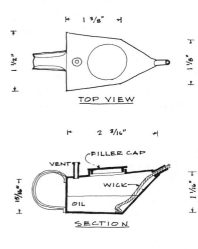

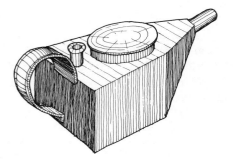

Although Lewis's light was a definite improvement over the former method of illuminating lighthouses, it was, in a way, an unfortunate development. Within a few years Augustin Fresnel was to perfect a lens system that was infinitely better than all systems developed until that time. Fresnel lenses were so good that even today, with our advanced technology in lighting, many lighthouses still are illuminated by these lenses and their light is just as effective as those possessing the most modern system. But because the United States adopted Lewis's lamps and reflectors, those who managed the nation's lighthouse establishment became so enamored of them that they ignored the Fresnel lens, thus causing this country to continue to lag behind others in the quality of its navigational aids.

In the meantime, Lewis patented his lamp and reflector system and offered to sell the patent to the government. The Lewis light impressed Henry Dearborn, the collector of customs in Boston, and after witnessing an official full-scale testing at one of the twin towers at Cape Ann, he urged the secretary of the treasury to take up Lewis's offer. In addition to his patent offer, Lewis proposed refitting all the country's lighthouses—then forty-nine in number—with his new system for the sum of $26,950.

The secretary of the treasury, Albert Gallatin, appealed to Congress, and in 1812 Congress appropriated $60,000 to pay Lewis for the patent as well as for outfitting the nation's lighthouses with his apparatus and maintaining them for seven years. Lewis went about his work with a will, and before the War of 1812 interfered, he had fitted out all but nine of the lighthouses. He finished the last lights in the fall of 1815.

Lewis placed a lens in front of each of his lamps. Unfortunately, the lenses had a greenish tint and as a result diminished rather than magnified the light. In time the lenses were removed, but it took twenty-five years before all were. Even this move did not increase the quality of the United States' reflector lights to the point where they could compare with England's or Scotland's. The fault was apparently due to the quality of the parabolic reflectors. One pharologist wrote in 1889 that Lewis's reflectors approached the paraboloid about as closely as did a barber's basin; forty-seven years earlier, an inspector of New England lighthouses referred to the reflectors as being of the wash basin design. The reflectors apparently were so thin that they did not hold up well under normal use and in many cases quickly became shapeless. In 1838, two examiners of lighthouses reported that some of the reflectors were actually spherical and others so bent out of shape that they no longer resembled the paraboloid. These reflectors were also apparently lightly silvered and normal cleaning wore the silver off the curved surface. The prescribed cleaner was tripoli powder, an abrasive that the Lighthouse Board outlawed in lighthouses in 1852.

### Lewis and the Fifth Auditor

One of the more revealing aspects of the 1838 inspection of lighthouses was the finding that several lighthouses had spherical reflectors in them. Stephen Pleasonton, fifth auditor of the Treasury Department, was in charge of the country's lighthouses, and this finding indicates how out of touch he was with actual conditions in the lighthouses. Just the previous year he had reported to Congress that all the United States' lighthouses were equipped with Winslow Lewis's *parabolic* reflectors.

Lewis remained active through the years in seeing that the lighthouse service retained the lamp and reflector system. His precise relationship to the fifth auditor is not fully understood at present, but there is no doubt that he did influence this government official. The correspondence of the lighthouse service shows that, from time to time at least, Pleasonton wrote Lewis seeking his advice on technical matters related to lighthouses. For example, at one light station Pleasonton decided to build a wooden keeper's quarters only after Lewis recommended that it be done. And at another time when the Whaleback lighthouse threatened to topple over, Pleasonton dispatched Lewis to the site to determine the problem and suggest a solution. Winslow Lewis's nephew, I. W. P. Lewis—a severe critic of Winslow Lewis, the fifth auditor, and the country's lighthouse system—said that Pleasonton had Winslow Lewis formulate the specifications for proposed lighthouses and then permitted him to be one of the bidders on the job.

Although not the ideal person, Lewis was not the worst one Pleasonton could have turned to for advice on matters relating to aids to navigation. Lewis did have considerable practical maritime experience, and he was gaining technical knowledge, not only through supplying the illuminating appara-

tuses, but also by the construction of some of the lighthouses.

Lewis's secure place in Pleasonton's scheme of things is illustrated by the fact that in 1835 Lewis changed the Mobile Point light from a fixed to a revolving light without first consulting the general superintendent of lights. Changing the characteristic of a light is a major step that should be taken only after adequate warning to seamen because of the confusion it causes when a mariner, expecting to see one light characteristic, suddenly discovers another, unfamiliar one. Lewis later explained his reason for this action and Pleasonton accepted it without argument. Shortly afterwards a number of ships' masters and the Blunts complained that the change was not a wise one, saying that now the Mobile Point light had the same characteristic as the Pensacola light just forty miles away. Pleasonton quickly came to the defense of Lewis and went about obtaining testimony from local pilots that the change was a good one. Two adjacent seacoast lights with the same characteristic can be confusing to the sailor who plies the ocean, but of little consequence to a local pilot. Years later, when the Lighthouse Board came into being, that body pointed out the error of these two lights having the same characteristic.

During the reign of the fifth auditor, only two firms in the United States possessed the forms necessary to mold the parabolic reflector: Hooper & Company of Boston and Winslow Lewis. Lewis, however, consistently obtained contracts to supply the illuminating apparatuses for lighthouses. Hooper & Company lost out so often that in 1847 when Pleasanton asked for bids to furnish the illuminating apparatuses for the Bodie Island lighthouse, Hooper & Company declined bidding against Lewis because Lewis always submitted a lower one. Lewis, Pleasonton said, "would work for nothing, I have understood from him, sooner than give up a branch of business in which he has been engaged for more than thirty years."

There is yet no "hard" evidence that there were any shady dealings between Pleasonton and Lewis. Indeed, the surviving records of the old lighthouse service do not hint at overt dishonesty. But that there was favoritism, at least unconsciously, there is ample evidence.

Lewis and Pleasonton were on friendly terms. At this stage of research, the historian can only charac-

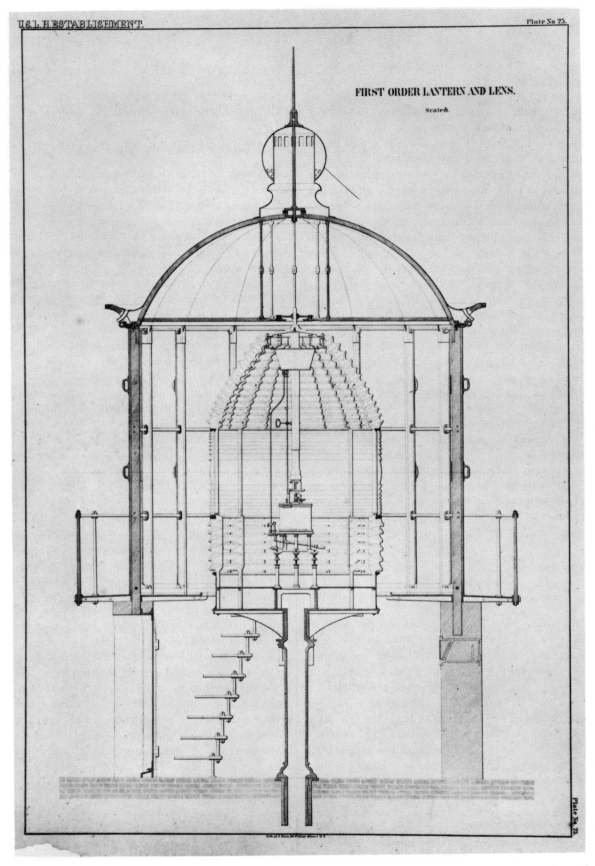

FIRST ORDER LANTERN AND LENS.

Scale¼

Vertical section of first-order Fresnel lens and lantern, with hydraulic lamp in the lens. *From Record Group 26, National Archives.*

terize the relationship as one between a sharp, but honest, Yankee businessman and an uninformed, naive, government bureaucrat. Lewis was doing everything to protect his business interests, and Pleasonton was so concerned with economy that he let this factor cloud good administrative practice: he let one firm develop a monopoly over a product the government needed. The important lesson here is the danger in slavish adherence to a regulation—namely, the government regulation that says an official always has to take the low bid. Always buying from one source discourages competition, and competition is the keystone of the capitalistic system, or so the businessmen tell us. In addition to discouraging competition, Pleasonton by default let the supplier be the judge of the quality of the product. Pleasonton had become so dependent upon the technical knowledge Lewis possessed that he defended Lewis, and did not keep as close an eye upon him as the best interests of the government would require. Pleasonton probably was smart enough to realize that any criticism of Lewis would be a criticism of his administration of aids to navigation.

There seems little doubt at this time that one of the prime reasons Pleasonton was reluctant to experiment with the Fresnel system was out of deference to Lewis. Certainly as far as the Fresnel lens was concerned, Pleasonton did a lot of foot-dragging.

## The Fresnel Lens

Augustin Fresnel, a French physicist interested in optics, had perfected a lens in 1822 that was to revolutionize the lighting of lighthouses by simplifying the maintaining of a good light. Fresnel's lens resembled a gigantic beehive that surrounded a single lamp. Prisms at the top and bottom refracted, or bent, the light so that it came from the lens in a narrow sheet. At the same time, the light was intensified at the center of the lens by a powerful magnifying glass. The result of this refraction and magnification was a bright, narrow sheet of concentrated light emitting from the lighthouse.

Fresnel devised seven orders, or sizes, of lenses, depending upon the power of light needed. The first-order lens was the largest and gave the most powerful light and would be used as a seacoast light. The smallest was a sixth-order lens for use in harbors. (There was a three-and-a-half-order lens.)

## The Fifth Auditor Drags His Feet

The countries with the more progressive lighthouse systems quickly saw the efficacy of the new lens and began adopting it. Pleasonton apparently ignored the lens. There is evidence, however, that in 1830 he wrote to France inquiring about it, but this apparently was a half-hearted effort without any serious intent.

The country's lighthouses often came under heavy criticism, and from time to time Congress felt compelled to take notice. In 1837, Edmund and George W. Blunt, publishers of the *American Coast Pilot* and long-time critics of the lighthouse service, launched a heavy attack upon Pleasonton. They contended that many of the lighthouse towers and dwellings contained inferior materials and poor workmanship; that lights were established, had their characteristic changed, and were temporarily put out of service without adequate notification to the mariner; and that in lighting lighthouses the United States was far behind more advanced nations such as England and France. They complained especially about the quality of the light, saying the Winslow Lewis's "patent lamps" were "nothing but the Argand lamp, with miserable arrangements." About the same time, Congress received a letter from a chamber of commerce, probably New York City's, stating that a committee it had appointed had heard testimony from ship captains, insurance inspectors, and others, and had concluded that the lights on the towers of France and Great Britain were superior to those of the United States.

In 1838, as a result of this criticism, Pleasonton wrote a congressional committee that he would experiment with a Fresnel lens, if Congress so directed. He also wrote that in his opinion the improvement principally in Fresnel's light was the use of the Carcel lamp, and thus he displayed his abysmal ignorance of the new system. Congress, however, perceived the need at least to experiment with the lenticular apparatus, and, accordingly, in 1838 sent Commodore Matthew C. Perry to Europe to examine lighthouses of that continent and to buy two Fresnel lenses: a first-order fixed lens, and a second-order revolving one.

Congress had these lenses installed at the twin

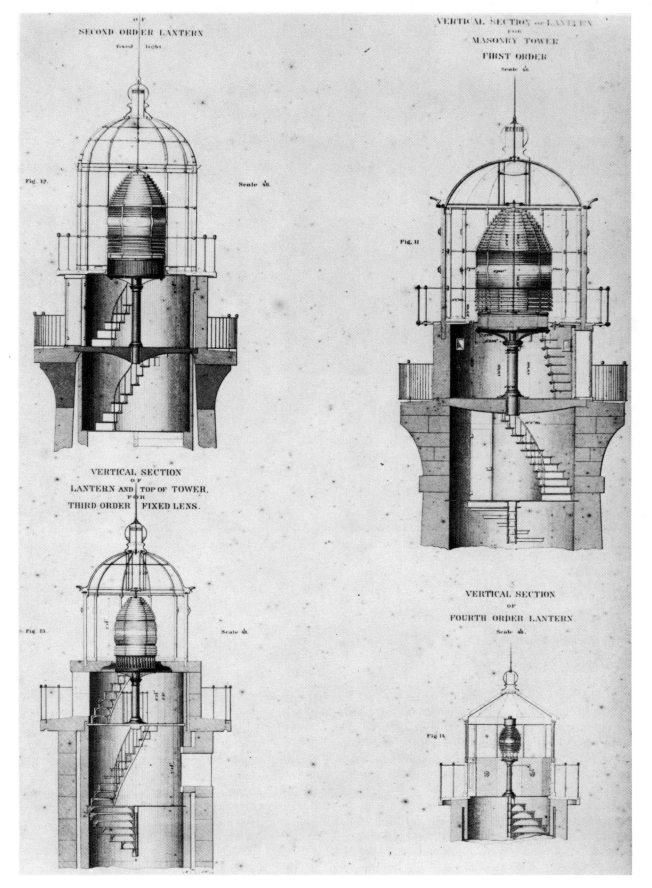

Vertical sections of lanterns and towers mounting (*starting at upper right and proceeding counterclockwise*) first- through fourth-order Fresnel lenses. The first- order lens was about ten feet tall, the fourth-order about three. *From Record Group 26, National Archives.*

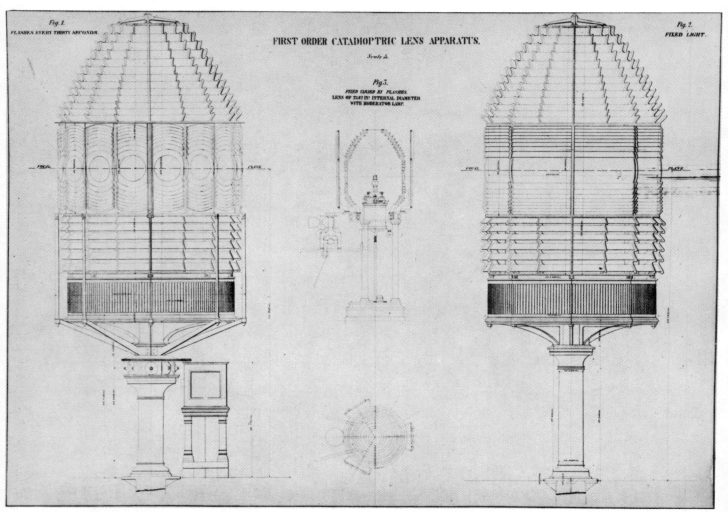

Fig. 1.
FLASHES EVERY THIRTY SECONDS.

FIRST ORDER CATADIOPTRIC LENS APPARATUS.
Scale ⅛.

Fig. 3.
FIXED VARIED BY FLASHES.
LENS OF 73.62 IN⁰ INTERNAL DIAMETER
WITH MODERATOR LAMP.

Fig. 2.
FIXED LIGHT.

First-order Fresnel lenses. The apparatus to the left, with its bullseye lenses at the center focus, emitted a flashing light, an effect achieved by mechanically rotating the six-feet-wide, twelve-feet-tall lens. The rotating mechanism, called a clockwork system because it was energized by a falling weight, was housed in the box to the right of the lens.

The smooth glass at the center focus of the apparatus to the far right made this a fixed lens that displayed a steady light.

The flashing effect of the fixed lens depicted in the center was achieved by rotating panels or solid sheets around the outside of the lens, thus blocking out the light every so often. If a colored, flashing light was desired, a red or green sheet of glass was substituted for the solid sheets, giving, for example, a fixed white light varied by red flashes. The exterior panels were rotated by a clockwork mechanism. *From Record Group 26, National Archives.*

towers of Navesink Light Station in 1840. Over the years this light proved an excellent one. In 1851, the board appointed to study this country's lighthouse system reported that although in poor condition at that time, the lighthouses with their lenses were "vastly superior to the Sandy Hook light, at equal and at greater distances."

There seemed to be no question, except in the fifth auditor's mind, of the superiority of the Fresnel lens. Nevertheless, by 1851 only three light stations in the United States were equipped with Fresnel lenses: Navesink, Sankaty Head Light Station on

Nantucket Island, Mass., and Brandywine screwpile lighthouse in Delaware Bay. Each had been authorized by a special act of Congress. Still, the fifth auditor was not convinced; he felt more testing was necessary and recommended to Congress that a Fresnel lens "be placed on the inward light in Boston Harbor, so that scientific and nautical men living in that city could examine it from time to time and determine its value."

## Congress Investigates

By this time, however, Congress had become completely dissatisfied with the administration of the country's lighthouses, and in 1851 it provided for a board of specialists to investigate all aspects of aids to navigation. Although the board's findings will be discussed in full subsequently, it can be mentioned here that the board found the lighthouses particularly and uniformly deficient in the quality of their lights. Indeed, they reported "that the lights at Navesink (two lenses) and the second-order lens light at Sankaty Head, Nantucket, are the best lights on the coast of the United States." Brandywine was not a coast light, but the board considered this third-order Fresnel lens equivalent to the best reflector light in the country. In general, the board felt the Fresnel apparatus to be "greatly superior to any other mode of light-house illumination, and in point of economy is nearly four times as advantageous as the best system of reflectors and Argand lamps."

In their comments on the old system of illumination the members of the board were specific and harsh. They found nothing good about the lighthouses they examined. The lanterns were poorly constructed and improperly ventilated; the lamps were, "with few exceptions, roughly and badly made"; the chimneys were generally too short for the lamps and reflectors used; the oil used in the lamps was consistently found to be below standard; the reflectors were "defective in form, materials, and finish"; some of the wicks were of fair quality, the others were inadequate; and the keepers, lacking training, for the most part did not know how to tend the lighting system. Moreover, the board went on, the fifth auditor supplied the keepers with tripoli powder to clean the reflectors. This powder generally was used for cleaning brass and copper and was much too abrasive to use on silver; consequently, many reflectors lost most of their silver after a few cleanings. Quite revealing was the finding that the majority of the reflectors were spherical and not parabolic. Generally, the investigators reported, "the illuminating apparatus in the United States is of a description now nearly obsolete throughout all maritime countries, where the best apparatus of that description was employed, prior to the introduction of the Fresnel lens, as substitutes." The lights were so bad, the board continued, that lighthouses south of Navesink were virtually useless to the mariner "for want of sufficient power and range." At this time one ship's captain said:

"The lights on Hatteras, Lookout, Canaveral and Cape Florida, if not improved, had better be dispensed with, as the navigator is apt to run ashore looking for them." And his was not an uncommon comment of seamen at the time.

*The Adoption of the Fresnel Lens*

Shortly after receiving the board's report, Congress reorganized the United States lighthouse service and provided for a Lighthouse Board to administer aids to navigation. Congress also stipulated that Fresnel lenses were to be placed in all new lighthouses and in lighthouses that needed new lighting apparatuses. Since the new board was composed essentially of the members of the investigating board, it is no wonder that it went about quickly converting the country's lighthouses to the Fresnel system. The board ordered these lenses from France, and by the time of the advent of the Civil War all United States lighthouses had been fitted with the Fresnel lenses.

Many Fresnel lenses are still in use in this country's lighthouses, and now with electric bulbs rather than oil lamps as the illuminant these lenses are still rendering excellent service. They are, however, not being placed in new lighthouses. The U. S. Coast Guard is putting the more powerful, airplane-type beacon in its new structures.

*Improving the Light*

Through the years there has been a constant search for a better illuminant, and this search has taken two tacks: seeking a better lamp and seeking a better fuel.

At the time Winslow Lewis introduced his Argand lamp and parabolic reflector, American lighthouses were using spider lamps, which had a number of wicks protruding from a common fuel reservoir. The Argand lamp remained in use until the introduction of the Fresnel lens. In the cases of the spider lamps and the Argand lamps, lighthouses required a number of them—from one to thirty—to provide a reasonably adequate light. The Fresnel lens, on the other hand, required only one lamp, but this lamp had one to four concentric wicks, the larger size of lens requiring the greatest number of wicks.

Several varieties of lamps were used in American

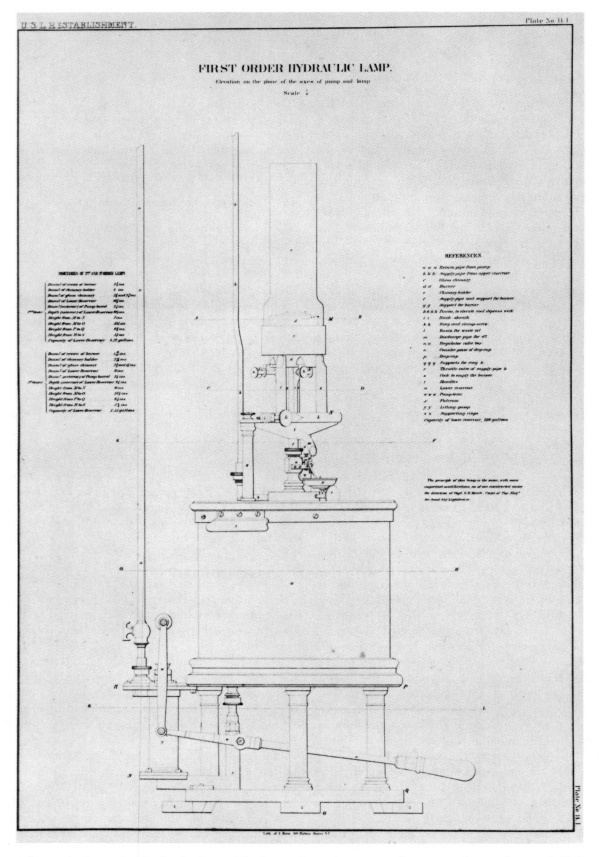

A five-wick, first-order, hydraulic lamp. The lamp shown here is similar to one designed around 1853 by George G. Meade, then assigned to the Corps of Topographical Engineers and later commander of the Union forces at Gettysburg. Meade's lamp was adopted and used in the lighthouse service. *From Record Group 26, National Archives.*

## Sperm oil and rapeseed oil

lighthouses with the Fresnel lenses in the nineteenth century. They all were of the concentric-wick type; their difference lay in the methods employed to get the fuel to the wicks. Carcel, Lepaute, and Funck were but a few of the names of the various lamps. The Funck lamp seems to have been the one most used, due perhaps to the fact that the inventor worked at the lighthouse service's principal supply depot.

One lamp used in American lighthouses with the Fresnel lens had been invented by George G. Meade, who during the Civil War rose to the rank of general and commanded the Union forces at Gettysburg. Meade devised his lamp when he was assigned to lighthouse duty as a young lieutenant in the army engineers.

The fuel employed in United States lighthouses from the beginning was whale oil. Two "strains" of this oil were used: a thick strain known as summer oil, and a thinner one for winter. In colder climates during winter even the thin oil tended to congeal, and it became necessary to keep a warming stove in the lantern of the lighthouse so that the oil maintained its proper viscosity to burn well.

In time the lighthouses used only sperm oil, as it was a high quality oil that burned evenly with a bright light. However, by the middle of the nineteenth century, the American whaler was taking fewer sperm whales, while at the same time the industrial use of this oil increased. The natural consequence was that the price of the oil rose steadily, and by 1855 sperm oil cost $2.25 per gallon, quite an increase over the 1840–41 price of fifty-five cents per gallon.

The Lighthouse Board began to look about for another and cheaper fuel. It turned first to the French lighthouse service and found that that country's lighthouses used colza or rapeseed oil, which France had found to be as good as sperm oil and only half the price. The board began to think that colza oil, which charred the wick very little, was the answer. Not deterred by the fact that wild cabbage, from which rapeseed was obtained, did not grow abundantly in this country, the board went about trying to encourage farmers to cultivate the plant. They hoped that by creating the market American farmers would respond by raising wild cabbage. The farmers, however, failed to heed the call and did not grow the plant in sufficient quantity to fill the needs of the lighthouse service.

In the meantime, the Lighthouse Board began in the late 1850's to introduce colza oil into the country's lighthouses. Within a few years it became apparent that there was not going to be an adequate supply to light all lighthouses, and the board would consequently have to find another fuel. Its committee on experiments, headed by Joseph Henry of the Smithsonian, resumed testing lard oil. Previous tests had been a failure, and Henry had found that lard oil burned badly. But with his new experiments, Henry discovered that if the oil was heated to a high enough temperature it burned well. Since this oil was cheap and in plentiful supply, the Lighthouse Board quickly adopted it. The board phased out colza oil in larger lamps, and in time used it only in lighthouses with smaller lamps. By 1867, lard oil exclusively was being used in the larger lamps.

In the 1870's, the Lighthouse Board once again undertook experiments seeking a better fuel. This time the committee on experiments examined kerosene, or mineral oil as it was then more popularly known. The tests were successful, and in 1878 the Lighthouse Board began introducing this fuel into lighthouses with fourth-order and lower lenses. The board then introduced it successively in third-, second-, and first-order lenses. The slowness in substituting mineral oil was due to the fact that the lens lamps had to be converted to use the new fuel.

The next change in the source of the light was the incandescent oil vapor lamp; this lamp was similar to the Coleman lamp used by campers today. Kerosene is forced into a vaporizer chamber where it strikes the hot walls and is instantly changed into a vapor. The gas goes through a series of small holes to a mantle where it burns like a glowing, bright gas ball. One writer summed up the value of this lamp when he stated: "With the I. O. V. type of lamp the candle power and brilliance are increased many fold as compared with the wick type, with no increase in the actual fuel consumption." This lamp was the final step in the refinement of the flame, and subsequent improvements in lighthouse lighting went beyond fire.

Around 1900, the Lighthouse Board began testing electricity to light lighthouses. In time the tests proved satisfactory, and the board began converting lights to electricity. The conversion could not be done with any great speed, since many lighthouses were not near power lines. Consequently, many

Lamps for Fresnel lenses. The concentric wicks used in these lamps were a modification of the wick developed by Ami Argand in 1781. *Left,* a two-wick lamp; *center,* a five-wick lamp; *right,* a three-wick lamp.   *U. S. Coast Guard photo 26-LG-16-38 in the National Archives.*

lighthouses had to await installation of generators. Generators were gradually introduced where power lines did not reach, and during the 1920's and 1930's the Lighthouse Bureau converted the bulk of the lighthouses to electricity. The advent of electricity eventually permitted the elimination of the jobs of many lighthouse keepers. The electric bulb requires little attention; turning it off and on and replacing it when it burns out is about all that is needed. Moreover, since it does not burn a fuel, the electric bulb emits no fumes or smoke to dirty lenses and lantern panes. By using a timer switch that turns the light on and off at the proper times, and by installing a multiple bulb holder that moves a new bulb into place when an old one burns out, the Coast Guard has been able to convert many formerly tended lighthouses to automatic ones that need visiting by a keeper but once a week.

Through the years, the lighthouse service experimented with other types of fuel, such as fish oil and olive oil. One interesting experiment occurred in 1803–1804 when the commissioner of revenue instructed the keeper of the Cape Hatteras light to test porpoise oil. The first results were quite favorable, but subsequent tests proved it not quite equal to sperm oil.

Several lighthouses have used natural and coal gas as the illuminant. Experiments with gas were

## From olive oil to automation

The interior of the first-order Fresnel lens at Bodie Island Light Station, North Carolina. Bodie's tower is now unmanned; when one of these 1000-watt electric bulbs burns out, another automatically turns on and rotates into position. *Photo by the author.*

undertaken by the fifth auditor when he had charge of lighthouses and later by the Lighthouse Board. Both found gas unsatisfactory.

The fifth auditor had three lighthouses in Delaware Bay equipped with furnaces and retorts to manufacture coal gas, but the keepers consistently let the furnaces and retorts burn through before announcing a need for new ones, thus forcing the lighthouse to fall back on its auxiliary system: lamps and oil. Even when Pleasonton installed two sets of furnaces and retorts at each lighthouse, he did not solve the problem. The keepers let both sets burn through before calling for replacements. Pleasonton felt the keepers deliberately let the damage occur, because they disliked making gas and favored using the lamps and oil.

During the same period, Pleasonton tested the use of natural gas at the lighthouse at Portland on Lake Erie. But this effort, too, proved unsatisfactory, since water tended to collect in the two miles of pipe leading to the lighthouse and gas would not pass through.

The Lighthouse Board, too, experimented with gas as an illuminant. At the Jones Point light on the Virginia side of the Potomac River, for example, the board sometime before 1866 installed pipes that ran from the Alexandria Gas Works to the lighthouse. Over the years these pipes proved a constant source of trouble from erosion and water, and in 1900 the board had the light converted to use an oil lamp in the Fresnel lens.

A few other lighthouses also used gas, but the Lighthouse Board found that gas was simply not satisfactory as an illuminant, and consequently, gas never really got past the experimental stage in American lighthouses.

# III

# A History of the Administration of Lighthouses

PRACTICALLY everywhere one looks today he will find the lighthouse as a symbol of some business or charitable organization. One of the country's largest newspaper chains, the Scripps-Howard syndicate, has a lighthouse on its masthead. The Lighthouse for the Blind is a well-known charitable group. And one of television's most popular "soap operas," "The Guiding Light," for many years used a lighthouse tower as its symbol.

The reason, of course, for the choice of the lighthouse is that it stands for integrity, constancy, reliability, and an aid when most needed. Such is the reputation the lighthouse has today. But this was not always the case in the United States. Indeed, by the middle of the nineteenth century, the country's lighthouses came under severe criticism for their poor lights, improper location, and poor administration. But to understand their decline and subsequent redemption, one needs an understanding of the changing administration of aids to navigation through the years.

## A Federal Responsibility

During the colonial period each of the thirteen colonies had been responsible for its own aids to navigation. The colonies established and placed lights to satisfy local needs and concerned themselves not with other lights on the coast.

Soon after its formation, however, the federal government realized that lighthouses and other aids to navigation were a national concern. As a result, on August 7, 1789, Congress passed an act assuming to the central government responsibility for all aids to navigation and took over all lighthouses then in operation, as well as four that were under construction.

Congress placed the aids to navigation in the Treasury Department and there they remained under the supervision of various officials until the twentieth century, when for a time governmental reorganization shoved them into the Commerce Department and in more recent years, after a brief return to Treasury, into the Transportation Department.

At first the secretary of the treasury, Alexander Hamilton, after administering them personally for several years, assigned lighthouses in 1792 to the commissioner of revenue. The country was small and high officials could take an interest in the operation of individual lighthouses. Presidents Washington, Adams, and Jefferson personally approved individual lighthouse construction contracts and passed on the appointment and dismissal of keepers. But as the nation's commerce grew so did the lighthouse establishment, and consequently, there were too many other problems facing the president for him to be concerned with the details of the operation of aids to navigation. Most of the president's larger lighthouse duties, such as the approval of contracts and the appointment of keepers, then devolved onto the secretary of the treasury.

## ADVENT OF THE FIFTH AUDITOR

The day-to-day operation of lighthouses and other navigational aids remained with the commissioner of revenue until 1802, when the secretary of the treasury, now Albert Gallatin, resumed direct superintendence of this activity. In 1813, the secretary returned aids to navigation to the commissioner of revenue, who continued to administer them until 1820 when they became the responsibility of the fifth auditor of the treasury.

At this time the fifth auditor was Stephen Pleasonton, a man who, as a government official, reflected his times. He was zealous, hard working, conservative, and an overly conscientious guardian of the public dollar. As fifth auditor he was one of the nation's principal bookkeepers, and he brought to the job of general superintendent of lights the bookkeeper's lack of imagination. He did not have a maritime background or any other experience that particularly suited him to take over the country's aids to navigation.

As fifth auditor Pleasonton was responsible for "the diplomatic, consular, and bankers accounts abroad, and all the accounts at home appertaining to the Department of State and Patent Office, as well as those of the census, boundary commissioners, and awards of commissioners for adjusting claims on foreign Governments." In addition, Pleasonton for a time performed the duties of the commissioner of revenue. In 1842, Pleasonton had working for him a total of nine clerks—five handling the work of the fifth auditor and four engaged in lighthouse business. At that time the lighthouse establishment consisted of 256 lighthouses, 30 floating lights, and a considerable number of beacons and buoys.

Pleasonton became popularly known as the general superintendent of lighthouses. His direct representatives were the local collectors of custom, and those collectors who had lighthouses in their districts were given the additional title of superintendent of lights. Under Pleasonton's supervision these collectors directly administered lighthouses. They handled virtually all personnel matters including the hiring, firing, and paying of keepers; the actual appointment of keepers was done by the secretary of the treasury. The collectors selected sites for lighthouses and purchased the necessary land. They generally saw to the supervision of contractors who erected lighthouses or related structures, and they authorized repairs to lighthouses and paid keepers who had legitimate expenditures. Also, they visited the lighthouses annually to see that all was right with them.

The general superintendent of lights kept a pretty tight watch on the activities of the local superin-

tendents of lights, letting them have little latitude for independent action. They could make only minor decisions without permission of Pleasonton. Prior to 1822, they had to clear all expenditures with Pleasonton, and after that date he allowed them to spend up to $100 without approval. Yet, despite this close watch upon their fiscal responsibilities, Pleasonton relied heavily upon them for knowledge of conditions of individual lighthouses. If he received a complaint about a lighthouse, Pleasonton invariably asked the local superintendent of lights to investigate, and he accepted as virtually gospel whatever the local superintendent reported. In payment for their lighthouse duties, the local collectors of custom received a commission of 2.5 percent on their expenditures for the lighthouse or lighthouses in their districts.

Pleasonton's lack of maritime experience apparently caused him to put a great deal of faith in and reliance upon the professional ability of Winslow Lewis, who did have a nautical background. The relationship between the two contributed materially to the lack of technical progress under the Pleasonton administration; particularly outstanding was Pleasonton's failure to support the adoption of the Fresnel lens in American lighthouses. Lewis, after all, had a vested interest in the lamp-and-reflector system.

*Economy vs. Effectiveness*

During his administration of lighthouses Pleasonton continually pointed with great pride to the economy with which he operated the lighthouse establishment. In 1842, he proudly showed Congress figures indicating that he ran United States lighthouses at less than half the cost at which the Trinity House operated English ones, and that he maintained lightships at one-fourth the cost of those in England. What he failed to mention, and probably did not even recognize, was that the English had a first-rate lighthouse system with first-class lights, while the quality of United States lighthouses left a lot to be desired. Indeed, in 1851 the investigating board that the secretary of the treasury appointed to look into the lighthouse establishment and its operation gave full credit to Pleasonton's zealousness in economy, but in its report issued the following year, the board filled something in the neighborhood of 750 printed pages criticizing the quality

Fourth-order Fresnel lens with incandescent oil vapor lamp. The stand on which the lens is resting contains a clockwork system used to rotate the bulls-eye lenses to achieve a flashing effect. This lens, which has a smooth glass center belt, was used at Fort Point around 1912. *USCG Photo 26-LG-64-34, National Archives.*

of lights, the lighthouses, and the personnel, as well as the general operation of the establishment. In retrospect, one wonders how many ships that wrecked during Pleasonton's thirty-two-year administration would have been saved had more effective lights been available.

From time to time Congress became dissatisfied with the lighthouse service. In 1837, it authorized a considerable number of new lighthouses, apparently at the request of the Treasury Department. Not fully assured in its own mind that the nation's interests required all the lighthouses asked for, Congress provided in the bill that a board of navy commissioners would examine the sites of these lighthouses and determine if the lights were really needed. As a result of the commissioners' work, Congress found that thirty-one of the proposed lighthouses could be eliminated.

### Congress Orders
### the Inspection of 1838

One outgrowth of this inspection was the introduction of professional seamen on a high level to look into the lighthouse situation. An act of June 7, 1838, divided the Atlantic Coast into six districts and the Great Lakes into two. The act designated that a naval officer be assigned to each district, and that he report on the condition of aids to navigation in his district and select sites for new lighthouses.

28

## A crumbling establishment

The officers inspecting the eight districts turned in reports varying in quality and thoroughness. Some of the officers were very conscientious and examined each of the aids to navigation in their districts, although one or two submitted general reports lacking in specifics. Their combined report is the best single picture we have of the country's aids to navigation in this period.

Some of the inspectors noted the bunching of lights. "In two different places on the [Maine] coast," said one, "there are nine lights to be seen at one time, which must confuse the navigator." This condition perhaps reached the ridiculous point at Nauset where the inspector found three lights being built 150 feet apart, a scheme he could not understand, since one light, he felt, would have done. Another inspector observed that whereas the comparatively safe shores of heavily populated areas were liberally dotted with lighthouses, the unsafe shores of unpopulated areas did not have many lights even though those shores saw heavy traffic.

The inspecting officers found the quality of the nation's lighthouses covered a wide spectrum, from very bad to very good. Although they noted structural flaws in some of the lighthouses, the most important and consistent defect they observed centered around the light. In some of the lighthouses, the keepers maintained the lights perfunctorily, and lackadaisically went about the task of cleaning the lamps and reflectors. In some cases the keepers had not shined the reflectors, and where they had, the silver had been worn away because of the abrasive cleaning powder used. At several lights, the inspectors saw Lewis's lenses in front of the lamps; some of these lenses were even cracked, but nevertheless still in use. They commonly found lamps and reflectors out of adjustment. And it was by no means unusual for them to find that the lights had been supplied with lamp chimneys so short they smoked the reflectors, thereby reducing their effectiveness. The reflectors were so thin that cleaning had bent them out of shape, and in some cases it was impossible to determine their original form. Although the lighthouses were supposed to be equipped with parabolic reflectors, the inspectors noted many spherical reflectors in use.

The inspecting officers found a number of towers badly constructed. The most general complaint was an improper fitting of the lantern on the tower which resulted in leaking during wet weather, causing, among other things, a rusting of the revolving machinery. One inspector observed that the best constructed towers were the old ones, while the recently built towers were generally poorly put together. Indeed, the inspector of the Fairweather Island light observed that the tower had pieces of wood, eight inches square and four feet long, inserted every so often among the stone. The mortar had not yet hardened at the twelve-year-old Stony Point light tower, nor at the eleven-year-old Great Captain Island tower. On his inspection of the Fourth District, Lt. William D. Porter observed the contractor building a house at the Sandy Hook light station using saline sand from near the site and not inland sand as called for in the contract. The keeper, who was superintendent of construction on the project, was reluctant to report the contractor; Porter, however, was not. Lt. James T. Homans, while inspecting lights in the Great Lakes, found the Grand River lighthouse contractor using shoddy material and faulty construction techniques. He reported these facts to the fifth auditor, who in turn asked the nearby collector of customs to investigate. The collector later reported that Homan's allegations were completely untrue, that he had found the walls sturdy and good lime and stone being used. Moreover, a number of residents of the area gave the collector a petition saying they had visited the construction site a number of times and had found good work and good materials going into the dwelling and the lighthouse. It is easy to understand why most of these inspectors wound up recommending that construction of lighthouses be supervised by a qualified engineer.

Lightships were not an exception, either, to the generally poor condition of aids to navigation. The inspectors reported that the lightboats, as they were then called, usually were badly built, inadequately rigged, and often too small for their station. Moreover, their anchors were too light, resulting in the ships being easily blown off station. The ships were apparently commonly lighted with compass lamps, each having ten wicks protruding from it. The crews were not always the most dedicated, for the inspectors found in several instances that the captain and the crew had left the ship en masse. In one case they had been gone a week and had left the ship in charge of a fourteen-year-old Negro lad, who did not possess the strength to raise the heavy light to the top of the mast.

Not all lighthouses and lightships were found to be in bad condition and improperly tended, but roughly 40 percent of the lights had serious defects, and that is a significant percentage. The report should have been a red flag of warning to Congress. But for some reason Congress did not then become alarmed enough to take action, and the lighthouses for the next decade or so rocked along pretty much as they had in the past. The report of the inspectors stands today as a preview of the investigation of 1851 when a lighthouse board of inquiry found the same faults, and many more, in the country's aids to navigation.

### Congress Considers a Reorganization

The next step Congress took came four years later and was entirely unrelated to the real problem of the nation's lighthouses: namely, how to obtain first-rate aids to navigation for the country. But the House of Representatives, composed as it is of human beings and political considerations, did not wrestle with this problem, but rather appointed a select committee to look into the operation of several departments of the government to determine whether a realignment of duties would not bring about a reduction in expenses and employment. In examining the Treasury Department, the committee concluded that customs duties should be taken away from the first comptroller and lighthouse duties from the fifth auditor and that these two activities be assigned to a to-be-established commissioner of revenue. Thus Congress, as it sometimes does, missed the point of what was wrong with the nation's aids to navigation; fortunately, the recommendations were not implemented. This move would simply have meant shifting lighthouses from one unknowledgeable administrator to another and would have done nothing about improving aids to navigation. At the same time the move would have acted as an escape valve for the pressure building up to improve these aids, thus postponing for some years the revolution that finally came in less than ten.

At this same time, the Commerce Committee was investigating whether the lighthouse establishment could not be operated more efficiently and less expensively under the supervision of the Bureau of Topographical Engineers. This study apparently was spurred by the report of the district inspectors of 1838, a report, interestingly enough, that the

committee regarded as generally favorable, which probably indicates the competence of the members of the committee to sit in judgment on anything affecting aids to navigation. Pleasonton obviously had kept up his relations with the Committee on Commerce, for the whole tenor of their subsequent report sounds as though Pleasonton himself wrote it. The committee decided that the system worked "tolerably well," and that Pleasonton's twenty-two years of experience as administrator of lighthouses gave him "a practical knowledge . . . which should not, for slight causes, be lost to the public." They concluded that about all that was needed was an improvement in the inspection system, and that transfer of lighthouse responsibilities from the Treasury Department "is not called for by the public good."

During this investigation Pleasonton had not been above exaggerating. He reported to Congress that he had a system for the classification of lighthouses. First-class lighthouses had lamps with eighteen-inch reflectors, second-class lighthouses had fourteen-inch ones, and third-class lighthouses used nine-inch reflectors. He didn't report a class for those lighthouses with bent reflectors. Pleasonton also reported a general classification of lighthouses based on the height of the tower. First-class lighthouses were sixty-five feet tall and had twenty-one lights, or panes, in the lantern; second-class were fifty feet tall and had a lantern with twenty-one panes one inch smaller than those in first-class towers; third-class structures were forty feet high and had lanterns containing eighteen panes; and fourth-class towers were thirty feet tall and held lanterns with eighteen lights one inch smaller than third-class lanterns. Actually, for all practical purposes there was no basis for a meaningful classification of United States lighthouses. Anyway, at about this time Pleasonton began introducing twenty-one-inch reflectors and modifying lanterns to hold much larger panes. Moreover, in 1851 Pleasonton said there was no formal classification of lighthouses. It would appear that the general superintendent of lights was exaggerating the situation in 1842, perhaps to give to an aroused Congress the appearance of more system to the lighthouse establishment than actually existed.

### Lighthouse Administration under Pleasonton

Pleasonton, during his tenure as general superintendent of lights, carried on the tradition of his

The lamp shop force at the Staten Island Depot, New York, the main service and supply depot of the light-house service, in 1890. *U. S. Coast Guard photo 26-LG-16-7 in the National Archives.*

predecessors; that is, he did not have a professional organization under his direction. Actually, he and his staff in Washington were clerical administrators contracting for everything needed to maintain aids to navigation. He contracted with a builder to erect the lighthouses, with shipyards to build lightships, with Winslow Lewis, usually, to install the lighting apparatus, with an oil merchant to supply the whale oil for the lights, and with builders for lighthouse repairs beyond the capability of the keepers. Toward the end Pleasonton did employ a vessel to visit the lighthouses and bring oil and other supplies—but he had just one tender to serve all the country's lighthouses and lightships. Master of the vessel was Captain Jonathan Howland, and he

visited each lighthouse once a year to deliver oil and supplies. Originally having worked for the oil contractor, Howland in 1839 hired his ship and crew to the government and thereafter engaged entirely in lighthouse business. Howland had aboard a lampist whose duty it was to see that the lighting apparatus of each lighthouse was in good working order.

During the construction of a lighthouse, the government's interests were protected by a supervisor hired by the fifth auditor. This supervisor was to see that the contractor followed the specifications outlined in the contract and that he did not use inferior material or substitute another ingredient for one called for in the contract, or take any short-cuts in construction. From the evidence presently available, it would appear that construction experience was not necessarily a prerequisite for being hired as a construction overseer. During the construction of the first Bodie Island lighthouse in 1847, for example, the construction supervisor was the former collector of customs at Washington, North Carolina. The ex-collector was not wholly without experience, since at one time he had been a local superintendent of lights. He obviously lacked construction knowledge, however, for at the time of building, the supervisor instructed the contractor to lay a brick foundation which was counter to the instructions of Pleasonton, who felt that a pile foundation was first needed. The result was that the brick foundation did not do the job, and within two years the lighthouse was canted to eastward, throwing the revolving light out of kilter and thus necessitating extensive and expensive repair work to the tower and the lighting apparatus. But even that work was a temporary repair, for within ten years after the completion of the lighthouse, Congress had to appropriate money to completely rebuild the Bodie Island tower.

The administrative organization that Pleasonton had when he took over administration of lighthouses was adequate to handle the small lighthouse service of fifty-five lighthouses that existed in 1820. But during his administration the lighthouse establishment grew considerably, and he, as well as Congress, clung to the original administrative arrangement, which was about like trying to run the modern United States Navy by the same methods and techniques employed during the Spanish-American War. The growth in size of the lighthouse establishment had been phenomenal. In 1800, the country had 16 lighthouses; by 1812 the number had grown to 49; and by 1822 there were 70. There were 204 lighthouses and 28 lightboats in 1838, and in 1842 the lighthouse establishment consisted of 256 lighthouses, 30 lightboats, 35 beacons, and nearly 1,000 buoys. By 1852, there were 331 lighthouses and 42 lightships. Pleasonton did not realize that this great growth demanded completely new thinking on how most effectively to administer lighthouses and provide the best light for the mariner.

Pleasonton's technique for selecting the site for a lighthouse was to have the local superintendent of lights gather a group of local pilots and active and retired seamen and go with them to select a site. This method did not always result in the best location of lighthouses, because the sites were often selected without regard to adjacent lighthouses or without knowledge of the adequacy of the spot as the foundation for a light tower.

There is no question that Pleasonton was a conscientious, hardworking bureaucrat, but in his administration of lighthouses he rather had his eye upon the hole and not upon the doughnut. He emphasized administration and economy in the operation of the lighthouse service; as a guardian of the public dollar, he is without a doubt one of the finest American bureaucracy has produced. In his quest for economy, all he sacrificed was quality. In Pleasonton's defense it has to be mentioned that he generally faced a parsimonious Congress, and undoubtedly the attitude of Congress influenced his emphasis on economy. Moreover, Pleasonton labored in the days when politics riddled the lighthouse service and most of the keepers were political appointees who, as a group, were not extremely conscientious.

Pleasonton failed to recognize that he was dealing with lives and that his responsibility was to the seaman in seeing that the best aid possible was available to him when he sailed in American waters. There are many examples of this attitude, but only one need be cited. In 1826, a particularly violent storm off the coast of North Carolina blew the Diamond Shoals lightship from its mooring, leaving the expensive anchor and most of its cable on the bottom of the ocean. Because the lighthouse service did not have a spare anchor and cable, the lightship was kept off station for about five months. For two of those months Pleasonton took no action because he had hoped to recover the anchor and cable by offering a $500 reward, thus encouraging private individuals to search for the items. He thought the reward would be less expensive than buying a new anchor and cable. In the end his scheme did not work, and he had to buy the anchor and cable. During this period Diamond Shoals remained unlighted. Although he had run a grave risk, present evidence indicates that Pleasonton's luck held; no ship piled up on the Diamond Shoals during the absence of the light vessel.

Pleasonton was not unaware of technological progress, especially concerning the development and adoption of the Fresnel lens. As early as 1830, he wrote to France inquiring about the new lens that the French lighthouse service had adopted. In a subsequent reply France informed him that a first-order lens cost $5,000 and a third-order one $2,000; he quickly decided they were too expensive for United States lighthouses. In 1838, Congress forced him to obtain two of the lenses, one of the first order and one of the second, and to place them at the two Navesink, New Jersey, lighthouses. A mechanic, imported from France and familiar with the Fresnel lens, completed fitting the two lenses in March of 1841. The two lenses, installation included, cost nearly $24,000, and the fifth auditor said, "The cost of these lenses, however, is nothing compared to the beauty and excellence of the light they afford. They appear to be the perfection of apparatus for lighthouse purposes, having in view only the superiority of the light, which is reported by the pilots to be seen in clear weather a distance of forty miles." After this gush of enthusiasm, his natural bureaucratic conservatism took over, and he said that the lamps used in the lenses were of the Carcel type and so complicated that most lighthouse keepers could not operate them; consequently, the lenses could be installed only in lighthouses near cities where adequately trained mechanics would be available as lighthouse keepers. Anyway, he later said, the portee, or reach, of the United States' reflector lights was equivalent to that from Fresnel lenses, although "the light from the lenses . . . is unquestionably better."

Despite what could be considered a favorable attitude toward the Fresnel lens, Pleasonton continued to act as a stumbling block, and in the next ten years the United States acquired only two other lenses.

For thirty-two years Pleasonton managed to hold on to the lighthouse service, and during that time his critics were vocal. A particularly sticky time came in 1842 when Winslow Lewis's nephew, I. W. P. Lewis, a civil engineer, publicly attacked his uncle's competence as a lighthouse expert. He stated that Winslow's lighting system had been copied from the apparatus at the South Stack lighthouse of Holyhead in England. He contended, moreover, that Winslow Lewis's reflectors only approached the paraboloid in form. His accusations were contained in a report he had been asked to make on the lighthouses of Maine and Massachusetts, and

in the report he went on to point out the deficiencies of individual lighthouses and the deficiencies of his uncle as a builder of lighthouses. Pleasonton quickly responded that the report contained "misrepresentations . . . made by persons who had no interest whatever in commerce or navigation. . . ." He maintained that the lights were quite good and that it was simply untrue that the lights could be seen only a short distance. He proudly stated that he consistently built lighthouses for less than Congress appropriated and that no bureau of the federal government turned back to the general fund more money than his did. Winslow Lewis's own reply, privately printed, was far more colorful and vituperative. He regarded his nephew's report as a personal attack, and so he, too, resorted to the personal. He called his nephew incompetent and a plagiarizer, thus calling his nephew the same things his nephew had originally called him. I. W. P. Lewis's report, he said, was filled with nothing but falsehoods. Winslow exhibited amazement that such an obviously untrained, unqualified person could have been selected to examine lighthouses. Lewis family reunions must have been cordial affairs in those days.

Through the years, Pleasonton's chief antagonists were E. and G. W. Blunt, who published the *American Coast Pilot*, the most useful aid then available to the mariner to help him navigate the coast of the United States and to help him identify lighthouses and other aids to navigation. The Blunts acted as a funnel for complaints about the country's aids to navigation, sending seamen's complaints on to congressmen and others.

## THE INVESTIGATION OF 1851

As time went on, the crescendo of complaints from this and other sources built up to a point where Congress felt it had to take firm action. In 1847, it took away construction of six lighthouses from the fifth auditor and placed them under the jurisdiction of the Corps of Engineers. But that action did not solve the basic problem, and in 1851 Congress took the final step. In the treasury's appropriation act of March of that year Congress "authorized and required" the secretary of the treasury to convene a board composed of two high-ranking naval officers, two army engineering officers, a civilian "of high scientific attainment," and a junior officer of the navy to act as secretary of the board. The secretary of the treasury, Thomas Corwin, appointed Commodore William B. Shubrick, Commander S. F. DuPont, Brevet Brigadier General Joseph G. Totten, Lieutenant Colonel James Kearney, Professor A. D. Bache, and Lieutenant Thornton A. Jenkins; the latter was the junior naval officer designated to serve as secretary. At the same time, Corwin instructed the board to look into every aspect of the lighthouse establishment, including methods of lighting, all phases of construction, management of the system, effectiveness of the lights, procuring of supplies, the way the lighthouses were operated, and efficiency and economy of operation. In other words, the board was to inquire into every minute detail of the country's lighthouse system. And in the end the board did just that.

It is doubtful that any agency prior to that time, or perhaps subsequently, went through such a searching inspection. The board's report consisted of 760 pages, plus numerous plates. The members literally poked their light into all the darkened crannies and corners of the lighthouse system, and in addition they compared this country's system of lighting with that of England and France. They examined the management of the system; personally inspected lighthouses from Portland, Maine, to Cape Fear, North Carolina; examined lighting apparatuses (including the oil and cleaning materials used); questioned keepers; studied the spacing of aids to navigation; inquired of numerous ships' masters what they thought of United States lighthouses; and looked into expenditures and methods of supplying the lighthouses and lightships. They found nothing right with United States lighthouses.

The board concluded that the lighthouse establishment was poorly managed from standpoints of both administration and economy. Moreover, it found that the towers were not tall enough to give proper range to the lights; that the spacing of the lighthouses was poor, that they were bunched in populous areas and widely scattered in sparsely settled areas; that keepers were poorly trained and many were incompetent; that lightships were "defective in size, model, and moorings"; that there was "no systematic plan adopted on any part of the coast of the United States for rendering navigation safe and easy by means of lights, beacons, buoys, &c., &c."; that the method of procuring and distributing supplies was inefficient and uneconomi-

cal; that light towers were badly constructed; and so on and on and on.

Perhaps most damning of all was the testimony of many seamen that they often could not see or distinguish the lights. The board was highly critical of the lighting apparatuses, saying that the lamps and reflectors were a type "now nearly obsolete throughout all maritime countries, where the best apparatus of that description was employed, prior to the introduction of the Fresnel lenses, as substitutes," and that they were "greatly inferior to the requirements of the service, being defective in form, materials, and finish." Moreover, the lamps and reflectors were poorly manufactured and badly maintained. The board found that the best lights were those fitted with Fresnel lenses, and those so equipped were the only lights in the United States that could compare favorably with European lights.

Almost as a sop, the investigating board recognized the tremendous growth in the number of aids to navigation that had occurred between 1820 and 1851, and it said that "great credit is due to the zeal and faithfulness of the present general superintendent, and to the spirit of economy which he has shown."

In conclusion the board said:

In investigating the subjects confided to them, [the members of the board] have endeavored to reach the truth from observation and research. That they have not done injustice to any one, they feel perfectly conscious; to have passed over palpable defects in the present management of our lights, involving great loss of human life and property, without pointing them out, would have been culpable and unpardonable; and that they have looked as leniently as possible on many points considered exceptionable, it is believed will be clearly shown by their report.

The board have not sought so much to discover defects and point them out, as to show the necessity for a better system. Commerce and navigation, in which every citizen of this nation is interested, either directly or indirectly, claim it; the weather-beaten sailor asks it, and humanity demands it.

To solve the problems of the lighthouse establishment, the board proposed a complete revamping of the system. Following the examples of England, Scotland, Ireland, and France, countries noted for

District lens-repair shop in Buffalo, New York, 1901. Note the fixed Fresnel lens standing near the workbench at the back of the shop. On the center bench are the wheels on which a rotating lens rested and turned, and also the "guts" of the clockwork mechanism. *U. S. Coast Guard photo 26-LG-43-43 in the National Archives.*

their fine aids to navigation and whose aids were guided by groups of people representing several professions, they suggested that a nine-member lighthouse board be established. In addition to the six composing the investigating board, it would have an additional civilian scientist and a second secretary drawn from the army engineers. The ninth member would be the secretary of the treasury, who would be the ex-officio president of the group. To provide on-the-ground professional supervision of lighthouses, the board recommended that an inspector be appointed in each lighthouse district; the inspector would be either an army engineering officer or a naval officer. The board would have complete control of the aids to navigation and would issue rules and regulations for the management of the lighthouse establishment and instructions to the keepers for the proper operation of a lighthouse. In addition, the board would devise a system of classification for lighthouses. Moreover, they urged the adoption of the Fresnel lens. In the appropriation act of 1851, Congress had authorized the secretary of the treasury to adopt the Fresnel lenses, if he thought "the public interest will be subserved thereby." It urged that the lens be adopted in the newly authorized lighthouses.

*The Creation of the Lighthouse Board (1852)*

Congress, with little hesitation, bought the proposed administrative system, and on October 9, 1852, created the nine-member Lighthouse Board. Commodore William B. Shubrick and Commander S. F. DuPont were the naval members; Brig. Gen. Joseph G. Totten represented the Corps of Topographical Engineers and Lt. Col. James Kearney the army engineers; A. D. Bache, superintendent of the Coast Survey, and Joseph Henry, first secretary of the Smithsonian and one of the country's leading physicists, were the civilian scientist members; Lt. Thornton A. Jenkins was the naval secretary; and Capt. E. L. F. Hardcastle was the engineering secretary. The secretary of the treasury was ex-officio president of the board. Shubrick was the chairman.

The new Lighthouse Board had a huge job ahead of it, and its members went about their work with the will of men dedicated to public service. Following its proposed organization, the board redivided the country into twelve new lighthouse districts. The First District began at the St. Croix River in Maine, and the Twelfth District embraced the west coast of the United States. They appointed an inspector in each district and he was "charged with building the lighthouses, with keeping them in repair, and with the purchase, the setting up, and the repairs of the illuminating apparatus." Although the local collectors of custom were retained as superintendents of lights, their responsibilities were reduced. Their duties were primarily fiscal and administrative; they saw to the appointing and paying of keepers and the disbursing of funds for routine lighthouse operation. As the years went on, the local superintendents' duties were further eroded, and in time they had no lighthouse responsibilities.

Within a few years, the Lighthouse Board found that the duties of the district inspectors had expanded so greatly that they felt it necessary to appoint in each district an engineer. The inspector, who was a naval officer, had general superintendence of the lighthouses in his district, being responsible for the disbursing of funds for salaries and supplies and seeing that the keepers were performing their duties adequately. He inspected each light station every three months and reported any deficiencies or repairs needed. The district engineer, an army officer, supervised the building of new light stations and the repair of old ones.

The Lighthouse Board also set up a central depot for the dispersing of supplies to light stations and light vessels. Located at Staten Island, the depot was under the aegis of the inspector of the Third Lighthouse District. In time, however, the board established a depot in each district, and these depots directly supplied the lighthouses and light vessels; the Staten Island depot shipped the supplies and materials to the district depots. For the Atlantic and Gulf coast districts, the supplies and materials were sent by a lighthouse tender, but for the West Coast and Great Lakes districts the goods were sent by rail. One of the principal duties of the central depot was to test the oil used in all the lighthouses.

Under the Lighthouse Board, aids to navigation in the United States improved dramatically. Most important, the board put the emphasis in the right place: their primary concern was that there would

always be a good light where the mariner needed a warning. Toward that end they lighted the darkened sections of the coast with new lighthouses, beacons, and lightships, and saw—indeed, demanded —that the keepers maintain a good light. The board didn't hesitate to fire a keeper who had to be warned a second time about keeping a bad light, unless there were mechanical or other difficulties beyond the capacity of the keeper to repair. The board raised many of the old light towers to give greater range to the light by overcoming a larger arc of the earth's curve. The members of the board brought their experience and knowledge to all levels of the lighthouse service, and, most important, they constantly sought good keepers and trained them to their task, giving them adequate and explicit instructions in writing. They experimented with new techniques of lighting and with different fuels. Although they were just as economy-conscious as the fifth auditor had been, they were not penurious. They kept spare equipment on hand; if a lens became damaged beyond repair, it was quickly replaced, and if a lightship was driven from its station and became too damaged to return, a relief vessel was immediately used until repairs could be made.

One of the board's more important contributions was the issuing of annual *Light Lists*, listing, describing, and showing the location of all the aids to navigation in service in the United States. It also set up a system of corrections called Notices to Mariners, telling the seamen of the establishment of new aids or changes in old ones that occurred between the annual issues of the *Light List*. It is a system that has continued down to today, and now is perhaps of even greater importance in this age of much faster sea transportation.

The board raised the reputation of the United States' lighthouses from the bottom of the heap to the top, and set the establishment on the road along which it has since led the world: developing and utilizing new techniques, equipment, and methods in providing the mariner with the latest and fullest aids to make his occupation safer.

*The Bureau of Lighthouses (1910)*

As time went on, though, the nine-member Lighthouse Board proved to be too cumbersome an administrative head to manage effectively and efficiently the country's aids to navigation. In 1910, Congress abolished the Lighthouse Board and created in its stead the Bureau of Lighthouses, headed by one man. The Bureau was retained in the Commerce Department, to which lighthouses had been transferred in 1903. In addition to eliminating the hydra-headed administration at the top, the act also had one other basic purpose: to do away with the distinct military cast of the lighthouse service.

From the very beginning, the Lighthouse Board had been dominated by the military. The act creating the board specifically stated that seven of its nine members would be from the army or navy. Moreover, the district inspectors and engineers were navy and army officers. Congress desired to eliminate this paramountcy of the military and create a civilian aura around this primarily civilian service. Consequently, the act specifically restricted the assignment of officers of the army and navy to the Lighthouse Service. The act, however, did state that the president could detail officers from the army engineers for consultative and/or supervisory duties related to construction. The commissioner of lighthouses gave a broad interpretation to this stipulation and assigned an officer from the Corps of Engineers to each district. This officer had virtually no role in the district's administrative hierarchy, although he had the title of superintendent. He reported solely to the civilian district inspector and concerned himself almost entirely with construction and repair work in the district.

The act also provided for a reorganization of the lighthouse service, and gave the commissioner permission to increase the number of districts to not more than nineteen; each district was to be headed by an inspector, who, two years after passage of the act, was to be a civilian. By August, 1912, civilians headed all but three of the districts, and these civilians for the most part were career lighthouse service employees. This reorganization reflects the tremendous growth in this country's aids to navigation from the time of the formation of the Lighthouse Board to the establishment of the Bureau of Lighthouses. In 1910, there were 11,713 aids of all types. By 1913, the lighthouse establishment consisted of 12,824 aids to navigation of all classes, including 1,462 lights above the status of river post lights, 51 lightships, and over 7,000 buoys of all types. In addition, the service had 46 tenders. Also, by this time, aids to navigation on the country's rivers had been added to the responsibilities of the lighthouse service.

The Bureau of Lighthouses inherited a far more efficiently functioning system than had the Lighthouse Board fifty-eight years before. Changes that the act of 1910 made in the lighthouse establishment did not alter the basic pattern of organization the board had created. The Lighthouse Board had rendered a distinct and valuable service to the nation and to humanity. It had taken a third-rate lighthouse system that was poorly organized and badly administered and transformed it into a first-class lighting system that ranked with the best in the world. This task was accomplished because of, rather than in spite of, the military dominance of the lighthouse service. Lighthouse duty attracted well-trained and dedicated military people, far better types than would have been found if the lighthouse service at that time had had only civilians to draw upon. The country owes a tremendous debt of gratitude to the Lighthouse Board and its military members.

The man selected to head up the new Bureau of Lighthouses was George R. Putnam, a man whose background was completely non-military. Putnam was a remarkable man. Born in Davenport, Iowa, on the Mississippi River in 1865, he first began the study of law, perhaps motivated by the fact that his father was an attorney. Within a year, however, he turned to engineering and attended Rose Polytechnic Institute in Indiana. On graduation he joined the Coast and Geodetic Survey and spent the next twenty years map making. He was on the survey to Alaska that established the southeast boundary of that territory and in the process denied a port to Canada which would have given her better communication with the Klondike gold strike region. He went to Greenland with Peary in 1896 to retrieve the large meteorite "Ahnighito" that had fallen near Cape York. Putnam's duties were to take magnetic and gravity measurements. The following year he was sent to the Bering Sea to survey the Pribilof Islands, and the next two years he participated in surveying and mapping the mouth of the Yukon River to make that area safer for the increased shipping traffic caused by the gold strike. In 1900, he was appointed director of coast surveys in the Philippines and for the next six years he supervised the surveying and charting of coasts of these islands, which, for the most part, had never been accurately mapped. While here, his path crossed that of William Howard Taft, who had been appointed governor of the islands. After Putnam completed a four-year tour of duty in the Coast and Geodetic Survey office in Washington, Taft offered him the newly created position of commissioner of lighthouses. He took the job, he said, on the understanding that politics would remain outside the lighthouse service, and during his long tenure of service he apparently was successful in this endeavor. When he selected the inspectors to head the districts, he chose career government employees, most of whom were veterans of the lighthouse service, although there was pressure to appoint friends of politicians. Edward C. Ruland and Ralph H. Goddard were both district superintendents who had long careers in the lighthouse service. Ruland entered the organization in 1887 as mate of a tender. In time he received his master's license and served as skipper of several tenders until his appointment as inspector of the fifth district in 1912.

Goddard started even farther down the ladder. He began his career as a fireman aboard one of the service's vessels in 1887. Later he became a ship's assistant engineer, and in 1904 he took duty ashore as a supply clerk in the Third District. After a tour of duty as assistant district engineer, he moved in 1910 into the position of general storekeeper of the Third District. Two years later, Putnam appointed him inspector of the Second District.

During Putnam's twenty-five years as commissioner, the lighthouse establishment continued to grow at a prodigious rate. The number of aids to navigation of all classes more than doubled, and at the same time the number of employees decreased by nearly 20 percent. This decrease was due in large part to an increased adoption of automatic aids to navigation and to technological advance, such as the use of electricity in lighthouses, that reduced the needed attention to lighthouses. By 1924, the United States lighthouse service was the largest such organization in the world; it had 16,888 aids to navigation. At the same time it had more automatic equipment than any other country.

During Putnam's tenure major advancements were made with the introduction of radio beacons to aid the navigator, the use of the electric buoy, and the application of electricity to fog signals. One of his finest administrative achievements came in

1918, when Congress enacted a retirement system for field employees and those serving on lightships.

### The Coast Guard Takes Over (1939)

Four years after Putnam retired, the Presidential Reorganization Act of 1939, in another one of those moves "in the interest of economy and efficiency" that aids to navigation had gone through so many times before, abolished the lighthouse service and incorporated its activities into the U. S. Coast Guard. On July 7, 1939, the Lighthouse Bureau went out of existence and its personnel moved themselves and their equipment to Coast Guard Headquarters from the Commerce Department building. Thus did lighthouses return to Treasury, the department they had been part of for so long.

Personnel in the lighthouse service were given the opportunity of remaining in a civilian status or of converting to a military position in the Coast Guard with no loss of pay. The personnel of the lighthouse service split about evenly on the two options, and down to July, 1969, there were still seven civilian lighthouse keepers. But even these men are nearing retirement, and with them will go the last vestiges of the lighthouse service as a separate entity.

The amalgamation of the lighthouse service into the larger Coast Guard organization has not been a bad move. Unquestionably, the bringing together of the nation's activities along the coast into one large organization has brought about greater economy and efficiency, in the same way that consolidation of related industries in the business world brings about cheaper products. Lighthouses, lightships, and other aids to navigation have not suffered, and the United States still ranks in the forefront of the nations providing reliable, first-rate aids to the mariner.

The Coast Guard has continued the progressive attitude started by the Lighthouse Board well over a hundred years ago. They have kept up with improvements in lighting lighthouses and lightships, and introduced loran (long-range navigation) and shoran (short-range navigation) by which the navigator receiving radio signals from Coast Guard stations is able to determine his ship's position. Perhaps the most exciting recent development has been the development of the technological capability to build lighthouses where once only lightships could be placed.

# IV

# The Keeper's Work

NOT MANY groups enjoy as fine a reputation for devotion to duty and heroism as the people who throughout history have manned the world's lighthouses. For the most part their reputation is well deserved.

*Appointments and Competence*

Although keepers are pictured as belonging to an almost heroic breed, they were not always so highly thought of in the United States, particularly in the early days. Too many of the light keepers looked upon their jobs as sinecures on which not a great deal of energy need be spent. This attitude was engendered by the fact that the position of light keeper was often subject to political appointment. The Lighthouse Board was distressed over this situation from its beginning, and did all it could to bring the jobs under a merit system. Despite its efforts and accomplishments, as late as 1874 a writer could lament correctly,

> It is hoped that civil service reform will make its way also into this department of the government service, for the petty though important place of lightkeeper has too often been made a political prize, and thus the service, which requires permanence, has been injured. The politicians of the baser sort have not seldom defeated the best intentions and desires of the [Lighthouse] board, and ousted a good man to put in one "useful at the polls."

Not all light keepers owed their jobs to political connections, but more than a few did, particularly in the years prior to the advent of the Lighthouse Board, and this factor was a handicap under which the fifth auditor labored and about which he could

do little. To a congressman or local politician, the building of a lighthouse in his district meant another plum on the bush of patronage. For example, when the Cape Hatteras lighthouse was authorized in 1794, the local congressman immediately recommended Adam Gaskins, a state legislator from that district, for the position of keeper. Although nearly nine years passed before the contractor completed the structure, Gaskins remained the nominee of the local politicians and got the job over another nominee of more education who wanted to open a school in the vicinity of the cape.

Over fifty years after the Cape Hatteras incident, little had changed in the appointment of keepers. The first keeper of the Point Conception lighthouse in California received his appointment through the efforts of United States Senator William S. Gwin, the chief dispenser of federal patronage in California. The keeper, for a time at least, virtually considered Gwin, in the person of the secretary of the treasury, as his employer, and barely recognized the authority of his immediate supervisor, the local collector of customs, or that of faceless bureaucrats in Washington. When difficulties later arose over his pay, he wound up taking his problems to his local congressman long before he had exhausted avenues available to him through the lighthouse service and the Treasury Department.

George R. Putnam, in his autobiography, mentions that one day while he was commissioner of lighthouses he ran across books of blank forms that were notifications to keepers that they had been replaced. These forms are still in existence in the National Archives and serve as a reminder of those days when politics played so important a role in the lighthouse service that blank forms for dismissing keepers added to the economy of the administration of aids to navigation.

Once the keeper had a job, particularly in the early days, there was no assurance that someone would not try to displace him, by fair means or foul. In 1816–1817, for example, the Cape Hatteras light had a notorious reputation, and some local people took advantage of this condition to undertake an assault upon the keeper's job. The most articulate wrote the secretary of the treasury complaining of the light, saying that it was burning bright and clear at the beginning of the night but was permitted to go out after a few hours. He implied further that the keeper was in collusion with wreckers on the Outer Banks. Moreover, he continued, the keeper was a vendue master (i.e., he conducted auctions of the goods of wrecked vessels), thus benefiting from the tragedy of shipwreck. The letter writer's motives had a false ring, since at the same time he questioned the integrity of the Cape Hatteras keeper, he was urging the appointment of a fellow townsman as keeper of the Cape Hatteras light.

Captain Bunker, keeper of the Nantucket light, underwent a similar experience in 1829. Someone circulated a petition accusing Bunker of "intemperate habits" and urging his removal. The petition, signed by a number of citizens and ship owners, recommended the appointment of one George Swain as keeper, thus indicating the probable instigator of the petition. On receiving the petition, the fifth auditor conducted an investigation that resulted in Bunker being retained.

Stephen Pleasonton, with rare exceptions, had all investigations to determine the correctness of charges of incompetence against keepers undertaken by the local collector of customs under whom the light came. Since the collector and the keeper were usually political appointees and presumably loyal to the party in power, the suspicious part of one's mind wonders if perhaps a prime motive of the investigation was to test the political climate to see if the keeper had fallen from grace politically.

The Lighthouse Board in its investigation of 1851 found the interest and ability of keepers "was very various" and advocated testing keepers prior to their selection. After the board took charge of the country's lighthouses, it did all it could to minimize the effect of politics on appointment of keepers. To a degree the board was successful, but the nomination of keepers continued to be the responsibility of the local collectors of custom, who were themselves political appointees. The collectors were a thorn in the side of the board, at times removing keepers and assistant keepers to make way for political favorites. Nevertheless, the board kept plugging away at improving the quality of the keepers. It set up standards that applicants for keepers' positions had to meet, and in time established a probationary period of three months, after which the district inspector or engineer tested the employee on his duties; failure of the probationer to pass the test meant dismissal.

*A Career Service*

The efforts of the board were helped considerably with the passage of the Civil Service Reform Acts of 1871 and 1883, but keepers' positions were not included in the classified civil service until President Grover Cleveland's executive order of May 6, 1896. Unquestionably, the board felt a great deal of glee and relief when President Cleveland issued his proclamation, and each member must have felt some elation when the board could later write to the district engineers:

The Board invites your attention to the rules for the government of Local Civil Service Boards, and requests you to take the proper steps to have eligible lists established in your District, so that, whenever vacancies occur in any positions coming under the jurisdiction of the Local Civil Service Boards, you will have a list from which to nominate a suitable successor.

In the meantime, the efforts of the board to create a career service had not been completely unsuccessful. As the second half of the nineteenth century progressed, an increased number of people rose through the ranks from lesser positions to that of keeper and transferred about from lighthouse to lighthouse, gradually rising in rank. It is interesting to look at the old ledgers in which the Lighthouse Board kept its list of keepers for individual lighthouses and peruse the column on the far right side which is entitled "How Vacated." In the 1850's and 1860's, this column is filled with either "Dismissed" or "Resigned," but in subsequent years the terms "Transferred" and "Promoted" begin to appear and gradually increase in frequency so that by the end of the century they are the dominant terms.

## Ten brass buttons and a badge

Another move the Lighthouse Board made to further the image of a career service was to introduce a uniform for male lighthouse keepers, as well as for masters, mates, and engineers of light vessels and tenders. The board prescribed dress and fatigue uniforms to go into effect in 1884. The dress uniform consisted of a coat, vest, trousers, and cap, all of "suitable dark indigo-blue jersey or flannel." A double row of five yellow metal buttons ran down the front of the double-breasted coat and a yellow metal lighthouse badge perched on the cap just above the visor. There was an optional canvas helmet for warm weather. The board gave the first uniform to affected employees, a task it finished in 1885. By that time there were some 1,600 employees in uniform.

By the turn of the century, the lighthouse service was a full-fledged career field. In the reorganization act of 1910 whereby Congress wanted to impart a civilian cast to the service, most of the civilian inspectors selected to head the various districts were career employees with long service in the lighthouse establishment, many of them having begun their careers at such tasks as seaman on board a lightship or as supply clerk in a district depot.

### Discrimination

Although the lighthouse service from its earliest days discriminated against Negroes (regulations in 1835 specifically forbade their hiring aboard lightships except as cooks), the Negro was nevertheless present throughout the history of American lighthouses. When George Worthylake, the country's first keeper, and his family drowned on their way back to the Boston lighthouse, a Negro slave died with them. At the time of the Seminole War, the Indians attacked the Cape Florida lighthouse which was manned by a keeper and a Negro companion; the slave subsequently died at the hands of the attackers. There are a number of recorded instances of Negro men serving aboard early light vessels as cooks.

It was a rare occupation that did not discriminate against the Negro in the nineteenth century, and lighthouse keeping was not one of those rare occupations. So far no evidence has turned up that a black man attained any position of responsibility, such as keeper.

An interesting contrast in attitudes toward the capability of non-whites is reflected by the keepers of the Gay Head lighthouse in Massachusetts and the Cape Hatteras lighthouse in North Carolina. At the former, the keeper hired nearby Indians in preference to Negroes because he felt the aborigines more competent, and at the latter, the keeper received his walking papers for using his Negro slaves to tend the light.

The advent of the Lighthouse Board did not mark the arrival of a more enlightened attitude. In fact, in 1862 the board issued an order that the hire of Negroes would require special dispensation from Washington. The board did on occasion give permission to hire blacks; for example, during the Civil War a short-lived lightship reestablished in South Carolina was manned solely by Negroes. The present evidence indicates, nevertheless, that throughout the nineteenth century and early twentieth, the lighthouse establishment was pretty much a lily-white organization.

It was not, however, an all-male organization, and there are numerous instances in the records of women serving as assistant keepers and even as keepers. The ledgers in the National Archives showing the lists of keepers and assistant keepers are generously sprinkled with names of women, usually the wives of keepers, who served as assistant keepers. In the 1870's, for example, Robert D. Israel, keeper of the Point Loma light in California, had his wife Mary as his assistant. According to family tradition, she stood her watches and when not actually tending the lamp, sat at the bottom of the spiral stairway and sewed by the light that beamed down through the clockwork weight hole in the deck of the lantern.

For many years, Mrs. Abbie Grant, herself the daughter of a lighthouse keeper, held an appointment as assistant keeper of the Whitehead Light Station in Maine. She began work at the same time the Lighthouse Board appointed her husband keeper. Both served in these positions for many years.

Mrs. Julia F. Williams succeeded her husband in 1865 as keeper of the one-man Santa Barbara lighthouse in California. Each night for forty years, the transplanted New Englander climbed the stairs of the tower about sundown to light the lamp, again at midnight to trim the wick and check the oil supply, and once more around sunrise to blow out the lamp. An immaculate housekeeper and marvelous

Mrs. Mary Israel, the wife of Capt. Robert D. Israel, long-time keeper of the Point Loma lighthouse in San Diego. Mrs. Israel served for three years as assistant keeper at her husband's light. *From the Israel Collection, Cabrillo National Monument.*

cook, the wiry, duty-conscious woman served until she was eighty-one, and probably would have worked longer had she not broken her hip.

Probably almost all of the United States' lighthouses whose histories go back at least to the 1800's at one time or another had female assistant keepers; and a surprising number had women as principal keepers. Point Pinos, today the West Coast's oldest active lighthouse, during its career has had two women who served as principal keepers. The Biloxi, Mississippi, light, Robbins Reef light in New York harbor, and Sambo Key light in Florida are but a few additional examples of lighthouses that had women as principal keepers.

The last of the lady lighthouse keepers was Mrs. Fannie Salter, who retired in 1947 as keeper of the

## Barely adequate

Turkey Point lighthouse in Chesapeake Bay. She had succeeded her husband in this position upon his death in 1925.

### Compensation

The pay of the keepers of lighthouses and lightships has never been munificent; it could perhaps be best described as barely adequate. Worthylake, the country's first lighthouse keeper, received £50 per year; at the same time he was permitted to serve as a harbor pilot. A few years later the keeper's salary was raised £20 and at the same time the colonial government designated the keeper as chief pilot of the port so that he would get preference on piloting jobs and thus supplement his income.

By the time of the arrival of the nineteenth century, the salaries were still low; they ran generally $200–$250 per year. In 1803, the Cape Hatteras keeper's salary was established at $250, and two years later the Treasury Department raised the Gay Head keeper's salary from $200 to $250 per year, and then ten years later added another $50 per annum.

Over the next several decades, the salaries of keepers steadily rose and by the mid-1840's the keeper's salary was in the neighborhood of $400. In the early 1850's, the salary for east-coast light keepers ran $400 to $600 per year while first assistant keepers received half those amounts. On the West Coast, however, where keepers were hard to come by because of the attraction of the gold fields, the keeper's salary was established at $1,000 and the assistant's at $650.

About this time, Congress set the average pay of light keepers at $600 per year, and it remained there until well into the twentieth century. The pay on the West Coast remained at $1,000 except for a brief period, 1859–1861, when it dropped to $800.

Despite the pay, which everyone except Congress acknowledged as being low, the Lighthouse Board remained scrupulous in holding keepers responsible for equipment supplied by the government. The board made the person in the service pay for equipment lost through his negligence. In 1891, for example, the board determined that the boat assigned to the Point Loma lighthouse had been lost through carelessness of the keeper, and, over protestations of the keeper, began deducting the cost of the boat —$50—from his salary.

For many years the Lighthouse Service had no retirement system. Congress remedied this situation on June 20, 1918, when it passed an act that permitted retirement at age sixty-five with thirty years of service and compulsory retirement at age seventy. Only field employees were affected, but they could get up to three-quarters of their annual salary.

### Keeping the Light

Through the years light keepers have had one common primary duty: to maintain a good light for the mariner to see. To perform this task effectively, the keeper, particularly in the early years, had to do many things. In the days of the spider lamp, his chores included keeping the oil reservoirs full, the wicks lighted, and the panes of the lantern free of the smoke that inevitably resulted from such primitive lamps.

When the Argand lamps and parabolic reflectors came into use the keepers' duties were not lessened; if anything, they were increased. In addition to tending a dozen or more lamps, the keeper had to keep the reflectors clean, which was a burdensome task, especially after the introduction of the shortened chimneys that so rapidly blackened the reflectors.

How did keepers in the years prior to 1852 perform? Some keepers were very conscientious and went about their duties with the seriousness and energy that so important a job deserved, while others performed perfunctorily. During the inspection of 1838, the investigators found some of the stations in good order and having a reputation for maintaining a good light. But in too many instances (empirically, it would seem, in the majority of cases) they found that by mid-afternoon the keepers had not prepared the lamps and reflectors for that night and/or that the reflectors had not been burnished in a long time. Poorly kept lights apparently outnumbered good ones.

There are a number of explanations for the poor lights of the period, one of the chief ones being the lighting system in use at the time. Another explanation, and perhaps the most important one, centers around the failure to provide the keeper with sufficient instructions in his work and adequate supervision in the performance of his duties. And, of course, one has to consider that the quality of the people hired to be keepers left much to be

Cleaning the illuminating apparatus aboard the Nantucket South Shoals lightship in 1891. *From* Century Magazine. *Reproduced from the collection of the Library of Congress.*

desired, especially in the realm of devotion to duty.

### Training the Keeper

The evidence indicates that the keeper received virtually no written instructions outlining his duties, although each lighthouse apparently was issued an instruction sheet on the operation of the lighting system, and this instruction sheet was to be posted in the lantern. In the investigation of 1851, however, the board found more lighthouses without this sheet than with it.

Today it is difficult to determine where the keeper learned the trade of lighthouse keeping. Undoubtedly he received some instructions, probably of a general nature, from the collector of customs. Perhaps he learned something of the operation of the lamps and reflectors from the outgoing keeper and/or from someone on the ship that brought the yearly supply of oil. At best the keeper's training was a hit-or-miss proposition, and this lack of adequate training goes a long way toward explaining

the poor lights in so many of this nation's lighthouses.

Lack of instructions and inadequate training were two things, among many, that struck the Lighthouse Board as being fundamentally wrong. So the board went about compiling written instructions, down to the minutest detail, for the keeper. Early in its career, the Lighthouse Board began doing everything possible to attract a better educated individual to the position of keeper, because it felt there were ample instructions for the keeper to run a good lighthouse, if he could read. Accordingly, the first two requirements the board established for the hiring of keepers was that the applicant had to be at least eighteen years of age and he had to be able to read.

In sharp contrast to the fifth auditor, the Lighthouse Board provided ample written instructions. Some of the publications the board issued were designed specifically for the keepers of lighthouses and lightships, and included: *Lighthouse Establishment Instructions; Instructions and Directions for*

44

the *Managements of Lenses, Lights and Beacons; List of Illuminating Apparatuses, Fixtures, Implements, and Supplies in General Use in the U. S. Lighthouses, Lighted Beacons and Light-Vessels . . . ; Instructions and Directions to Guide Lighthouse Keepers and Others Belonging to the Lighthouse Establishment;* and *Management of Lens Apparatus and Lamps.* In addition to all these items, the keeper also received each year the latest copy of the *Light List.*

It might be added parenthetically here that the Lighthouse Board issued written instructions for the operation of the administrative unit in Washington. Entitled *Routine Duties,* the booklet outlined the day-to-day activity in the Lighthouse Board office.

To perform effectively their main task of keeping the light burning from sunset to sunrise, the light keepers had to maintain the lighting equipment in good shape, and the Lighthouse Board instructed the keepers to have the lantern and lens in order by ten o'clock in the morning for lighting in the evening. In carrying out this admonition, the Lighthouse Board divided work at light stations with two or more keepers into two "departments." The person performing the work of the first "department" had to clean and polish the lens, clean and fill the lamp, dust the framework of the apparatus, trim carefully the wicks of the lens lamp, and, if required, put new ones in, and see that everything connected with the apparatus and lamp in general was perfectly clean and the lamp ready for lighting in the evening. The keeper in carrying out the work of the second "department" had to clean the copper and brass fixtures of the apparatus as well as the utensils used in the lantern and watchroom; clean the walls, floors, and balconies, or galleries, of the lantern; and sweep and dust the tower stairways, landing, doors, windows, window recesses, and passageways from the lantern to the oil storage area. In performing their work in the lantern, the keepers were further instructed by the Lighthouse Board to wear linen aprons, to prevent the possibility of their coarse clothes scratching the lens.

The various printed instructions, of course, spelled out not only the daily, but also the periodic routine of a keeper's job. The books directed him to perform such tasks as washing the lens every two months with spirit of wine (alcohol), polishing it annually with rouge, and alternating the lamps inside the lens every fifteen days. The keeper could find the answer to any question about his work by carefully perusing the instructions available. If a keeper dropped oil on the lens, the book told him to use spirits of wine in cleaning it off. If he did not know how to trim a wick or adjust a lamp, he could find a step-by-step detailed description, including a picture of what the lamp flame should look like. The Lighthouse Board left little to the discretion, or the imagination for that matter, of the keeper, and a keeper could maintain a neat, workable lighthouse with only a modicum of intelligence and initiative. Intellectually, all he needed was the ability to read and to comprehend what he read. Physically, he needed to bring to the job a certain amount of energy.

Once the keepers had finished the routine daily work connected with the light, they turned their attention to maintenance, which for the most part consisted of repairs of a minor nature to the equipment and structures at the station. A not-so-minor task the keepers performed was painting the tower, a job female keepers were exempted from. Normally a work force in the employ of the district engineer took care of major repairs, and Congress usually provided specific appropriations for these as requested by the Lighthouse Board.

## Performance of Duty

There was a tremendous difference in performance between the light keepers under the fifth auditor's administration and the ones under the Lighthouse Board. This difference cannot be explained wholly by the fact that under the Lighthouse Board the keepers had written directions. Ranking along with the availability of written instructions in importance was the fact that the Lighthouse Board set high standards of performance and saw to it that keepers maintained this high level by instituting a program of close supervision. Moreover, the board was not very tolerant of mistakes. It did its best to be fair and to determine where guilt lay, but once it had determined guilt, the board, or its agents the inspectors, meted out stern justice.

In 1855, the inspector for the Pacific Coast found the keeper of the Alcatraz lighthouse absent from his post on several occasions. He reprimanded the keeper severely and contemplated dismissing him, but the keeper appeared so contrite that the inspector, Major Hartman E. Bache, decided to leave him in his position. But six months later the Alcatraz keeper committed another offense, and Bache, without hesitating, dismissed him for "unfitness" and "neglect of duty."

Sleeping on duty was an intolerable offense to the Lighthouse Board. In the 1880's, the keeper of the Cape Hatteras light reported that he had found the second assistant keeper asleep on duty. Without pause or an investigation, the board ordered the dismissal of the man.

Keeping a station in good order was also important to the board. In the 1890's, the Lighthouse Board wrote the keeper of the Point Loma Lighthouse informing him that the district inspector had found the light station in unsatisfactory order and firmly instructed him to correct the errors. A second offense, the board admonished him, would result in dismissal. Several months later the lighthouse had not been brought up to satisfactory condition, and the board fired the keeper, despite his more than twenty years of heretofore satisfactory service.

The Bureau of Lighthouses continued the standards of performance established by the Lighthouse Board, and, so that there would be no misunderstanding on this point, the bureau's service newsletter, the *Lighthouse Service Bulletin,* in its early issues published warnings and punishments meted out, but did not name the malefactors. Listed are such punishments as dismissal of a keeper for being intoxicated on duty, warning to a light vessel skipper "for failure to show proper interest in his work," and dismissal of another keeper "for oppressive and capricious conduct and for failure to forward an official communication. . . ." One keeper was reduced to assistant keeper "for not keeping his station in proper condition, and on account of his slovenly appearance." Another keeper was reprimanded "for misstatement of facts in connection with charges, and for nagging his assistants." And another keeper, who headed a four-keeper station, was transferred to a single-keeper station "for incompetency in maintaining his station and its discipline in the proper manner."

The Lighthouse Board had taken a distinctly non-professional group of people and molded and hammered them into a thoroughly dedicated and hard-working corps who were responsible for the country's aids to navigation being among the finest in the world. Probably a chief cause for the board's success was the military background of its members and their sense of military justice: fair, stern, and swift.

THE BETTMANN ARCHIVE

46

# V

# The Keeper's Life

WE THINK today how nice it would be to escape from our world of constant hustle and noise and seek a lonely seashore where the loudest noise is the splash of a wave as it rolls shoreward or the caw of a sea gull as it searches the near shore for food. We close our eyes and imagine we are standing on a beach, the sun warming us and the wind blowing through our hair. We look up and down the beach for miles and see no one. And we think, how sweet the loneliness. We think of a light keeper a hundred years ago on some isolated shore or island and envy him the peace and tranquility, wishing we could magically swap places with him.

But if we really knew the life of such a keeper and how he felt, it is doubtful anyone would long retain a desire to exchange places; certainly not on a permanent basis.

In the literature about the more isolated lighthouses, the two words most commonly used are *loneliness* and *monotony*. The historian of the Colchester Reef lighthouse in Lake Champlain chronicled the deadly monotony of life on a lighthouse over a mile from shore. A visitor to the Minot's Ledge light in the 1890's noted the monotony of the keepers' existence and quoted the principal keeper as saying, "The trouble with our life here is that we have too much time to think." Another writer who visited lighthouses on the West Coast in the early 1900's said, "The life is monotonous, and is one of great vigilance and exposure to the severest weather." One long-time keeper on the Maine coast said that the isolation of a lighthouse was hard on a keeper, but it was particularly hard on the women. The man at least got to see other peo-

ple when he went to town on occasion to pick up the mail or buy supplies; the woman was confined to her home over much longer periods than the keeper.

## Educating the Children

Some stations were more isolated than others, but it was the rare one that did not have some degree of isolation, particularly up to World War I. And this isolation affected all aspects of the keeper's life. Perhaps the most sensitive effect was in the area of the education of his children. In cases where the light was not near enough to a school, the keepers on their own worked out different solutions to get their children educated. When a keeper's children began to reach school age, he did what he could to get a transfer, in many cases working out a swap with a keeper from another station that was nearer a school. At other times the keeper boarded his children with someone in town, or simply arranged living quarters for his family in a town. Undoubtedly, both of these arrangements put a severe financial drain on the resources of the average keeper, who did not receive a high salary.

In some instances the light may have been near enough to a school that with extra exertion the keeper could get his children educated and at the same time have them with him. The keeper of the Kennebec River light in Maine, for example, rowed his children across the river each morning so that they could attend the school at Phippsburg Center. But in some cases, such as at the St. Croix River Light Station in the early part of this century, the ice was too thick in the river to permit rowing to and from the mainland, and one lady who spent her seventh to twelfth years at the station recalls that her schooling ceased when the ice began to thicken in the river. She admits that for this reason she received a sketchy education.

The education of keepers' children was long a problem, but not too many people were concerned about it. One who exhibited distress at the problem was Alexander P. MacDonald. In 1908, MacDonald, a missionary in the Maine Sea Coast Missionary Society, became interested in the education of these children. He felt light keepers were "far above average," and were anxious "to do the best for themselves and their families." He reported that in his area there were over 100 children of school age "who are growing up without school privileges, some of them in lamentable ignorance." The state took a rather provincial attitude, contending that the federal government sent them there and, therefore, had some responsibility for their education. But the Lighthouse Board was not too sympathetic. In response to a query from MacDonald, Admiral George C. Reiter, chairman of the board, replied: "I beg to say that the condition . . . in the Lighthouse Service is inevitable, has always existed and always will exist, but I am fully satisfied that the inspectors take this into consideration and do all they can to remedy it." Anyway, the admiral continued, the board did not have any funds to apply to the problem, since Congress barely appropriated enough money to keep the lighthouse establishment running.

Miffed at the attitude of the Lighthouse Board, MacDonald concluded that the condition may have always existed, but that was no reason it should continue to exist. Nevertheless, it did continue to exist and light keepers made the best arrangements they could for the education of their children. As late as the 1930's, the keepers of the Bodie Island light sent their families to Manteo, N. C. for the winter so their children could go to school daily. By 1937, the keepers were not satisfied with the arrangement; they wanted their families with them year around. They decided to use the private car of one of the keepers to haul the children daily to the main highway where they could catch a school bus. The keepers asked the Lighthouse Bureau to help with some of the expenses, such as a tire allowance and payment of damages to the car that

might occur incidental to transporting the children. In the meantime, the local school board had agreed to pay for the gasoline, some eighty gallons, used in carrying the children to the bus stop. The Lighthouse Bureau later replied that current legislation would not permit payment of such expenses. They did agree, however, a year later to pay for fourteen gallons of the fuel used in transporting the children.

## Lighthouse "Farming"

The degree of isolation varied from station to station; the severest, perhaps, could be found on the rocky islands off the coasts of Maine and California. On these islands the keepers and their families faced not only loneliness, but also frustration. Man may have evolved from sea creatures and the sea may exert an instinctual pull on him, but man, having been out of the sea a long time, has just as strong a feeling about land, and when he goes to sea he feels the pull of the shore and usually wants to see something grow, especially plants. There are a number of inhospitable places for growing plants, but none quite as bad as Mount Desert Rock, Saddleback Ledge, or Boon Island. At all three places the keepers have tried to grow things, despite the fact that none of the sites possesses soil. At Saddleback Ledge the keeper had a few pea vines, hills of potatoes, and sprigs of oats growing in his trash, and he nursed them tenderly. On Mount Desert Rock and Boon Island the keepers hauled dirt from the mainland to their homes in barrels and boxes just to have small gardens in which they could grow flowers. And they did their work knowing full well that the first good storm would sweep the island and probably carry everything away, including the soil. But for a while, at least, they could watch things grow.

Although many light stations did not have the soil, either in quantity or quality, to raise flowers or vegetables, there were many stations that did. The Farallon Islands off the coast of California at San Francisco had for hundreds of years been a nesting area for a variety of sea birds, and these creatures had fertilized the Farallones, including South Farallon where the lighthouse was situated. The keepers grew turnips, radishes, and onions. They planted lettuce also, but it would not, for some reason, make a head.

At Point Loma, near San Diego, the keeper and

Interior of the dwelling of an Atlantic-coast lighthouse in the 1880's.    *From* St. Nicholas Magazine.

his family kept a potato patch for a few years. The constant wind and salt spray there do not create an ideal condition for a vegetable garden. It was only with diligent attention and care that the principal keeper's wife kept a tomato vine growing for several years near the lighthouse.

The keeper of the Colchester Reef lighthouse in Lake Champlain maintained a garden on an island about a half a mile from the lighthouse. His children tended the garden. The captain and crew of the Carysfort lightship in Florida, in the years before the Lighthouse Board, maintained a garden, the evidence indicates, on one of the keys near this station and rowed to the site periodically to cultivate their plants.

During World War I, the Bureau of Lighthouses encouraged keepers to grow gardens, "in order," the bureau said, "to relieve as much as possible the shortage of food." The bureau even encouraged the use of their land by non-lighthouse people for gardens. One enterprising keeper, L. A. Borchers of the Turn Point Light Station, "gardened" the sea. He canned salmon, sardines, grayfish, and caviar. The Bureau of Fisheries inspected his stock of canned fish and pronounced them of high quality. Borchers's enterprise even received praise from Herbert Hoover, then United States Food Administrator.

The lighthouse service did not stipulate that keepers could not engage in outside work. It did establish certain rules for the keepers, such as maintaining the station in good order and being present to light the tower at sunset. In the absence of rules to the contrary, however, keepers engaged in a variety of outside occupations to supplement their income. In New England, some of the keepers fished and lobstered. In other places keepers engaged in boat building. The first keeper of the Point Loma lighthouse, for example, also ran a shipyard and in 1857 launched the first vessel built in San Diego. In later years another keeper of the Point Loma light supplemented his income—or at least his children did —by signalling the pilot station when a ship needing a pilot neared the harbor. They also signalled the shore whaling station when a whale was passing. They boys received proper remuneration for these "favors." The keeper's wife was also enterprising. She and the children gathered shells from the tidepool area below the lighthouse. With these shells they formed designs which they encased in frames decorated with other shells; they sold these shell pictures to tourists who visited the lighthouse to view the magnificent panorama of ocean, islands, mountains, rolling countryside, and harbor.

On South Farallon Island the keepers shot seals for their oil, bristles, and other valuable parts. Among the Chinese of nearby San Francisco, powdered seal whiskers were rumored to be a sure cure for impotence. The mounted heads of large bull seals were popular ornaments. In addition, the keepers engaged in egg-gathering. Cormorants, sea gulls, murre, and other sea birds used the islands as a nesting area, and thousands of their eggs lay about on the ground. For a time the keepers picked up the eggs and sold them in San Francisco for twenty-five cents per dozen. Bakers used the eggs in cakes and bread dough. This egg-gathering made tremendous inroads into the bird population and so alarmed conservationists that they were able to get the practice halted.

### Fighting Monotony: The Lighthouse Library

Recognizing the loneliness of many of the light stations, and the fact that keepers engaged in "monotonous routine duties," the Lighthouse Board in 1876 began distributing small libraries to isolated light stations. These libraries consisted of about forty books which were enclosed in a case that folded open to display their contents. Each library was different, for the board envisioned transferring the boxes among the lighthouses, at first leaving a library at each station for about six months. Specifically, the Lighthouse Board wanted the libraries sent "to isolated light-houses of the higher orders, where there are keepers with families, who will read and appreciate the books the Libraries contain."

Each library contained a mixture of novels, histories, biographies, adventures, religious works, and magazines. Titles found in some of the libraries included *Newcomb's Astronomy; The Battle of Mobile Bay; Voyage of the Paper Canoe from Quebec to the Gulf of Mexico; The Five Little Peppers and How They Grew; Memoirs of Commodore David Porter; A Christmas at Sea;* and the eight-volume set *The Library of Choice Literature.* A popular magazine often in the libraries was the *United Service Magazine.* The board constantly replaced books and magazines in these libraries; some it bought, while others came by donation from people who found sympathy for the lonely keeper.

In the first year the board collected 50 libraries. Within two years it added 100 more, and by 1885 there were 420 libraries in circulation. The libraries were generally exchanged at the time of the quarterly inspections. The board required that the keeper sign out each book as he took it from the library; the board wished to determine the type of reading matter the keepers liked so as to guide further acquisition of books. When a book was no longer serviceable for circulation, the board instructed district inspectors to give the book to a "deserving keeper."

How long the circulating libraries remained in use is not known, but as late as 1912 the Bureau of Lighthouses reported having 351 libraries, enough for all light-vessels and isolated lighthouses.

### The Keeper's Family Pitches In

Lighthouse keeping was often a family endeavor, and one or more members of the family knew how to operate the light, filling in when the keeper was away or during times of emergency.

The Lighthouse Board recognized the family nature of the work and on more than one occasion turned it to the benefit of the lighthouse establishment. For example, the Colchester Reef lighthouse was originally a two-man station with the families living ashore. But before long the Lighthouse Board eliminated one position and moved the family of the remaining keeper out to join him at the light-house. Thereafter it was a one-man station. There are many examples of wives of keepers serving as assistant keepers, thus saving the lighthouse service from having to supply additional quarters for another family.

The history of the lighthouse service is replete with examples of wives or sons or daughters filling in for the absent keeper. The daughter of the keeper of the Matinicus Rock Light Station is a good example. Samuel Burgess had been appointed keeper in 1853, and he took his invalid wife, one son, and four daughters to this island twenty-five miles off the coast of Maine. His oldest daughter, Abbie, was housekeeper and assisted her father in his light-house duties, since the son was away much of the time fishing to help supplement the family income. In January, 1856, the father had to be away, and on the nineteenth of the month a severe storm struck; it was the same storm that toppled the Minot's Ledge light tower. Since her father was away, Abbie tended the light. Water swept completely over the thirty-nine-acre Matinicus Rock. Soon the keeper's dwelling became flooded and Abbie, her mother, and sisters had to seek sanctuary in the light towers which were at each end of the dwelling. Despite the violence of the storm and the threat of catastrophe, Abbie went on with her work of keeping the light burning. The sea remained rough and for four weeks Abbie and her sisters, without any male help, kept the lights burning, and not once did the light fail.

A little over a year later Abbie's father had to go ashore to get his pay and pick up supplies. The sea kicked up, and he could not return for three weeks, but Abbie kept the lights going. The food began to run out, and the women were reduced to eating one cup of cornmeal and one egg each day. Despite these vicissitudes Abbie faithfully performed her duties.

Abbie, incidentally, continued in lighthouse service for many years. In 1861, she married the son of the new keeper of Matinicus Rock Light Station, and in 1875 when her husband was transferred to the Whitehead Light Station in Maine, she went as assistant keeper. She was still there in 1889.

A similar story is told of the son of the keeper of the Saddleback Ledge light. The keeper went ashore and before he could get back a storm came up that continued for days. Each night the fifteen-year-old boy lighted the lamp. He had little food at the light, but nevertheless he stuck to the job. Meanwhile, ashore, the father peered anxiously each evening toward the light to see if it would come on, thus letting him know his son was all right. After three weeks the sea subsided enough for the keeper to return to the station. He found his son in a weakened condition, but otherwise all right. The father was thankful and very proud of his son's achievement.

Wives, too, were often called upon to fill in for their husbands. Mrs. Kate Walker, long-time keeper of the Robbins Reef light off Staten Island, became keeper by substituting temporarily for her husband. The Walker family transferred to this light station around 1885. Kate, who had qualified as an assistant keeper while they served at Sandy Hook, assisted her husband. When he caught pneumonia and had to be transported to the hospital on the mainland, he admonished Kate to mind the light. She tended the light faithfully, and when her husband died, several potential keepers came to look over the job, but each decided it was too remote for him. With no one willing to take the job, the Lighthouse Board had little choice but to appoint Kate keeper. For about thirty years she minded the light, in the meantime raising two children. She estimated during her tenure that she rescued fifty people, most of whom were fishermen whose small boats, from sudden storms or carelessness, cracked up on the rocks around Robbins Reef. In 1919 Mrs. Walker retired.

Situated as they were, light keepers and their families were subjected to greater danger than most people. The most common threats to safety were storms that swept the coasts. The keepers on the more exposed light stations, such as the ones on the islands off the coast of Maine, feared not so much the winds of storms as they did the green water that might wash across their station during particularly violent periods. As mentioned previously, the family on Matinicus Island had their house flooded from a storm. The keeper of the Tillamook Rock lighthouse must have felt his blood turn cold when in 1882 he saw green water sweep over the top of his light tower, 150 feet above sea level. And on another occasion he must have blanched when storm-created waves ripped rocks from the tiny island and tossed them through the metal dome of the lantern. Of course, no one will ever know the thoughts that passed through the heads of the keepers of the first Minots Ledge lighthouse as that terrible storm whipped against the tower, bending it over until it snapped from its moorings, and carried the two men to their wet grave.

It was during such storms that ships were likely to crash against the rocks, particularly in the days of sail. Fred Kreth, one of the keepers at the Point Reyes lighthouse north of the entrance to San Francisco Bay, rescued three seamen from the craggy shore at the base of the Point. Their loaded fishing vessel was returning to port in a heavy storm when the wind, the sea, and the waves drove her on the rocks. The sailors left their vessel to find they faced a sheer precipice that rose over 300 feet into the air. It was at this place hours later that keeper Kreth found them clinging desperately to the rocks and being buffeted by the strong winds and spray. Realizing these seamen could not survive long, Kreth went over the cliff's edge to attempt to save them. The keeper slowly descended from rock to rock, being careful of his footing in the wet and wind. When the footing gave out he lowered a rope to the exhausted men below. Although his exertions must have pushed him near exhaustion, Kreth pulled the men from their perilous perch one by one.

Some years before, Keeper Marcus A. Hanna of the Cape Elizabeth Light Station in Maine performed a similar feat. The time was January 28, 1885, and a snow storm was lashing the Maine coast. The schooner *Australia* smashed onto the ledge near the light station's fog signal. By the time Keeper Hanna reached the edge of the shore, a huge wave had swept the captain overboard and only two of the ship's hands remained, both clinging for their lives to the icy rigging. Time after time Hanna tried to toss a weighted line aboard the schooner, but each time he failed. Then the sea tipped the ship over on its beam ends, and Hanna threw the line once again. This time one of the seamen gripped the line, tied it around his waist, and jumped into the icy water. Hanna struggled to pull the man through the churning sea. Finally he was able to get the seaman to the rocky ledge where he stood. As the rescued seaman huddled near him, Hanna tossed the line to the second man. He, too, tied the rope around his waist and jumped into the sea. By now Hanna was nearly exhausted, but he mustered reserve energy from the depths of his body and hauled away. But just as this extra

strength waned, the assistant keeper and two neighbors arrived to relieve Hanna, and they easily pulled the sailor ashore. For his heroism, the government, six months later, awarded him a gold medal.

Bravery of light keepers was not limited to the male sex. Mrs. Ida Lewis Wilson, keeper of the Lime Rock Light Station in Rhode Island, for example, received a gold medal in 1881 "for saving lives at the imminent peril of [her] own." And during her thirty-two years as keeper of the Lime Rock lighthouse at Newport, Rhode Island, she reportedly rescued thirteen people from drowning. At Angel Island in San Francisco Bay, the female light keeper on July 2, 1906, struck the fog bell by hand for over 20 hours when the machinery became disabled, and two days later she stood all night pounding the bell with a nail hammer.

## *"Humane and Gallant Services"*

Canada on at least two occasions expressed its gratitude to United States light keepers. C. R. Dobbins, keeper of the Moose Peak, Maine, lighthouse, received a gold watch "in recognition of his humane and gallant services to the shipwrecked crew of the British schooner *Ashton*." C. E. Marr and E. H. Pierce, keepers of the Cuckolds, Maine, fog signal station, received silver watches for rescuing the captain and crew of the schooner *Aurora* on January 4, 1896.

Other perils, too, plagued the light keepers. During lightning storms the metal spiral stairway in the Bodie Island tower became heavily charged with electricity. The keeper discovered this fact when he was standing on one of the metal landings and received a severe jolt from the lightning. For some time thereafter the lower half of his body was numb. The problem was solved seven years later with the installation of a more effective lightning conductor.

One problem, and potential danger, the lighthouse keeper faced was from birds. The light attracted various species and it was not uncommon for flocks of flying birds to smash against the lantern. Not much damage occurred when smaller songbirds crashed into the lantern; the keeper just had a mess to clean up. But when ducks and larger fowl flew the suicide route, they did considerable damage. Often they shattered the glass in the lan-

Part of the interior of the Point Loma lighthouse, Cali-
fornia, refurbished to look as it did around 1885. *Above,* the bedroom; *below,* the kitchen. *National Park Service photos by Fred Mang, Jr.*

Captain David Splaine, who served for some years as assistant keeper at several West Coast lighthouses. In 1894 he became the first keeper of the Ballast Point lighthouse at the entrance to San Diego Harbor. *From the Grace Killeen Collection, Cabrillo National Monument.*

problem that the Lighthouse Board ordered a screen made of heavy wire strung on the exterior of the lantern.

Light keepers through the years have experienced storms, hurricanes, earthquakes, and cyclones. Sometimes they had their material possessions damaged or destroyed and on a number of occasions their nerves were severely tested. During the months of January and February of 1918, the east coast of the United States saw an unusual build-up of ice in its bays and sounds, and lighthouses, lightships, and other floating aids to navigation felt the brunt of drifting ice. Lightships were dragged from their moorings and badly damaged; in some instances they were driven aground. Ice piled up around light towers in the water and threatened to push them over and in other instances floating ice bumped into lighthouses, rattling everything inside. At Green Point Shoal Light Station, the ice tipped over the lamp and lens, shattering the latter. That year ice did damage as far south as the Cape Fear Light Station in North Carolina. Especially hard hit were Chesapeake Bay and the sounds of North Carolina. In the face of this danger, when their nerves must have been strung tighter than a cheap guitar, the keepers at the lighthouses and on the lightships maintained their lights. The Hatteras Inlet light, a screw-pile structure well into the inlet, and the Long Point Shoal light, at the mouth of a river in North Carolina, were in especially vulnerable positions because of floating ice, but their keepers remained on duty, lighting the lamps at dusk and snuffing them out at sunrise.

The light keeper led a lonely and monotonous life. His job possessed a great deal of routine and was so spelled out in written instructions that he had little opportunity to exercise his imagination—a characteristic of three-quarters of the jobs in this modern age. Perhaps as a consequence, the light keeper did not consider himself as being of an especially heroic breed. He was, for the most part, a person devoted to his duty. He did what he felt the job called for, whether it was to remain on his station in severe weather, or to go to the water's edge at the height of a storm and rescue someone in distress. In essence, the light keeper symbolizes what we think of ourselves as doing in our better moments: when the situation calls for that extra bravery or devotion to duty, we can rise to the occasion and not be found wanting.

terns and their bodies came hurtling through to smash against the lens. There are a number of instances in the records of the lighthouse service of lens prisms being cracked and broken by these flying missiles. Moreover, if a keeper were inside the lantern when these birds came crashing through, he stood a good chance of suffering injury from flying glass, if nothing else.

At some lighthouses the birds became such a

# VI

# The Lightship

COMPARED to the lighthouse, the lightship is a newcomer among aids to navigation; yet today it is already disappearing. Developed to be placed where lighthouses could not be, the lightship during its career has served usefully and effectively, but technological advances are permitting its replacement by, of all things, lighthouses.

The lightship goes back only to 1731, when a British entrepreneur received a patent which permitted him to place a lightship at the Nore Sandbank in the estuary of the Thames River and collect duties from ship owners. This first lightship was a single-masted sloop, and its light consisted of two ship's lanterns suspended twelve feet apart on a crossarm attached to the mast. The lightship proved an immediate success and was most popular with navigators.

Although the Nore lightship can be considered the beginning of this type of aid to navigation, one has to remember that the light vessel had an ancestor in the days of the Roman Empire. Evidence indicates that, several hundred years before the birth of Christ, a Roman galley patrolled the coast to protect merchant ships from becoming the victim of pirates. At night the galley carried a lighted fire basket at its masthead as a signal to both merchants and pirates that the galley was on duty as an aid to commerce. But from then until the advent of the Nore lightship, no record has survived of the use of this form of navigational aid.

## Lightships under the Fifth Auditor

The United States' first lightship was established at Willoughby Spit in Virginia in 1820; this position proved too exposed for the seventy-ton vessel, however, and Pleasonton had it moved to Craney Island near Norfolk, Virginia. The following year, four more were placed in Chesapeake Bay. The first "outside" lightship—that is, a station in the ocean outside the shores of the United States—was the one placed at Sandy Hook, New Jersey, in 1823. This light vessel station, incidentally, remained until it was replaced by the Ambrose Channel lightship on December 1, 1908.

Although manned by a number of seamen and usually weighing well over 100 tons, these early light vessels were called lightboats. Just when they began being called lightships is not known precisely, but it apparently occurred within a few years after the Lighthouse Board took charge of the lighthouse service. In their 1851–52 investigation report, the board referred to these aids to navigation in various places as lightboats, light vessels, and lightships.

By 1837, this country had twenty-six lightboats in use, and in 1852, when the fifth auditor relinquished control of aids to navigation to the Lighthouse Board, the number had grown to forty-two. In 1889, however, the country's light vessels numbered only twenty-four, all of them being on the east coast or in the Great Lakes. The reason for this reduction was that many of the "inside" lightships—that is, those in bays and sounds—had been replaced by lighthouses, mostly of screw-pile construction. But in subsequent years, other "outside" lightships were established, including several on the West Coast, and in 1917 the commissioner of lighthouses reported fifty-three lightship stations.

## Diamond Shoals Lightship (1824)

During the period Stephen Pleasonton administered aids to navigation, lightboats appeared to have suffered from the same malady as lighthouses—that is, the accent was on economy, not purpose. For many years there were no relief lightships to take the place of those that had to leave their stations for repairs or other reasons. Moreover, equipment on the light vessel was at a minimum and no provision was made for spares. The career of the first Diamond Shoals lightship is not an atypical example of one of these types of aids to navigation. Built in New York in 1823–24, the light vessel in late June, 1824, assumed its station some thirteen miles east-southeast of the Cape Hatteras lighthouse. It remained there until the following February when a severe storm parted the vessel's moorings and did considerable damage to the ship itself. Captain Lief Holden, the skipper of the lightboat, steered his vessel for Norfolk where it stayed for ten months under repair. In the meantime, Diamond Shoals was without a light.

Back on station in late December, the ship remained there for five months, until May, 1826, when another storm snapped her moorings. Without a spare anchor or chain, the captain had no choice but to head for Norfolk again. Damage to the vessel was negligible, but Pleasonton became disturbed over the loss of the anchor and cable, and he kept the ship in port while another vessel under Captain Holden's guidance went out to the shoals in search of the anchor. This search proved fruitless, and Pleasonton, in an effort to stimulate private enterprise, offered a $500 reward to anyone who found and returned the anchor. Again, no results were forthcoming, and Pleasonton ordered another anchor and cable made. The ship finally resumed its station in November, 1826. Nine months later, in August, 1827, another storm parted the moorings of the vessel, and this time the severe winds drove the lightship ashore, six miles south of Ocracoke Inlet. Too far up on the beach to be worked into the water again, the ship was broken up for salvage. Seventy years were to pass before Diamond Shoals saw another lightship.

## Lightship Equipment and the Ability to Maintain Station

During the decade following the abortive effort to light Diamond Shoals, little change occurred in the equipment of the country's light vessels. They still carried no spare equipment, and when repair work or replacement of equipment was needed, the sta-

tion remained vacant while the lightship was in port. The important Sandy Hook lightboat was blown off station on September 12 and on the fourteenth of the following month it was still in port awaiting a cable and anchor. The Michilimackinac lightboat spent virtually the whole shipping season in port being repaired.

One can imagine the anger a navigator must have felt when he suddenly realized a lightship was not where he had come to expect it to be. One local superintendent of lights retorted that when light vessels were taken off station, public notice was given of its removal. Unfortunate was the mariner who failed to subscribe to the local newspaper, or who had been away on a long voyage. In 1837, Pleasonton purchased a relief lightboat and stationed it at Norfolk to be used when necessary. But one light vessel hardly seems adequate for the number of lightboat stations then in existence. The relief vessel still worked out of Norfolk in 1851, and it was still the only relief vessel in the lighthouse service.

In 1838, the majority of the lightships were in good condition and manned by reasonably competent seamen. But a sizeable percentage had serious faults ranging from bad lights to untrustworthy keepers. Several of the ships were rotting and leaking, and on at least four of the light vessels the inspectors found the captain and crew absent. At one, a fourteen-year-old Negro lad had been left in charge, and he did not possess the strength to hoist the lantern to the masthead. The naval officer who examined aids to navigation between New York City, and Norfolk, Virginia, including the huge Delaware and Chesapeake bays, observed that most of the lightboats were kept by local farmers "who have either employed others at low wages to attend their duties, or wholly neglected them."

Two classes of lightboats were in use during this period: large and small. The distinction in size is not clear from records presently available. It would seem that a "small" vessel weighed in the neighborhood of 100 or 120 tons and a "large" one in the vicinity of 200 tons. But there was a considerable disparity in the size of light vessels. The ship at Bartlets Reef in 1838 was of 41 tons, while the Cape Hatteras or Diamond Shoals lightship in 1825 topped the scales at 300 tons. A large-class lightboat rated a master (who received $700 per year), a mate, five or six seamen, and a cook, while a small-class vessel had a master ($500 per year) and three or four hands. The mates received $350 per annum and the seamen the going rate in the merchant marine plus twenty-five cents per day subsistence.

These vessels carried one and two lanterns and each lantern contained either a compass or a common lamp from which protruded ten to twelve wicks. The lanterns varied in size. The Diamond Shoals lightship had two lanterns, each three feet square and five feet high. On the other hand, the first lightship at Brandywine—a small "inside" light vessel—had a lantern measuring two feet square and two and one-half feet high. The lanterns aboard lightships were often poorly situated so that the mast obscured the light when seen from certain angles. The records are reasonably clear that some of these early lightboats also carried fog signals, usually a fog bell. The Diamond Shoals lightboat

during its 1825 repair work had a six-pound cannon installed; unquestionably, the cannon was to serve as a fog signal.

*Lightships under the Lighthouse Board*

After taking over the nation's aids to navigation, the Lighthouse Board went about better equipping the lightships. Spare equipment, such as anchors and additional cable, was installed and the lights in lanterns were changed to Argand lamps and parabolic reflectors. The board also began replacing lightships with lighthouses. By 1860, the country's lightships had been reduced by three to thirty-nine.

One of the first lightships built under authority of the board was, upon completion in 1854, assigned to Minot's Ledge. It replaced an older and

Martin's Industry lightship, Georgia, in 1914. Stationed off Port Royal, this ship is typical of the older, wooden-hulled light-vessels. Her smooth bilges do little to prevent rolling in heavy weather. *U. S. Coast Guard photo 26-LG-69-58 in the National Archives.*

temporary light vessel that had been stationed there when a storm toppled the recently completed lighthouse.

Another of its lightships built about this same period had a different history. According to lighthouse service records the vessel that later became Lightship No. 8 was built in the Philadelphia Navy Yard in 1854–55. Navy records state that she was built in 1853 in New Jersey as the *Thomas C. Haight*. But whatever her origin, the vessel was acquired by the navy, which renamed her the *Arctic* and dispatched her north to search for Dr. E. K. Kane whose ship had become stranded in the ice. The rescue expedition was a famous one at the time. The screw steamer, in company with the *Release,* reached Godhavn on Disko Island in Davis Strait, loaded the arctic explorers aboard, and returned home. Afterwards, the vessel remained in the navy until 1859, when the Lighthouse Board received the ship minus her propulsion machinery, and converted her into a light vessel. In May, 1860, she assumed duties as relief lightship of the Sixth District.

As a light vessel the former *Arctic* typifies what happened to aids to navigation in the south with the advent of the Civil War. The rebels destroyed lighthouses and beacons and sank or confiscated lightships. They seized the former *Arctic* and sank her in the Cape Fear River, where she remained until the end of the war. They destroyed the Smith Point vessel in Chesapeake Bay, and, down in Georgia in the Savannah River, sank the lightship from Martin's Industry. In 1862, the Lighthouse Board lamented: "All the light-vessels from Cape Henry southwards, including the two in the Potomac River and those in Chesapeake Bay (except Hooper's Straits and Jane's Island), have been removed and sunk or destroyed by the insurgents."

But the Lighthouse Board did not simply sit on its backside and wring its collective hands in despair. As soon as conditions permitted, the board replaced the lightships. In 1862, the board purchased the five-year-old, 203-ton brig *A. J. W. Applegarth* and altered it to a lightship for the Smith Point station in Chesapeake Bay. Lightships Nos. 21 and 24 were built originally in 1863 for upper and lower Cedar Point in the Potomac River. At the same time, the board had a new ship built and placed at Rattlesnake Shoal near Charleston Harbor. Fearful that the Confederates might return, the

army, at the request of the Lighthouse Board, stationed guards aboard re-established light vessels.

The Lighthouse Board displayed ingenuity in fulfilling its mission under wartime conditions. When it became evident that Port Royal Harbor—a center of federal military activity—needed a lightship, the Lighthouse Board purchased the schooner *Ascension* at a prize auction in Key West, Florida, in May, 1863. After some quick alterations the board placed the vessel in Port Royal Harbor on July 5, 1863. The navy eyed the ship covetously and seized her in a few weeks. The board notified the navy to either return the vessel or pay for it. The navy returned the vessel and it was back on station at Fishing Rip at least by the first of March, 1864, manned by four Negroes—contrabands, as the military liked to term ex-slaves. Within a few months, however, the wooden-hulled vessel showed signs of severe worm damage, and the board moved it to a quiet creek and used it as a hulk to store lighthouse supplies. Meanwhile, the board assigned another vessel to Fishing Rip.

When the federal monitor *Weehawken* sank in Charleston Channel, the board secured a ship that had started life as a James River tug and at the beginning of the war had been converted to a Confederate gunboat named the *Lady Davis*. By 1865, it was devoid of its machinery and owned by private persons. The board acquired the ex-tug, converted her quickly to a lightship, and placed her near the wreck of the *Weehawken* to warn other vessels of the hazard. She remained in service until 1871, when her hull was found to be too thin and the board had her sold at auction.

After the war, a wrecking party raised the Sixth District relief light vessel—the former *Arctic*—and the Martin's Industry lightship from their respective resting places in the Cape Fear and Savannah rivers. Finding the relief vessel in good condition, the Lighthouse Board had her repaired and refitted and dispatched in 1867 to Hen and Chicken Shoals, where she served faithfully, but unspectacularly, for nine years. Found to be "old and worn out" and not worth repair, the valiant ship was removed from service in 1876 and sold at public auction three years later. The Martin's Industry vessel was also repaired, but a closer examination showed her to be in an advanced state of dry rot. The board had her stripped and sold at public auction in 1868.

In 1867, the Lighthouse Board began numbering

its lightships so as to keep better track of them. Thereafter, no matter how often the ships were moved from station to station, they still retained their numbers. The ships at first were not numbered according to age, as one would think. The board began numbering from north to south. Lightship No. 1 was assigned to New South Shoal off Nantucket and had been built in 1855. Lightship No. 25 was built in 1827 and at the time of numbering was assigned to Hooper Straits in Chesapeake Bay. In time, however, the number came to have chronological meaning, because as new vessels were built, the board assigned them the next highest number not in use.

Through the years the lightships continued to serve a most useful purpose, and stations were established or eliminated as need dictated. In 1890, for example, the board placed the first lightship on the west coast—No. 50—at the Columbia River. Over the years it added others on that coast. At the same time, the board replaced, where possible, the lightships with lighthouses, particularly those in Delaware and Chesapeake bays.

## Lightship Duty

Unquestionably, duty aboard a lightship was the most dangerous and most uncomfortable in the lighthouse service. Yet despite the discomfort and danger, lightship duty was characterized by monotony. A visitor to the Nantucket New South Shoal light vessel stationed twenty-four miles off Sankaty Head in 1891 wrote his observations of life aboard a lightship, and his remarks fitted pretty closely most of the lightships in service during the nineteenth century.

The New South Shoal station was a particularly rough one, and much of the time the ship was pitching and rolling, causing the most experienced seaman on occasion to become seasick. Work, however, was not difficult or demanding. The crew rose at 6:00 A.M. and after sunrise lowered the lantern. They then had breakfast, which lasted about forty minutes, and afterwards turned to preparing the lantern for the evening lighting. On a calm day this chore took about two hours. With this primary duty out of the way, the men concentrated on cleaning the ship. A good portion of the day was left, and since the crew were not readers (evidenced by lack of use of the ship's library), the men turned to man-

ual activities, such as whittling, to pass the time. The crew also supplemented their income with a sideline business: they made rattan baskets and sold them ashore.

In the evening, with the exhibiting of the light, the crew went on watch. There were two alternating watches aboard ship: the captain's watch, and the mate's watch. The isolation put the crew under considerable emotional stress that was only partly relieved by two long periods ashore each year. Each watch between spring and winter went ashore twice for two-month periods, which meant each man spent eight months a year aboard ship.

Food aboard ship often consisted of scouse and duff. "Scouse," the visitor wrote, "is a wonderful commingling of salt beef, potatoes, and onions, with varied trimmings. Duff seems substantially like the dumplings served in Yorkshire pudding with a sauce of melted brown sugar. Plum duff—with raisins—is a great luxury; but often the plums are nothing more than 'Nantucket raisins'—in plain English, dried apples."

At times the crew took the ship's boat and went to the rescue of a foundering vessel or castaway on a raft. Although not expected to perform such tasks, since their primary responsibility called for them to keep the lightship on station displaying a light, innate humanity would not let them ignore a seaman in distress, no matter how stormy or dangerous the ocean.

Such was life aboard the lightship: monotonous, repetitive, dangerous, and above all, lonely.

## Lightship Design

One of the principal reasons for the uncomfortableness of the light vessel was the design of the ship. The captain of the Sandy Hook lightship wrote of his vessel in 1851:

If you will but look at the model of this ship, you will at once perceive that her broad bluff bow is not at all calculated to resist the fury of the sea, which, in some of the gales we experience in the winter season, break against and over us with almost impending fury. . . . The model of the present ship and her bottom, is similar to a barrel; she is constantly in motion, and when it is any ways rough she rolls and labors to such a degree as to heave the glass out of the lanterns, the beds

The wharves at Staten Island Depot in 1912. Two lightships (one of which is numbered 44) are tied up to the vessel at the dock in the left foreground; it is just possible to discern the foremast lantern hoisted part way up the mast of the left-hand lightship. A lightship is moored to the dock at the right. *U. S. Coast Guard photo 26-LG-16-41 in the National Archives.*

out of the berths, tearing out the chain-plates, &c., rendering her unsafe and uncomfortable.

Much of the crew's discomfort stemmed from the nature of the job the lightship performed; but in the early days, as the captain indicates, the design of the vessel needed considerable work. Not until the second half of the nineteenth century did the nations of the world begin to think of lightships as having a special duty and therefore requiring a special design and construction. England, France, Ireland, and the United States were active in studying lightships to improve their design, construction, propulsion, lighting apparatus, and living accommodations. Marine architects began to flatten the bottom of the hull and to install bilge keels to inhibit rolling. They reduced the metacentric height (to twelve inches for United States lightships) so that the vessel would sit steadier in the water. Some of these studies and discoveries extended well into the twentieth century. For example, it wasn't until 1911 and 1912 that the lighthouse service of Ireland first published information on the effects of bilge keels on rolling.

Today, United States lightships are rather ungainly looking vessels. They do not possess the sleek lines of a cruiser or a cutter. But then, lightships are not assigned the same task that those vessels are. The modern lightship is designed for its purpose: to stay on station when the sea gets rough.

Sea-keeping ability, then, is an important ingredient in the design of the lightship. In the early days this fact was not appreciated, or perhaps even understood, and the country's first light vessels were designed similarly to regular ships.

For many years lightships were constructed of wood, and in 1851 the fifth auditor stated that because of this fact, lightships usually lasted five to ten years, depending upon the latitude and the timber used. The reference to latitude concerned the presence of a certain type of marine worm in southern waters, from about Charleston, S. C., southward. This borer was a bane to the Lighthouse Board. "A whole plank is completely riddled with worm-holes," the board said, "before the least indication is visible on the skin of the ship inside. A small leak is a sure warning that the vessel must be docked right away." To combat this insidious foe, the board recommended in 1886 substituting iron-hulled vessels for the wooden ones as they needed replacing.

Even with the presence of the marine worm, one still wonders about the fifth auditor's statement. It was not the experience of the Lighthouse Board to have its lightships last only ten years. The records in the National Archives of ninety-four lightships—a number of which had been purchased in the days of the fifth auditor—reveal that the average vessel lasted in the neighborhood of forty years and it was not unusual for a wooden-hulled light vessel to be still in service sixty years after construction. The shortest-lived light vessel of which there is extant record was the one assigned to Carysfort Reef in the 1820's; it succumbed to dry rot after five years of service. Another short-lived new light vessel during the administration of the Lighthouse Board was No. 30. It came off the ways in 1863; but after only eight years of routine duty in the vicinity of Charleston, S. C., the board declared the vessel "unfit for service," and had it sold at public auction for $916. The Carysfort Reef light vessel and No. 30 were unusual, however; it was the rare lightship that served less than twenty years. It is difficult to understand the fifth auditor's statement, unless he really meant that the ships remained on station five to ten years before they had to be taken to the yards for major work.

Although through the years there had been an occasional metal-hulled lightship—one in 1874 at Merrill's Shell Bank in Mississippi, and the ex-Confederate gunboat *Lady Davis* in Charleston—naval architects were convinced for many years that metal hulls could not withstand the shocks of the rough seas that wooden hulls absorbed. Moreover, these people argued that a metal-hulled vessel would suffer more damage if driven ashore, that a metal-hulled lightship would be too expensive, that the metal bottom would foul more rapidly than the wooden one, and further "that the interior of the hull would sweat and become damp and unwholesome."

So the United States continued to build wooden light vessels. But in 1881 the country began to ease into metal-hull construction with the building of composite—part metal, part wood—hulls. Lightship No. 43, the first such vessel, had a hull of metal plates sheathed over with yellow pine planking. Lightships Nos. 68–71, built in 1897, exemplify another type of composition hull. They had steel frames covered partly by planks and partly by metal plates. By 1900, all but a few people had come to recognize the superiority of metal hulls, but as late as 1902 the Lighthouse Board ordered an all-wood light vessel, No. 74.

## Lightship Propulsion and Equipment

Propulsion machinery was late in coming to light vessels. The steamer *Arctic* had been equipped with an engine, but when it became a lightship, the machinery was removed, and the vessel had only sails to rely upon for motive power. The first lightships built with engines were Nos. 55, 56, and 57; the board authorized them in 1891. A tender towed the three vessels to their new stations in Lake Michigan in October, 1893, which indicates the power of the engines. Later lightships received more potent engines which could move the ship along at ten knots.

As naval architects worked on the design and motive power of these vessels, they also improved the habitability of the lightship. Originally, lightships were single decked, and the crew lived on a lower deck below the water line. The first steps to improve quarters involved building up the sides of the forward portion of the ship and decking it over so that quarters could be placed there. In later vessels the designers extended the forecastle, and in 1894, for the first time, a light vessel, No. 58, was constructed with a full upper, or spar, deck. Thus the quarters for all the crew were on the main deck, well above the water line. With this extra space each officer, usually four to a vessel, had a stateroom, and the crew had two-man rooms.

Ostensibly, during the days of the fifth auditor, the lightship crew was expected to keep its vessel on station in the severest of weather. But in view of the rather light anchor (1,200 lbs.) and the comparatively small cable of these early day lightships and the absence of spare equipment, the crew had a degree of protection. When a storm became very severe, the anchor dragged or the cable snapped and the captain had no choice but to head the ship for port.

The Lighthouse Board provided spare equipment, such as anchors, and, as time went on, heavier anchors and chains. In 1894, for example, three of the smaller-type light vessels, Nos. 55–57, were each moored to a five-ton sinker. And at least by 1917 the Diamond Shoals lightship, on one of the most exposed points of the east coast, was held on its station by an anchor and chain together weighing fourteen tons. The result of the heavier mooring gear, of course, was that fewer and fewer light vessels were blown off station. With the addition of engines as propulsion power in lightships, there were few justifiable reasons, in the eyes of the administrators, for a lightship to leave its station, and bad weather was not one of them. In 1892, the

The Nantucket Shoals, Massachusetts, lightship in 1956. Part of the ship's bilge keel, to lessen rolling, is visible just below the lettering on the hull. Here, a Coast Guard helicopter picks up a seriously ill seaman from a small boat, an example of the excellent physical access provided to this ship, on one of the most exposed lightship stations in the world. Early lightships would have had to leave station under similar circumstances. *U. S. Coast Guard official photo.*

three Lake Michigan light vessels left their stations without orders a few days before the close of the season. The Lighthouse Board was incensed at this "dereliction of duty" and fired the crews of the three lightships with the exception of one man.

In January, 1912, Lightship No. 25 left its station on Nantucket Shoals after parting its moorings and headed for port to pick up new equipment. The Bureau of Lighthouses thought so little of this decision that it publicly reprimanded the captain in the *Lighthouse Service Bulletin,* saying:

> In such cases it is expected that a light vessel with power, when her spare moorings and her hawser cannot be used, will remain on her station

by means of her engines, unless conditions are such that this is impossible. This vessel should have remained on her station and sent a wireless message to the lighthouse inspector to send a tender with extra moorings. Officers in charge of light vessels are cautioned that it is most important that the vessels remain on station during bad weather.

## Lightships Against the Sea

There were instances, however, when a skipper was considered justified in leaving his station. In a hurricane in September, 1889, the master of the Five Fathom Bank lightship, No. 24, found his twenty-

## "She was considerably hogged"

six-year-old ship "laboring heavily and leaking." He slipped his moorings and sought the shelter of Delaware Bay. Later, a close inspection of the ship at the district depot revealed "that she was considerably hogged, that her starboard rail was broken, that the seams of the spar-deck forward had opened during the storm, and that her hawsepipe would in short time have worked out had not the moorings been slipped." The ship was beyond repair, so the Lighthouse Board condemned her and six months later sold her at public auction for $200. Seldom had a lightship captain's decision been so utterly correct.

To maintain their stations in stormy weather, lightships took fearful poundings. In the fall of 1913, a hurricane swept the North Carolina coast

and passed over the Cape Lookout lightship, damaging davits, life boats, and life rails, as well as snapping the port chain to her rudder. A few months later Lightship No. 88 at the Columbia River station off Oregon experienced a severe gale. To hold the vessel on station the captain had "to steam strongly ahead from 5 A.M. to 4 P.M. during the worst part of the gale." In the morning a large comber came aboard the starboard side of the vessel and swept the deck of ventilators and smokestacks, smashed in the side of the pilot house, snapping the steering compass, bending the wheel shaft, and carrying the wreckage, along with the seaman on duty in the wheelhouse, across the deck. The seaman saved himself from going overboard by grabbing the life line. The sea ripped off deck bolts,

"THE LIGHT-SHIP FOR MINOT'S LEDGE. The light-boat represented [below], is a first class vessel of two hundred and thirty-two tons burthen, being ninety-eight feet in length, twenty-three and one-half in breadth and eleven feet in depth, and built by James H. Hood, Esq., of Somerset, Mass., under the superintendence of Capt. E. Jones. The appropriation for its construction was made by Congress, March 3d, 1853, the amount being $22,000. The total cost, however, will reach about $27,000. It is painted cream color, with the words 'Minot's Ledge,' in large black letters on each side. It now takes the place of the old light-vessel that has been moored there since the destruction of the ill-fated light-house which formerly occupied the ledge. There are two lamp masts; the mastheads rising sixty-one feet above the level of the sea. She is fitted with two lanterns, each having eight lamps and twelve inch reflectors, and displays

two lights forty-one feet and six inches above the level of the sea. The lighting apparatus was manufactured by H. N. Hooper & Co., of this city. The vessel is built in the most substantial manner of white and live oak and locust—well found with chains, anchors, water tanks and every necessary and convenience. She is copper bolted and copper fastened. She was fitted at the Charlestown navy yard, under the direction of John Southwick, Esq., agent of the light-house board. Capt. Joseph Battles, of Cohasset, keeper of the old vessel, is to take charge of the new. This fine vessel reflects great credit on the parties concerned in its construction and fitting, and the promptitude with which the provisions of Congress and the lighthouse board have been executed, are worthy of commendation [from *Gleason's Pictorial,* November 18, 1854]."

a coal bunker plate, smashed the engine room sky-light, and flooded the galley and engine room. After the storm passed, the captain assessed damages and coolly concluded that his vessel could wait for its annual trip to the yards for repairs. In March, 1924, the Pollock Rip lightship suffered through an easterly gale that forced her to keep full steam up for over thirty-six hours in order to stay on station. The seas battered her, at one time stoving in the whaleboat, at several other times rolling the ship over on her beam ends, and at another time washing several ventilators over the side, breaking the engine room skylight, and snapping the main signal mast. The severity of the storm can be measured by the fact that the seven-masted schooner *Wyoming* and a five-masted schooner, both of which were anchored in the vicinity, foundered, all hands being lost.

Other vessels trying to remain on station were not so fortunate. In November, 1913, Lightship No. 82, assigned to a station thirteen miles southwest of the north entrance to Buffalo Harbor, New York, disappeared in a storm with six men. Six months later the ship was found nearly two miles from its station in sixty-three feet of water; a year after the sinking, one crewman's body was found about thirteen miles from where the ship sank. A diver reported the ship's hull in good condition, but the interior of the vessel was wrecked. Investigators surmised that the vessel went down when the sea smashed the lantern house and poured water into the interior of the ship. The Lighthouse Bureau employed a contractor to raise the ship, but he failed; it was nearly two years after the sinking that another contractor delivered the raised vessel in Buffalo Harbor. In 1918, the Cross Rip light vessel mysteriously disappeared. Fifteen years later, a government dredge picked up wreckage in the vicinity of the station and local people speculated that it was part of the lightship, which had probably been crushed by the ice. This vessel was the second lost from this station. In 1866, the ship assigned there broke its moorings and drifted to sea, where her crew abandoned her. And in 1944, the Cuttyhunk lightship disappeared in a hurricane. The whole crew was lost. Although two bodies later washed ashore, no one has ever been able to determine what happened.

The accident that perhaps rattled the Lighthouse Board most was the loss of Lightship No. 37 at Five

Fathom Bank off the entrance to Delaware Bay. On August 23, 1893, the seas were rough at the bank; the captain was ashore and the mate had charge of the vessel. As the afternoon wore on the winds began to blow and increased as night fell. As midnight approached green water began to break over the ninety-eight-foot, 240-ton vessel. A little after midnight the seas carried away the ship's two boats. The crew noticed that after each swamping the ship listed a little more to port. At 1:45 A.M. a particularly vicious wave rolled the lightship over on her beam ends. She paused there for a moment and then slid sideways into the sea. The crew was thrown into the water. The assistant engineer was trapped below deck, but he managed to free himself after the ship went down and popped to the surface where he grabbed the scuttle of the main hatch and held onto it until rescuers reached him sixteen hours later. Meanwhile, the other crew members secured what wreckage they could find and held on. But four of the crew could not withstand the rough seas and succumbed before rescuers arrived.

"This was the first instance in the history of the United States Light-House Establishment," the board lamented, "in which a light-ship has foundered at her moorings." The board promptly dispatched an investigating committee to the area to find out what happened. After questioning the two survivors the committee concluded that the main hatch had been improperly secured and the sea had worked the covering loose. A succession of waves poured water into the interior of the vessel through this opening, as well as through the companionway and the forward ventilator. The committee concluded that had a more experienced man been in charge of the ship, he would have found a way to close the main hatch securely. Thus the mate received the blame, but he wasn't there to defend himself, since he was one of the four lost.

The sunken light vessel was now a hazard because a portion of her upper works protruded above the surface of the water. Feeling that it would not be practicable to raise the ship, the board asked the navy to blow her up. On October 16, 1893, the U.S.S. *Vesuvius* destroyed the wreck of Lightship No. 37.

These were unusual instances. A more typical case involved Lightship No. 1 when it was assigned to Martin's Industry off Tybee. In October, 1894,

## Wreck at Five Fathom Bank

the forty-year-old vessel was blown off station by a "cyclone"—a term used in those days that usually meant a hurricane. The sea swept over the ship taking all her boats and breaking three of the captain's ribs. The mate and the crew with much difficulty worked the ship back on station where she remained until the weather improved.

Even with the improved moorings the Lighthouse Board introduced, there were many instances through the years of lightships snapping their chains and winding up on the beach. Most often these vessels, with the aid of tugs, could be worked off, repaired, and put back on their regular stations. Repairs usually were expensive. Lightship No. 11, assigned to Nantucket Shoal, went ashore in 1855, just one year after coming off the ways, and cost 90 percent of her original price to get ready for return to duty. Ten years later a storm blew her on the rocks from her station at Brenton Reef, Rhode Island, and extensive repairs at "heavy expense" were needed to put the vessel back into shape.

The first lightship on the West Coast, No. 50, went aground several times and each time was an expensive burden to the Lighthouse Board to get her back on station. Built in 1891–92 at Union Iron Works in San Francisco, the vessel took up station near the mouth of the Columbia River on April 11, 1892, and was held in place by a 5,000-pound mushroom anchor. She performed faithfully and unspectacularly until November 28, 1899, when a gale with winds up to seventy-four miles per hour slashed at the Oregon coast. All day the ship strained at her moorings and in late afternoon the two-inch chain snapped, putting the vessel "at the mercy of wind and sea." Hauling in the remaining chain, about forty-five fathoms, the captain moved the ship off-shore about twenty-five miles and waited out the night. The next morning the skipper headed his vessel for the Columbia River. By now many on shore knew the predicament of the lightship, and the lighthouse district inspector dispatched two tugs and the district tender to help her get to port. One of the tugs, the *Wallula*, got a line to the lightship, but hardly had a strain been put on the manila when it parted. Then the tender *Manzanita* shot over a hawser, but it broke and fouled the tender's propellers, putting her in a perilous condition. Then the *Escort*, the second tug, moved in and succeeded in taking the lightship in tow. The tug had pulled the vessel nearly over the bar of the

The Nantucket New South Shoal lightship, on station and rolling heavily (note her smooth, round hull), in 1891. Her lanterns, which encircle the masts, have been raised from their deck housings into position as night falls. *From* Century Magazine. *Reproduced from the collection of the Library of Congress.*

river when the hawser parted. The captain had to make a quick decision, and he had few options; he could beach the vessel or see her pounded to death on the rocks either at McKenzie Head or at the southern end of Cape Disappointment. The captain chose beaching the vessel, and aimed the lightship for a sandy shore between the other two evils. Before running up on the beach, the skipper adroitly maneuvered the vessel so that her bow pointed toward the sea, thus using the high forecastle to prevent the sea from rolling the ship over. Having safely beached the vessel, the crew disembarked in an orderly manner via breeches buoys.

The Lighthouse Board immediately laid plans to refloat the ship. In July, 1900, it entered into a contract with a firm to haul the ship off her perch, but the task proved more difficult than the board or the contractors imagined. Several subsequent efforts also were unsuccessful. The board then decided to haul her overland—some 700 yards—to Bakers Bay. On February 14, 1901, a company agreed to pull the vessel to Bakers Bay within thirty-five days. First, the contractor's crew cleaned the sand out of the partially filled ship and then swung her bow around so that the ship headed toward shore. Next they laid tracks and pulled the vessel on to this temporary railway. By dint of will and strength they inched the vessel across the land and through woods to Bakers Bay. Depositing the ship in the bay, the contractor had finished; it was now up to the board to get her ready for sea again. The Lighthouse Board spent $14,000 on repairs, and towed the light vessel back to her station on May 26, 1902.

Three years later the ship was back on the beach, this time just north of Cape Disappointment. She was hauled off, repaired, and put back on station a year and three days after grounding.

Next to storms, the greatest danger a lightship faced was collision with another vessel. Usually these rammings were not too serious and damage was slight. Barges under tow and sail vessels seem to have been involved in the majority of these accidents, and many of them occurred in the New England area where traffic was thicker. Lightship No. 5, while stationed at Cross Rip, experienced collisions with fifteen barges and schooners over a twenty-one-year period that began in 1886. Generally, damage was not heavy. The cost of repairing damages to the lightship was always borne by the colliding vessel, since the lightship was at anchor and could not maneuver out of danger. That is, the offending vessel paid damages if it could be identified. The barges and schooners that caromed off lightships and faded into the fog without giving identification are legion.

The most serious collision occurred on April 24, 1919, when a Standard Oil Company barge under tow struck Relief Light Vessel No. 51 while it was temporarily assigned to the Cornfield Point station off Connecticut. The ship went down within eight minutes of being rammed, but the crew abandoned ship in an orderly manner and no lives were lost.

The Diamond Shoals lightship also was sunk, but not accidentally. Lightship No. 71 was occupying the station on August 6, 1918, when the crew noticed a German submarine attacking a merchant vessel. The lightship's radio operator sent a message crackling over the wireless to warn other shipping in the area. Apparently the submarine picked up the signal, for the Germans turned their attention toward the lightship. They did permit the twelve-man crew to abandon ship, and then fired six shots at the immobile vessel. About this time, though, a richer target in the form of a merchant vessel hove into view, and the submarine broke off the attack on the lightship. Disposing of the merchantman, the submarine turned its deck gun once again on the light vessel and this time poured shells into her until the vessel sank onto the shoals she had guarded other vessels against. Nevertheless, her demise had not been useless; the warning her radioman sent out saved about twenty-five other vessels whose masters had received the message and took refuge in the bight of Cape Lookout. Rather than risk another vessel on the shoals while hostilities existed, the Lighthouse Bureau used buoys there until March 30, 1919, when Relief Lightship No. 72 took up the position of her sunken sister vessel.

In addition to serving as a warning to the navigator of a dangerous hazard, the lightship has on more than one occasion been a haven to the seaman who had been the victim of shipwreck. The crew of the British steamship New Castle City undoubtedly felt the finest Christmas present they had ever received was Lightship No. 1, assigned to what was then called Nantucket New South Shoal. On Christmas Eve of 1887, the New Castle City foundered in a storm a few miles from the lightship. Able to launch the steamer's boats, the officers and men pulled for the lightship, and, fortunately, all reached her safely. The weather remained bad, and the survivors had to stay aboard the light vessel for over two weeks before other ships could get out to take them off. In 1916, the Blunts Reef lightship off Cape Mendocino hosted over 150 men, women, and chil-

The Blunts Reef lightship off Cape Mendocino, California. A typical modern lightship, her masts not only display her light but bristle with sophisticated communications and meteorological devices. *U. S. Coast Guard official photo.*

dren, all passengers of the liner *Bear* which had run afoul of the northern California coast. Although the survivors remained less than half a day, the resources of the little lightship were considerably strained providing blankets and food. Once, the San Francisco lightship served as a haven of refuge for birds. In 1902, forest fires in northern California caused a thick smoke to hang over that section of the state, apparently driving many birds from their normal habitat. These land birds, including species ranging from owls to hummingbirds, took refuge aboard the lightship. When the smoke cleared, the birds flew off.

## Improving the Lightship

Over the years the lighthouse service continued to work on lightships to improve their effectiveness as aids to navigation. Shortly after the Lighthouse Board took charge, it introduced an improved type of lamp and reflector into the lighting apparatus of the light vessel, replacing the lamp that had the solid cylindrical wicks. Lanterns aboard lightships at this time usually encircled the mast and were lowered each morning into houses built around the mast. The lamps and parabolic reflectors in the lantern were tended to and readied for exhibiting that night. At sunset the lightship crew raised the lantern to its normal height on the mast, about twenty-five feet above the deck. In the 1890's the board began the use of electricity in the lighting apparatuses of the lightships. No. 51, built in 1892, was the first vessel to use this new source of light. At first stationed at Cornfield Point off Connecticut, it was moved in 1894 to the more important station off Sandy Hook.

As time went on, of course, better fog signals were added to the ships. Radio, too, was added to lightships as soon as that medium proved practical. The board first experimented with radio aboard

The Ambrose lightship surrenders her station off New York harbor to a Texas tower in 1967. The first "outside" lightship, stationed off Sandy Hook in 1823, was replaced by the Ambrose Channel lightship in 1908.

Contrast the easy accessibility of this station, via helicopter and electronic communications equipment, with the almost complete isolation of most early lightships. *U.S. Coast Guard official photo.*

lightships in 1901. As it turned out, the first commissioner of the Lighthouse Bureau, G. R. Putnam, had a special interest in radio and encouraged its use throughout the service.

The lightship has served well through the years—whether as a haven of refuge or as an aid to navigation—and has been a most useful instrument. Lightships could be placed where no lighthouses could be built or where no buoys would remain. But from the beginning the lightship was doomed, especially in the United States.

Americans from the earliest days thought in terms of lighthouses. As early as 1806, Congress ordered an examination of Diamond Shoals to see if a lighthouse could be erected there, and when a negative reply resulted, Congress did not then turn to lightships, but instead lost interest. Americans were slow to realize the unique value of lightships and did not introduce them into this country until nearly a century after England proved their effectiveness. About thirty years after the first one was positioned, the country's lighthouse service, through the Lighthouse Board, revived the emphasis on lighthouses and made it a policy to replace lightships with lighthouses where possible. The board directed its efforts first toward replacing the "inner" lightships—that is, the ones located in bays and sounds—with screw-pile lighthouses. This endeavor proved successful, so it was inevitable that in time the country would attempt to replace outside lightships.

In the 1880's and 1890's, the Lighthouse Board tried placing a lighthouse on the rough and tempestuous Diamond Shoals. But the currents and storms halted efforts in the first stages of construction, and the board settled for a lightship on this dangerous shoal. Technology simply had not progressed enough to erect a lighthouse at such a violent place.

Also, where possible, the lighthouse service has tried to replace lightships with buoys. The Heald Bank lightship, for example, was placed on station in 1905 and remained there until 1938 when a buoy replaced it. Today buoys occupy numerous spots, particularly off the New England coast, where full-crewed lightships once strained at their moorings. As of 1971, New England had only three lightships remaining, at Portland, Boston, and Nantucket Shoals; Cross Rip, Pollock Rip, New South Shoal, and the others have all been replaced by buoys.

As time went on, technology in the construction of buildings on the water advanced, and by the 1960's for such places as Diamond Shoals the United States Coast Guard had the answer: the Texas tower. The Coast Guard began erecting these huge four-legged towers to replace such well-known vessels as the Ambrose lightship and the Diamond Shoals lightship.

The sun is setting on the red-hulled lightship as an aid to navigation. Texas towers or improved buoys have replaced all the country's lightship stations except one.

# Lighthouses of the North Atlantic Coast:

## *Maine through Delaware*

FOR MANY years the bulk of the country's lighthouses clustered in New England. In 1825, for example, nearly two-thirds of them were located between New York City and West Quoddy, Maine—a distance of less than 600 miles. There were several reasons for such heavy concentration in this relatively small section of the coast. The basic one was that the shipping industry centered at that time in New England. Of course, no one would deny that the area's rock-bound coast, liberally dotted with offshore islands and shoals, called for aids to navigation; no one begrudged New England a single lighthouse, buoy, or light beacon. Moreover, the system of establishing lighthouses in use at that time—that is, responding principally to local agitation—favored New England because its population, heavily centralized along coastal areas, was deeply interested in shipping activities.

The pattern for this concentration of lighthouses had been set during the colonial period; after all, nine of the colonies' eleven lighthouses were located from Delaware Bay northward. Indeed, seven of them were situated on the coast between New London, Connecticut, and Portland in southern Maine.

After the Revolution, New England retained its preeminence in maritime activity, and as a result, the number of lighthouses increased overwhelmingly along her coast. Of the fourteen lighthouses built between the end of the war and 1799, all but four were north of New York City. And the following twenty years saw little change in this ratio. Only six of the twenty-six lighthouses erected in

the 1801–1820 period guarded shores south of Delaware Bay. In other words, in 1820 the coast from Delaware Bay northward possessed 75 percent of the nation's lighthouses.

One should not draw any inference of sectional rivalry from these statistics. There is no evidence that the southern states felt any discrimination in the lighthouse field. These figures reflect only greater seafaring activities in the northern states.

The foundation and nucleus of the lighthouse service in New England were, of course, the colonial lighthouses. At the end of the Revolution, less than half these lighthouses were still operating; consequently, the various ex-colonies went about repairing these lights and making them operable.

### *Boston Light (1716)*

Boston lighthouse on Little Brewster Island received immediate attention. In 1783, the Massachusetts legislature provided over £1,400 to rebuild the war-damaged tower and to secure a suitable light. The workmen erected a conical stone tower seventy-five feet tall, and the keeper lighted its several lamps in December, 1783. The state operated the light until June 10, 1790, when, in accordance with recently enacted federal law, it turned the station over to the central government. The colonial practice of letting the keeper also serve as a harbor pilot continued under federal government rule, and in 1838, a naval officer inspecting lighthouses at the request of the Treasury Department

\* Not lighted        †Not standing

1. Boston
2. Brant Point
3. Beavertail
4. New London
5. Sandy Hook
6. Cape Henlopen†
7. Plymouth
8. Portsmouth
9. Cape Ann
10. Nantucket
11. Newburyport Harbor
12. Portland Head
13. Seguin Island
14. Montauk Point
15. Baker's Island
16. Cape Cod
17. Gay Head
18. Eaton's Neck
19. Annisquam Harbor
20. Chatham Harbor
21. Franklin Island
22. Whitehead Island
23. Black Rock Harbor†
24. Clark's Point†
25. Butler Flats
26. New Haven Harbor\*
27. Cape Poge
28. Point Judith
29. West Quoddy Head

30. Falkner's Island
31. Little Gull Island
32. Sands Point†
33. Scituate†
34. Long Island Head
35. Tarpaulin Cove
36. Race Point
37. Boon Island
38. Petit Manan Island
39. Libby Island
40. Owl's Head
41. Pemaquid Point
42. Dice Head
43. Fort Tompkins†

44. Long Point
45. Windmill Point
46. Isle of Shoals
47. Monhegan Island
48. Moose Peak
49. Cape May
50. Fire Island
51. Matinicus Rock
52. Cape Elizabeth
53. Navesink\*
54. Baker Island
55. Brandywine Shoal\*
56. Morgan's Point\*
57. Whaleback
58. Ipswich
59. Nauset Beach

60. Robbins Reef
61. Bear Island
62. Marblehead
63. Mount Desert Rock
64. Saddleback Ledge
65. Barnegat\*
66. Minots Ledge
67. Sankaty Head
68. Absecon\*
69. Ship John Shoal\*
70. Cross Ledge\*
71. Fourteen Foot Bank
72. Bass Harbor Head
73. St. Croix River\*
74. Statue of Liberty\*
75. Derby Wharf

The present Boston light tower in 1966. This tower was erected in 1783 at the site of the first, which had been blown up by the British in 1776; in 1859 the tower was raised to its present height of 89 feet. Here and at Cape Ann, Massachusetts, Winslow Lewis so successfully demonstrated his Argand lamp–parabolic reflector system that the federal government adopted it in 1812. The site of this light is the oldest still in use in the United States, and today its second-order Fresnel lens gives a light rated at 2-million candlepower. *U. S. Coast Guard official photo.*

complained that the keeper's piloting duties caused him often to neglect his lighthouse responsibilities. This practice apparently ceased prior to 1851, for in their report the Lighthouse Board did not mention it; and that sort of thing the Lighthouse Board would not have overlooked. Also, sometime prior to 1851, the wooden interior tower stairway was removed and a metal stairway installed. By that time the tower had been recently equipped with new twenty-one-inch English parabolic reflectors, and seamen considered Boston light the best of the reflector type on the United States coast—which doesn't speak well, however, for the American-produced reflectors. Nevertheless, the board felt the tower was too short, and in 1859 it had the tower raised fourteen feet so that the top of the lantern was eighty-nine feet above ground. At the same time, the tower, which the board had previously noted as being cracked, was strengthened with a lining of brick. In addition, where the outer masonry bulged, workmen removed stones and patched the tower with brick. A new second-order Fresnel lens completed the renovation. Since then, the light has served faithfully, except for a period during World War II when the Coast Guard extinguished it for security reasons.

Until the late 1840's, the cannon remained the station's fog signal. Around 1850, a fog bell, weighing nearly three-quarters of a ton, was installed. In 1872, the Lighthouse Board installed a more modern fog trumpet, and fifteen years later had a steam siren placed at the station.

Despite the warning supplied by the light and the fog signal during inclement weather, several ships have come to their end virtually at the doorstep of the Boston light. In 1861, the *Miranda,* a square-rigger, ran on the rocks near Brewster Island in a snow storm and left but twelve survivors. The schooner *Calvin F. Baker* during a gale in 1898 also smashed onto rocks near the lighthouse; she lost at least three crewmen, who froze to death in the rigging.

The Boston light is the country's first, and therefore oldest, light station. Its *tower,* though of an early vintage, is *not* the country's oldest—Sandy Hook rates that honor. The Boston tower of colonial days was destroyed by the British when they evacuated Little Brewster in 1776. According to some accounts, the British placed their charge of black powder *under* the structure when they blew it up.

The state of Massachusetts rebuilt the tower on the same island in 1783. There is no documentary evidence that the builders reconstructed the tower on the undamaged portion of the old tower, if there was even any useable portion left. The only time the tower seems to have been built on was in 1859 when the Lighthouse Board raised the tower to its present height.

*Brant Point Light (1746)*

The Brant Point light at the entrance to Nantucket Harbor survived the Revolution, but not for long. In 1783, it burned, and the local people erected a fourth light that same year. Cheaply made and simply erected, this light became known to mariners as a "bug" light because of the dimness and smallness of its beam. Unsatisfactory, the "bug" light was replaced by a stronger one in 1786. This light survived two years, when a storm blew it down. Some time between 1788 and 1795, when Massachusetts turned the Brant Point light over to the central government, a more substantial structure rose up on the point. This building resisted the blows of Nantucket for thirty or more years, but by 1825 it had become unsafe, and the government condemned it. This time the fifth auditor erected a frame tower on top of a dwelling. Completed in 1826, this tower lasted for thirty years. In 1837, an inspector found that the light consisted of eight lamps with twelve-and-a-half-inch reflectors. Its light was poor, and no wonder: the interior of the lantern was smoked, as were the chimneys, and the reflectors were black and spotted.

By the time the Lighthouse Board arrived on the scene the structure had deteriorated badly, and in 1853 the district engineer felt the lighthouse was beyond repair and recommended rebuilding it. Completed and lighted on December 10, 1856, the new tower, located on the west side of the entrance to Nantucket Harbor, was constructed of brick and stood forty-seven feet above the ground. It was equipped with a fourth-order lens.

During the last half of the nineteenth century the channel into Nantucket Harbor shifted, thereby reducing the effectiveness to vessels of the Brant Point light. A temporary light was installed at the extremity of Brant Point in 1900 while a new cylindrical, wooden tower was built nearby. Lighted on January 31, 1901, this tower has survived to the

Beavertail Light Station, Rhode Island, in 1884. Although this tower was built in 1856–57, the station itself dates back to colonial times. Note the drawn shades inside the lantern, a standard practice in the nineteenth century to protect the lens against discoloration by the sun's rays. *U. S. Coast Guard photo 26-LG-11-17 in the National Archives.*

present, and is the lowest lighthouse in New England; the focal plane of the light is but twenty-six feet above sea level. The old brick tower was left standing and was there at least as late as 1945.

### Beavertail Light (1749)

New England's third—the country's fourth—light station, situated on the southern end of Conanicut Island, has through more than two centuries marked the east and west entrances to Narragansett Bay. Burned by the British in 1779, the station, better known as Beavertail, was later relighted by the state of Rhode Island. The state turned the lighthouse over to the central government in 1793.

The keeper's dwelling, built too near the water and on a poor foundation, collapsed in 1815, and the government built a new one the following year.

Although better located, it was poorly put together, according to Lt. George Bache's report twenty-two years later. Bache also reported that the tower, sixty-four feet tall, was built of rubble stone and contained a spiral wooden stairway. The light, ninety-eight feet above sea level, consisted of fifteen lamps with nine-inch reflectors, some of which were bent out of shape.

In 1851, the Lighthouse Board said that the Beavertail tower was the worst built one the members had seen to that point. Furthermore, they found the station to be poorly maintained and in a "wretched condition." The keeper was Mrs. Demarius H. Wheaton, the widow of the former keeper who had died in 1848, but her twenty-year-old son actually did the work of tending the light. The lamps and reflectors were also in a run-down state.

The board built a new light tower at the station

New London Harbor Light Station, Connecticut, about 1884. The keepers take time out from a game of croquet to watch offshore activity. *U. S. Coast Guard photo 26-LG-13-20 in the National Archives.*

in 1856–57 and placed on it a third-order lens exhibiting a fixed white light. The square granite tower has survived to the present. The board installed a fourth-order lens, flashing white, in 1899; today the light is a fourth-order lens converted to hold an electric bulb.

### New London Light (1760)

Located at the entrance to the Thames River and placed to guide vessels in and out of the harbor, the New London light was turned over to the federal government in 1790. No longer useful, the 1760 tower was replaced in 1801 with a stone, octagonal

Sandy Hook Light Station, New Jersey, about 1890. This tower still stands and is today the oldest light tower in the United States. *U. S. Coast Guard photo 26-LG-15-1 in the National Archives.*

shaped tower, eighty feet tall. In 1838, Lt. Bache reported the light, whose focal plane was 111 feet above the sea, was "in very good order." The workmen obviously built a good tower in 1801, for it has survived through the years. But its fourth-order lens, first installed in 1855, is today only eighty-nine feet above the water.

### Sandy Hook Light (1764)

The oldest light tower in the United States (although its height may have changed) is at Sandy Hook, New Jersey, at the entrance to New York Harbor. Despite the vicissitudes of the Revolution, the tower survived, still a credit to its builder. In 1838, the lighthouse was found to be in good order, and in

1852, the Lighthouse Board reported it in a remarkably fine state of preservation with a light adequate as an entrance light. In addition to the tower, the station had two beacons, and the one keeper was expected to take care of all three lights. He was given a small sum to hire help, but the paucity of the amount permitted him to hire only poor quality assistance. The keeper expressed his independence by lighting and putting out the lamps when he saw fit, usually at dusk and dawn respectively, not at sunset and sunrise as the fifth auditor instructed.

In 1856, the board placed a third-order lens on the tower, where it has remained. Although threatened by erosion in the 1870's, the octagonal tower has lasted through the years, a remarkable monument to its builder, Isaac Conro.

The Cape Henlopen, Delaware, light tower around 1925. Erosion slowly ate at the foundation of this historic colonial tower and toppled it in the spring of 1926. Note that the lens had already been removed when this picture was taken. *U. S. Coast Guard photo 26-LG-19-18B in the National Archives.*

## A battle with erosion

### Cape Henlopen Light (1767)

Down the coast on the south side of the entrance to Delaware Bay, the Cape Henlopen light for years guided shipping along the coast and into the bay. During the Revolution, the British burned the tower nearly to the ground, but with the return of peace the Pennsylvania Board of Wardens went about repairing the structure and in 1784 relighted the tower. The workmen must have done a good job, for almost seventy years later it was regarded as a well-built tower.

In 1838, the light consisted of thirteen lamps with spherical reflectors. Although the tower was in good condition, the lantern had many broken panes that had been replaced by sheets of copper and wood, thus reducing the quality of the light.

By 1851, conditions had improved and the lantern now had eighteen twenty-one-inch parabolic reflectors with "Lamps and burners not good; though better than usual." In 1856, the board replaced the light with a first-order Fresnel lens to make Cape Henlopen an effective seacoast light.

The nemesis of the lighthouse was erosion. For over 160 years the tower waged a constant battle with the forces of nature. When construction of the tower began in 1765 the shore line was one mile away; 150 years later the shore line was within 150 feet of the tower.

Erosion first lifted its head in 1788, when the Board of Wardens noticed that sand was blowing away from the foundation of the tower, thereby threatening to undermine the structure. The Wardens apparently controlled erosion by planting bushes and weeds.

Many years later nature put in motion a sand dune that bore down on the light station. During the Civil War measurements showed the dune was moving at the rate of eleven feet per year. By 1863, the sand had banked up to the second floor of the keepers' dwelling, and the Lighthouse Board had to build a new home for the keeper and his family. Five years later the same dune posed a threat to the security of the light tower, and the keepers worked diligently shoveling the sand away as fast as it piled up around the tower.

In 1883, a storm drove the sea up on the beach so that water lapped at the foundation of the tower, causing considerable anguish and concern for the safety of the tower. A year later the bark *Minnie*

*Hunter* went ashore north of the tower, and the beach and the shore line began to build. Out of the tragedy of shipwreck came an answer, so the board thought. Feeling that the bark was a good breakwater, the board ordered brush and stone jetties laid. For the most part, tides swept away the jetties about as fast as workmen installed them.

In 1899, the erosion pattern changed, and the sand dune around the lighthouse began blowing away, exposing the foundation. The Board put in a brush cover to stop the wind erosion, but that only slowed the movement of sand. By the fall of 1924, it had become apparent that the tower was doomed, so the Bureau of Lighthouses discontinued the light. On April 13, 1926, a severe storm undermined the tower and toppled it.

### Plymouth Light (1764)

Plymouth, or Gurnet Point, lighthouse, situated on the north side of the entrance to Plymouth Bay, easily survived the Revolution and apparently performed its job throughout that conflict, despite having been near the scene of a battle between a nearby fort and a British frigate and having been struck by a stray cannon ball. The state repaired the war damage in 1783, and in 1790 turned the light station over to the central government. With the station came the keeper, a Mrs. Thomas, the widow of the first keeper.

Fire consumed the Plymouth light tower in 1801, and in 1802–1803 the federal government erected twin towers, so that navigators could distinguish that station from the single light station at Barnstable. The double lights were each but twenty-two feet tall and thirty feet apart. "Their elevation," an inspector reported in 1838, "is 70 feet above the level of the sea, enabling them to be seen . . . all the way across to Race point [*sic*], a distance of nineteen miles." The inspector pointed out that the towers were too close together and at a short distance appear to be a single light. In 1842, the government rebuilt the Plymouth light towers. Like their predecessors these two wooden towers were too close together to be effective. Nevertheless, they continued to function, although their importance steadily declined as Plymouth lost its maritime traffic. With the opening of the Cape Cod Canal in 1914, the light resumed importance as a coastal aid. Ten years later, the Bureau of Lighthouses discon-

Nantucket (Great Point) light in 1969. This light station was the first (1784) of only two lighted by any state government after the United States declared its independence and before the federal government assumed responsibility for navigational aids. *Photo by Jack Boucher for HABS.*

tinued one light. The one left was described in the 1951 *Light List* as being a white, octagonal, pyramidal tower whose fourth-order electric light was 102 feet above sea level.

## Portsmouth Light (1771)

The Portsmouth Harbor, New Hampshire, tower survived the Revolution easily, and in 1791 the state turned over to the nation the tower and "one and three-quarters acres of a neck of land in New Castle, on Great Island, at the entrance of Piscataqua River, commonly called Fort Point." By 1804, the original wooden tower had deteriorated, compelling the government to erect a new one, also of wood, on a granite foundation. In 1838, Lt. T. J. Manning, U.S.N., reported the lighthouse as being in "fine order," and in 1851 the investigating board found the tower in good condition, but they noted that the tower was lighted with lamps and spherical reflectors "old and much worn." The interior of the lantern was "very dirty." This octagonal tower, eighty feet tall, lasted for twenty-six years, and in 1877 the Lighthouse Board built an iron tower 1,000 feet east of the old tower. This white tower still stands, emitting a green flashing light, the focal plane of which is fifty-two feet above sea level, from an electrified fourth-order lens.

## Cape Ann Light (1771)

The tradition of twin lights on Cape Ann at Thatchers Island has been continued through the years. In 1790, when the state turned over the station to the federal government, the two towers were forty-five feet tall, but their lights were ninety feet above sea level, giving them a range of sixteen miles. The towers were 300 yards apart. In 1851 the Lighthouse Board considered this station "very important," and felt that it should be increased in power and range. At that time its light consisted of eleven lamps with twenty-one-inch reflectors.

In 1860–61, the Lighthouse Board rebuilt the towers of stone and fitted them with first-order Fresnel lenses. The towers were 124 feet from base to the top of their lanterns, but their lights were 166 feet above sea level.

In 1865 the assistant keeper became very ill. The keeper felt he had to get the man ashore for medical attention and on the day before Christmas rowed the sick man to the mainland. While ashore a thick snowstorm came up and the disappointed keeper had to spend Christmas Eve away from his family. Meanwhile, his wife and children, mindful of the importance of this station, lighted the two towers and every so often throughout the cold night trudged through the snow to tend the lights. The next morning the storm had not let up, but the keeper wanted to spend at least part of Christmas Day with his wife and children. Early in the morning he began rowing for Thatchers Island. It was impossible to see the island in the cloud of snow flakes, but he pulled in the direction he thought the island lay. On he rowed, not knowing for sure which lay across his track, the island or the open sea. Then in the distance he saw the distinctive twin lights, and with relief he pulled in their direction. Soon he felt the warmth of his kitchen, smelled the odors of the cooking Christmas meal, and, most important, heard the happy noises of his children.

The station on Thatchers Island was instrumental in averting a tragedy of monumental proportions in 1919. The S.S. *America,* returning from Europe with President Woodrow Wilson and his staff aboard, was unknowingly steering for Thatchers Island in a thick fog. At the last minute the sound of the fog signal at Cape Ann was heard aboard ship, and the captain altered course in time to prevent disaster.

The station has continued to function through the years, but today only the southern tower is lighted. The Bureau of Lighthouses discontinued the northern tower in 1932.

These surviving colonial lighthouses were the nucleus for the formidable system of aids to navigation that came to line the United States shore from St. Croix River in Maine to Cape Henlopen in Delaware—a system that was never static, but from the close of the Revolution to the present underwent continuous growth and change as technology permitted advances.

## Nantucket (Great Point) Light (1784)

Of course, the greatest growth and change came under the administration of the federal government, and Massachusetts was the only state that effectively continued providing lighthouses prior to 1789, when the central government assumed to itself responsibility for aids to navigation. Hardly had the

Newburyport Harbor Light Station on Plum Island, Massachusetts, in 1914. This light station was the last (1788) lighted by any state government before the federal government took over responsibility for lighthouses in 1789. *U. S. Coast Guard photo 26-LG-8-80 in the National Archives.*

dust of the Revolution settled when the Commonwealth of Massachusetts planned a lighthouse for Great Point on Nantucket Island. Established in 1784 and known through the years as the Nantucket light, the station has had a remarkably stable existence. The first light tower was wooden, and a fire in 1816 consumed it. Rebuilt of stone two years later, this second structure, with a brick lining as reinforcement installed in 1857, has survived to the present. Numerous shipwrecks occurred in the vicinity of the light in the latter part of the nineteenth century because vessels confused the light with the Cross Rip lightship. For some reason the Lighthouse Board was uncharacteristically slow in responding to this problem, but in 1889, it placed in the light a red sector covering Cross Rip Shoals. Although not entirely halted, shipwrecks occurred with less frequency thereafter.

### Newburyport Harbor Light (1788)

Four years after establishing this light, Massachusetts had two towers erected at Newburyport Harbor to mark the entrance to the Merrimack River. Originally set up on Plum Island, these lights have been moved many times to conform to the shifting channel of the river. The two towers have been rebuilt several times. The present light comes from a single tower which was built in 1898.

### Portland Head Light (1791)

In the 1790's, with lighthouse building now the responsibility of the central government, there was an increase in the construction of lighthouses in New England. In 1791, Maine received its first light tower. In 1790, the partially completed tower lo-

Portland Head Light Station, Maine, about 1940, and *(below)* as drawn for the Historic American Buildings Survey, National Park Service, in 1965. Although the keeper's dwelling has undergone minor changes and the station has acquired a new foghorn, the tower is essentially the same as originally constructed in 1790. *U. S. Coast Guard photo 26-LG-4-1 in the National Archives.*

Montauk Point Light Station, New York, in 1884. Built in 1797 on the east end of Long Island, this tower is today threatened by erosion. Note that the lens is draped with a cloth cover, another precaution to pro-tect the lens from being scratched and from the sun. *U. S. Coast Guard photo 26-LG-12-68 in the National Archives.*

cated at Portland Head was turned over to the federal government. Congress appropriated $1,500 to complete the work, and the tower was lighted in 1791. In 1855, the tower was lined with brick, received an iron stairway, and had placed on it a fourth-order Fresnel lens. Ten years later, in order to provide adequate warning to mariners of Alden's Rock and Bulwark Shoals, the Lighthouse Board raised the light twenty-one feet by installing a second-order lens. Lowered again in 1883 by re-install-ing the fourth-order lens, the light regained its per-manent height two years later with the return of the second-order lens. Although extensively repointed in 1900, the tower survives to the present, at least on the exterior, essentially as it was originally built.

### Seguin Island Light (1797)

Five years after completing the Portland Head light, the federal government erected a light on

The first-order Cape Cod (Highland) light, Truro, Massachusetts, in 1959 *(left; photo by Cervin Robinson for HABS)*, and as it appeared in 1859, when it mounted a Fresnel lens. *U. S. Coast Guard photo 26-LG-6-3 in the National Archives.*

Gay Head Light Station on Martha's Vineyard, Massachusetts, about 1890. The squat appearance of this 47-foot tower tends to hide the fact that its light is 160 feet above the sea. *U. S. Coast Guard photo 26-LG-6-76B in the National Archives.*

Seguin Island about twenty-five miles east of Portland, Maine. Lighted in 1797, the tower was rebuilt in 1820 and again in 1857, and was considered by the Lighthouse Board as "one of the most important positions on the eastern coast." To dispel rumors of buried treasure on the island, the Bureau of Lighthouses in 1936 authorized one Archie Lane to hunt for one year on the island. After nine months of unsuccessful digging, Mr. Lane gave up his quest.

### Montauk Point Light (1797)

In 1797, John McComb, one of the United States' earliest famous builders and architects, and the son of a well-known builder and architect, completed the lighthouse at Montauk Point on the eastern tip of Long Island, New York. In compliance with his contract with the government, McComb erected an 80-foot tower of "Chatham freestone, fine hammered." The light was 160 feet above sea level. This tower has survived through the years, continuing to be a significant mark to those vessels entering and leaving Long Island Sound. In the mid-nineteenth century the Lighthouse Board called this station "a very important light, especially for navigators bound from Europe to New York." The Lighthouse Board greatly increased the effectiveness of the light in 1858 when it installed a first-order Fresnel lens on the tower. The Montauk tower today is threatened by erosion, and efforts to stop the encroachment of the sea have so far been to no avail.

### Bakers Island Light, Massachusetts (1798)

Also in the 1790's, the government built a lighthouse on Bakers Island at the entrance to Salem Harbor to replace a beacon, apparently an unlighted daymark, put up there by the Marine Society in 1791. Lighted January 31, 1798, the station at one time consisted of two lights, but since about 1870 the station has exhibited only one light.

### Cape Cod (Highland) Light (1798)

Toward the end of the eighteenth century, the central government erected two other lighthouses in Massachusetts. One of these was the first lighthouse on Cape Cod. Located in 1798 on high land near Truro, the tower's light was 160 feet above sea level. The Cape Cod tower was rebuilt in 1833 and again in 1857. At the time of the latter construction, the Lighthouse Board had a first-order Fresnel lens placed on the tower to make this aid more visible to the mariner; the light, after all, was usually the first sighted by traffic from Europe bound for Massachusetts Bay. Today, the short brick tower, with its light 183 feet in the air, still gives its warning to the seamen plying these hazardous waters.

*Above,* the old twin masonry towers of Chatham Light Station, Massachusetts, about 1884. *U. S. Coast Guard photo 26-LG-6-17 in the National Archives. Below,* the original (1816) Race Point Light Station, Cape Cod, Massachusetts, about the time of the Civil War. *U. S. Coast Guard photo 26-LG-9-21, National Archives.*

## Harbor lights and seacoast lights

### Gay Head Light (1799)

The following year, in 1799, Martha's Vineyard received its first lighthouse. Located on the western tip of that island, the Gay Head light was a wooden, octagonally shaped tower on a stone foundation. Though the tower was but 47 feet tall, the focal plane of the light was nevertheless 160 feet above the level of the sea. Not content with the effectiveness of the light, the Lighthouse Board built a new tower and placed a first-order lens on it. The new light was exhibited on December 1, 1856, and could be seen nineteen miles. A brick double dwelling completed the station. Although the Coast Guard donated this first lens to the Dukes County Historical Society in 1953, the light with a different apparatus has continued to serve its function both as a guide to the entrance to Vineyard Sound and as a seacoast light.

### Eatons Neck Light (1799)

Deep in Long Island Sound the government erected a lighthouse in 1799 on Eatons Neck at Huntington Bay, Long Island. Fifty feet tall, the tower, with only renovation in 1868, has lasted through the years. Today its third-order lens exhibits a flashing white light that is 144 feet above sea level.

### New England Lights (1800–1810)

During the first decade of the nineteenth century, New England continued to receive the bulk of new lighthouse construction. Of approximately nineteen lighthouses erected during the period 1801–1810, sixteen were located between New York City and the Canada–United States border. Nearly half of these lights were situated to mark entrances to harbors or bays. Annisquam Harbor on Wigwam Point, Gloucester, Massachusetts (1801); Chatham Harbor, Massachusetts (1808); Franklin Island at Muscongus Bay, Maine (1807); and Whitehead Island at the entrance to Penobscot Bay (1807) are several examples of light stations established in the first decade of the nineteenth century to mark bays and harbors. Several harbor lights built at this time have not survived to the present day. Black Rock Harbor light not far from Bridgeport, Connecticut, built in 1809 and rebuilt in 1824 after a gale toppled it; a light at Clark's Point, New Bedford Harbor,

built in 1804 and replaced by the Butler Flats light in 1898; and the New Haven Harbor light, erected in 1804 and discontinued in 1877 with the lighting of the Southwest Ledge light, are today nothing but memories.

Cape Poge light (1802) served not only to guide shipping into Edgartown Harbor on Martha's Vineyard, but also to help seamen clear the shoals to the southward. Point Judith light (1809) guided ships into Narragansett Bay as well as past it. West Quoddy Head lighthouse (1808), with its distinctive red and white horizontal stripes, marked the Quoddy Roads and served to guide vessels along that stretch of the Maine coast.

### Lights in Long Island Sound (1800–1810)

Lighthouses established in Long Island Sound during this decade included Falkner's Island (1802), Little Gull Island (1806), and Sands Point (1809). This latter light, whose tower dated back to 1868, was superseded in 1922 by a new structure out on the reef beyond this point. About the same time, Mrs. Oliver H. P. Belmont built an estate nearby. Offended by the traffic that passed over the government road, Mrs. Belmont purchased the property, reportedly for $100,000, and demolished the old light tower.

### Increase in Seacoast Lights (1811–1830)

The second decade of the nineteenth century saw a greater emphasis put upon the erection of lighthouses south of Delaware Bay, although the majority of new construction occurred north of the bay, especially in Maine and Massachusetts. Although several of the northern stations had harbor light functions, such as Scituate (1812), Long Island Head (1820) at Boston, and Tarpaulin Cove (1818) on Naushon Island, Massachusetts, other lights with broader duties were being constructed. Race Point Light Station on the northern tip of Cape Cod, for example, served as a guide to both Boston Bay and Cape Cod Bay. When originally established in 1816, the tower was of stone, but in 1876, the Lighthouse Board erected a cast-iron tower that is still in use. Boon Island light, a gray granite tower on a bare rock six and a half miles off the coast of Maine, was lighted in 1812, and functioned as a coastal light and as a guide to Ports-

Owls Head Light Station, at the entrance to Rockland Harbor, Maine. This light was established in 1825 under the superintendency of Stephen Pleasonton. The metro-nome-shaped structure on the point is a daymark. *U. S. Coast Guard official photo.*

mouth. Tall for its day, some seventy feet, the Lighthouse Board considered the tower too short for a first class light and on January 1, 1855, lighted a new stone tower whose focal plane was 133 feet above sea level. The scene of a sad instance of shipwreck and cannibalism in the eighteenth century, Boon Island has been regarded as one of the most isolated stations on the coast of Maine, which is saying a great deal, since Maine is abundantly endowed with islands off her coast that are little more than rocks. And on many are light stations. Celia Thaxter, whose father was keeper at the Isle of Shoals Light Station in New Hampshire, wrote the poem "The Watch of Boon Island," which tells of the responsibility these light keepers felt.

Like the Boon Island station, the lighthouse on Petit Manan Island, Maine, erected in 1817, was intended as a coast light, but the board considered its height, fifty-three feet, to be hardly adequate for a "first class seacoast light." In 1855, the board constructed a new stone tower and surmounted it

with a second-order Fresnel lens, thus raising the focal plane of the light to 123 feet above sea level.

The 1820s saw the advent of Stephen Pleasonton as general superintendent of lights, and a tremendous spurt in lighthouse construction. In the period 1821–1825, the nation erected at least twenty-nine lighthouses. Many, of course, were lights designating entrances to harbors, bays, and rivers, such as Libby Island (1822) at the entrance to Machias Bay, Maine; Owl's Head (1825) at Rockland Harbor, Maine; Pemaquid Point (1827) at the entrance of Johns Bay, Maine; Dice Head (1829) at the entrance to Penobscot River in Maine; and Fort Tompkins light (1828) at the entrance to New York Harbor. This latter light, incidentally, was moved in 1903 to Fort Wadsworth near what is now the south end of the Verrazano Narrows Bridge.

Long Point, near Provincetown, Massachusetts, was established in 1827 and rebuilt in 1875. Today it is viewed annually by thousands of visitors to

Dice Head Light Station, Maine, about 1900. The curtains are drawn in the lantern to protect the lens against discoloration by the sun. *U. S. Coast Guard photo 26-LG-1-92 in the National Archives.*

Cape Cod National Seashore. The light station at Stonington, Connecticut was established in 1824 on Windmill Point. In 1840, the stone tower and dwelling were torn down and relocated on the east side of the harbor. This combination tower–keeper's dwelling served until the establishment of the Stonington Breakwater light in 1889. The old lighthouse is preserved today by the Stonington Historical Society, which has opened it to the public.

More significant was the continued proliferation of lights that served other than local traffic. The Isle of Shoals light was erected on White Island off the mainland of New Hampshire south of Portsmouth in 1821 and was last rebuilt in 1859, when it received a second-order Fresnel lens. Monhegan Island light, some eleven miles off the Maine coast, went into service in 1824, and in 1857 received a second-order Fresnel lens. The Moose Peak Light Station in Maine began operation in 1827, and its remodeled tower received a second-order lens in

1887. Second-order lenses were not designed to serve harbor or other local traffic; fourth- and fifth-order lights were usually quite adequate for that work.

The 1820's saw the advent of a number of lighthouses that in time became well known. In 1823, the Cape May, New Jersey, light located on the north side of the entrance to Delaware Bay went into service. Rebuilt in 1847 and again in 1859, the tower, with the light from its first-order lens visible nineteen miles, still guides shipping into Delaware Bay.

### Fire Island Light (1826)

The Fire Island lighthouse came into use in 1826, and, with the focal plane of its light eighty-nine feet above sea level, marked the entrance to the Bay of New York. The height was not enough for a principal coast light and in 1852 the Lighthouse Board

Stonington Harbor lighthouse in 1929. Moved from its original site to the town of Stonington, Connecticut, this old structure is now preserved by a local historical society as a historic house. *U. S. Coast Guard photo 26-LG-17-10 in the National Archives.*

felt that it would be "clearly necessary to increase its height, and place in the tower the most powerful lens apparatus that can be found." In 1857–58, the board erected a new tower rising 150 feet into the air and situated 200 yards northeast of the original tower. Lighted November 1, 1858, the lens's focal plane was 167 feet above sea level. The tower was first painted with its present black and white bands in 1891. The Lighthouse Board regarded the Fire Island light as the most important one on the coast for transatlantic steamers bound for New York. These vessels aimed for this light, and, generally, it was the first one they made.

### Matinicus Rock Light (1827)

To the north, in Maine, two important lighthouses went into service in the latter part of the 1820's. Matinicus Rock has been described as having "neither tree nor shrub and hardly a blade of grass. . . .

The surface is rough and irregular and resembles in a large way a confused pile of loose stone. Portions of the rock are frequently swept by the waves which move the huge bowlders [*sic*] into new positions." On this inhospitable site the fifth auditor had built a light station composed of two wooden towers. Lighted in 1827, the towers lasted until 1848, when it became necessary to rebuild them, this time using stone. Rebuilt ten years later and equipped with third-order lenses, these two towers, located about twenty-five miles from the mainland, served through the years to guide ships along the Maine coast as well as into Penobscot Bay.

### Cape Elizabeth Light (1828)

On the mainland just south of Portland, the government built at Cape Elizabeth in 1828 two rubble stone towers, one equipped with a fixed white light and the other a flashing light. Serving both as a

Institutional gingerbread: Fort Tompkins lighthouse, New York, about 1900. In 1903, the Lighthouse Board moved this light to Fort Wadsworth at the Verrazano Narrows. *U. S. Coast Guard photo 26-LG-11-69 in the National Archives.*

Fire Island Light Station, New York, in 1898. The original tower was replaced by the present tower *(right)* in 1858. *U. S. Coast Guard photo 26-LG-11-62 in the National Archives.*

coastal light and as a mark to enter Casco Bay and Portland Harbor, the Lighthouse Board regarded this station as one of the most important on the east coast, a rather extravagant claim. Two cast-iron towers 300 yards apart replaced the stone towers in 1874, and in the 1920's the west iron tower was taken down. Since then the station has had only one light, and that coming from a second-order lens 129 feet above the water.

*Navesink Light (1828)*

In 1828, two years after the establishment of the Fire Island light, the government erected the Navesink light to mark the western entrance to New York Bay. The Highlands of Navesink had seen lights as early as 1746, but these were signal lights designed to warn New York of the approach of enemy vessels. A militia unit took up station on the Highlands

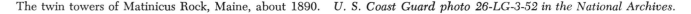

The twin towers of Matinicus Rock, Maine, about 1890. *U. S. Coast Guard photo 26-LG-3-52 in the National Archives.*

with explicit orders to light the fires only upon sighting the enemy. The decision to touch off the fire could be made only by the militia officer present. The fire would be seen by an observer in New York who would then spread the word. For a while everything went fine; the militia was on duty, standing its regular watches to seaward. One night a soldier accidentally touched off one of the beacons. Unable to put out the fire, the militia unit envisioned the people of New York in a state of panic as they fumbled to meet the invasion. They need not have worried; no one in New York noticed the fire, not even the person assigned to keep an eye out for the warning beacon.

The Navesink station consisted of twin towers, and David Melville of Newport, Rhode Island, supplied the lighting apparatus—one of the rare times when Winslow Lewis did not get the contract. The first Fresnel lenses used in this country were the ones Commodore Matthew C. Perry purchased and the fifth auditor had installed at Navesink. The first- and second-order lenses were placed on the twin towers and lighted in 1841. In 1852, the Lighthouse Board called these lights "the best on the coast."

By 1857, the twin towers were in bad condition and the Lighthouse Board decided upon erecting replacements. The board erected two brownstone towers, one octagonal and the other square, and connected them with a dwelling. The keeper lighted the new lights, both first-order lenses, on May 1, 1862.

In 1883, the Navesink towers became the initial first-order lighthouses to use mineral oil, and in 1898 the south tower became the first electrically lighted lighthouse in the United States when an electric arc bi-valve lens was installed. About the same time, the board discontinued the north tower, and in 1954 the Coast Guard turned the Highlands of Navesink Light Station over to the Borough of Highlands for development as a historic site.

### Baker Island Light, Maine (1828)

Lighted also in 1828, the Baker Island lighthouse, near what is now Maine's Acadia National Park, was primarily a harbor entrance light guiding vessels into Frenchman Bay. The light's first keeper was William Gilley, a long-time resident of the 123-acre island. He remained keeper for twenty-one

years and was removed for some reason now lost to history. His sons resented the dismissal of their father, and they continued to live on the island, harassing the new keeper at every opportunity. Even though they were squatters, Joseph and Elisha Gilley virtually prohibited the keeper from free access to the island's landing. And what is more, they collected grazing and other fees for use of the island.

When the district inspector learned of their activity, he recommended in 1853 that the Gilleys be forcibly ejected from the island. The Lighthouse Board started legal action to remove the squatters, but the Gilleys entered a countersuit contesting ownership of the island. In attempting to prove it indeed owned the land, the government found there was a defect in the title that went back to a land transfer in 1806. Unable to prove clear title, federal attorneys effected a compromise with the Gilleys whereby the government received nineteen acres of land on which the light station stood, a road access from the landing to the lighthouse, and pasturage for the keeper's cattle.

About this time the old tower had become worthless, so the Lighthouse Board in 1855 built a new tower and fitted it with a fourth-order lens. It hasn't been rebuilt since.

Some forty years later the question of trespassing arose again, and government attorneys, after examining the record, concluded that it would work undue hardship to reopen the question of ownership at this late date, and that the lighthouse service really could claim only the plot of land on which the light station stood. The whole thing was finally settled when the courts ruled that in addition to the light station land, the lighthouse establishment should have free access to the landing and a right of way to the light station. The light still beams from the 1855 tower to guide shipping into Frenchman Bay. In addition, many visitors to Acadia National Park journey over to the island.

### Brandywine Shoal Light (1828)

Down the coast at Brandywine Shoal in Delaware Bay, the fifth auditor had a pile lighthouse built in 1827–28. Not long afterwards it was "demolished by action of the sea," and a lightship resumed its place at the shoal, where one had been first placed in 1823.

## Harbor Lights (1830–1840)

In the 1830's, harbor lighthouses were erected at such places as Morgan's Point near Mystic, Connecticut (1831); Whaleback near Portsmouth, New Hampshire (1831); Ipswich, Massachusetts (1838); Nauset Beach on Cape Cod (1839); and Robbins Reef in upper New York Bay (1839). Bear Island light near Acadia National Park went into service in 1839, and was last rebuilt in 1890. The light at Marblehead, Massachusetts, was established in 1836. Its tower was low, but adequate for the time. But as the years rolled by, houses rose up around the station and obscured the light. After more than a decade of suspending the light from a 100-foot mast, the Lighthouse Board erected a new tower, 100 feet tall, on the site of the old one and lighted it April 17, 1896.

## Mount Desert Rock Light (1830)
## and Saddleback Ledge Light (1839)

Mount Desert Rock light, about twenty-five miles south of Mount Desert Island, was erected in 1830. Rebuilt in 1848, it was raised to sixty feet in 1857 and equipped with a third-order lens.

Saddleback Ledge light in Maine was lighted in 1839 and has survived through the years, due to its fine construction. In 1842, I. W. P. Lewis said it was the best-constructed lighthouse he had seen on his inspection trip and (still sniping at his uncle, apparently)[1] was "the only one ever erected in New England by an *architect and engineer.*"

## Barnegat Light (1835)

Barnegat Light Station, New Jersey, came into existence on July 20, 1835, and had been built by Winslow Lewis. Located on the south side of Barnegat Inlet about forty-five miles south of Sandy Hook, the light was apparently primarily a guide to the inlet; the tower was but forty feet high. In 1851, the Lighthouse Board found that the lamps had fourteen-inch reflectors and figured the light was equivalent to a fifth-order lens. But if the fifth auditor had intended it also as a coastal light, it had a miserable reputation. Lt. David D. Porter,

[1] See pp. 16 and 33. The history of Barnegat Light (above) indicates that I. W. P. Lewis's criticisms of his uncle's skill may have had some substance.

U.S.N., commanding the mail steamer *Georgia,* said the light could be seen about ten miles in clear weather, but "when the weather is at all hazy, (as in Indian summer,) the light cannot be discerned, or if seen, it is impossible to tell whether it is a ship's light or a lighthouse." Similarly Captain H. K. Davenport, U.S.N., skipper of the mail steamer *Cherokee,* said, "Barnegat light is but an indifferent one; is frequently mistaken for a vessel's light. . . ." At the same time, he recommended upgrading the light to first order, since ships "bound to New York from the South generally run for this light. . . ."

Although desiring that Barnegat be a first-order light, the board installed as its first Fresnel lens on the tower one of only the fourth order.

In 1855, the board dispatched Lt. George G. Meade to look at the light and make recommendations as to its fate. Meade quickly perceived that

The first-order Barnegat lighthouse, New Jersey, about 1865. This light, 175 feet above sea level, was lighted in 1859 in an attempt to lessen the frequency of shipwrecks along the treacherous New Jersey coast. *From Frank Leslie's Illustrated Newspaper.*

BARNEGAT LIGHT-HOUSE.

The triple lights of Nauset Beach on Cape Cod, Massachusetts, about 1884. This is a good example of the "overlighting" revealed by the inspection of 1838. Apparently, this instance was allowed to continue. *U. S. Coast Guard photo 26-LG-8-69 in the National Archives.*

Mount Desert Island Light Station, Maine, as depicted in an 1839 engraving. *U. S. Coast Guard photo 26-LG-4-5 in the National Archives.*

the light's primary duty should be that of a coastal light and that it served little purpose as an inlet light, since the channel was so twisting that only a foolhardy skipper would attempt to bring his ship in at night. Moreover, he found the Barnegat tower to have been poorly constructed with inferior materials. The mortar was falling out in places, and ten feet below the lantern the wall bulged out, causing a number of bricks to fall away. Meade, as had others before him, noted the number of shipwrecks along that coast and said that had there been a better light many disasters could have been avoided. In order to have an adequate aid to navigation at this point, Meade proposed erecting two towers. The principal tower would be 150 feet tall and placed on a rise 30 feet above the ocean; thus, the focal plane of the light would be 180 feet above the sea. A second tower of lesser order, he said, should be placed nearby and it would be 80 feet tall.

Agreeing with Meade about the real role of this lighthouse, and concluding that it was probably more important than the one at Sandy Hook, since it was usually the first one sighted by vessels from Europe and from the south, the Lighthouse Board in 1857 began construction of a new tower 900 feet south of the old one. Exhibited January 1, 1859, the new first-order light was truly a seacoast light, since its focal plane was 175 feet above sea level. Through the years the light tower was often threatened by erosion, but brush jetties slowed the progress of the abrasion.

In 1926, the Bureau of Lighthouses gave the station, except for the tower, to the state of New Jersey. The bureau continued to maintain an automatic light in the tower until January 1, 1944, when it decided to discontinue the light because the same job was being done by the Barnegat lightship, which had been established in 1927. The old tower still stands, and is viewed annually by thousands of seashore visitors.

## Sankaty Head Light (1850)

The year 1850 saw three significant lighthouses go into operation: the Sankaty Head light, the Minots Ledge light, and the screw-pile lighthouse on Brandywine Shoals. Benjamin F. Isherwood, later to achieve fame as chief engineer of the United States Navy during the Civil War, supervised construction of the brick tower at Sankaty Head on the southeast corner of Nantucket Island. Its light, a second-order Fresnel lens, was 150 feet above the sea, and was considered by the Lighthouse Board an excellent light. Isherwood built well, for the tower has never been rebuilt, and is today, with a broad red band around its middle, a prominent daymark, as well as a prominent light. It is equipped with a first-order lens.

## Minots Ledge Light (1850)

The Minots Ledge light, on the outermost of the Cohasset Rocks about twenty miles southeast of Boston, achieved its first fame through tragedy. Cohasset Rocks and vicinity had seen many shipwrecks, forty recorded between 1832 and 1841. The need for a light here was recognized by I. W. P. Lewis and other engineers, as well as ship's masters and owners. Lighted January 1, 1850, the light tower was the first one the United States built that was exposed to the full force of the ocean. Pleasonton, on advice of Captain William H. Swift of the Topographical Bureau, had built an open skeleton wrought-iron tower. The iron piles, or legs, of the structure were sixty to sixty-three feet in length. The workmen sank each leg into the rock five feet and "a cement formed of iron filings held each in place." Horizontal braces held the eight outer legs together. Braces radiated out from a ninth leg, a centerpole, to further strengthen the tower. At the top of the legs rested the dwelling and lantern.

Pleasonton and his staff felt that the tower could be thrown over only if the sea topped the dwelling. But then that was an unfounded fear, they reasoned, since the dwelling was perched on high legs and beyond the reach of the ocean. The first keeper did not have such confidence in the pile lighthouse, and, denouncing the structure as unsafe, he quit. His successor, John W. Bennett, a former sea captain who had experienced storms and had little fear of a riotous sea, scoffed at the first keeper's attitude. But it wasn't long before the ex-sea captain changed his mind, and after his first storm in the tower, he reported it unsafe. A committee from Boston investigated the light, but did nothing. In March, 1851, a severe storm swept that portion of the coast and thoroughly shook and rattled the iron frame structure, creating so unstable a platform that the keepers were unable to go about their work. A visitor to the light tower went through one of these

Sketch of the first Minots Ledge lighthouse, Cohasset, Massachusetts, lighted 1850. The pilings were sunk five feet into the rock and were cemented in place. *U. S. Coast Guard photo 26-LG-8-47, National Archives.*

Artist's conception of the destruction on April 17, 1851, of the first Minots Ledge lighthouse. *From* Century Magazine. *Reproduced from the collection of the Library of Congress.*

storms with Captain Bennett and reported the tower "vibrated and trembled with every shock" of the wind and sea. The tower shook and turned and the visitor noted: "The lighthouse shakes at least two feet each way. I feel as seasick as ever I did on board a ship." After the storm had passed, the visitor remarked, "The [bracing] rods put into the tower section are bent up in fantastic shapes; some are torn asunder from their fastenings."

A month later another and more intense storm descended upon the New England coast. The principal keeper left the lighthouse on April 11 and attempted to return the next day, but the sea was too high for the mile-and-a-quarter trip in a small boat. The storm continued to build and by the sixteenth it was raging at its fullest, already having

swept several houses on the shore into the sea. Around 1:00 A.M. on the morning of April 17 people on the shore heard above the howl of the wind the Minots Ledge fog bell being pounded furiously. Then there was silence. When the dawn came and visibility cleared, the people on the shore no longer saw the spidery thing on the Outer Cohasset Rocks. The site was as clean as it had been in 1847 before construction began. When people rowed out to the site, all they saw were iron stubs bent to leeward. The two assistant keepers manning the station died. The body of one washed ashore at Nantasket, and the other one was found to have reached Gull Rock, where he died of exhaustion and exposure.

Almost immediately afterwards, a lightship arrived to assume the duties of the vanished tower.

Laying the twenty-seventh course of stone on the present Minots Ledge light tower in 1859. The vessel moored to the left of the tower carries stone for construction of the new tower. *U. S. Coast Guard photo 26-LG-8-25 in the National Archives.*

It remained on duty until the new light tower displayed its light in 1860.

The Lighthouse Board decided a stone tower should go up on Cohasset Rocks in the same location as the old skeleton tower, and General Joseph G. Totten of the Lighthouse Board submitted drawings that were followed almost to the letter in final construction. On June 20, 1855, work on the new edifice began. The workmen removed the stumps of the old tower and cut away the ledge to prepare a foundation for the stone base of the tower. Eight iron poles sunk in the old holes and running through the lower courses acted as a frame to hold the foundation stones in place. Two-inch, galvanized-iron bonding bolts and cement further held the courses of granite stones in place. This solid foundation rose up to forty feet, and an additional forty feet comprised the living, working, and storage space of the lighthouse. The new lantern and lens were installed and test lighted on August 22, 1860. Regular display of the light did not occur until November 15, when the keepers reported for duty. The Lighthouse Board built homes for the keepers and their families ashore. Since then the tower has withstood the worst storms, the only effect being vibrations. In 1947, Minots Ledge, whose focal plane is eighty-five feet above the sea, was made an unmanned station.

The Minots Ledge tower was probably the single greatest engineering achievement of the Lighthouse Board. The original Minots Ledge tower was probably the single greatest construction mistake of the fifth auditor's administration of lighthouses. On the other hand, probably the finest construction contribution during the fifth auditor's reign was the introduction of the screw-pile lighthouse into the United States.

*The Screw-Pile Lighthouse:*
*Brandywine Shoal (1850)*

The screw-pile lighthouse is similar to other pile-type lighthouses except that the end of each pile is equipped with a broad-bladed screw. The screw is twisted into a sand or coral bottom much as one twists a screw into a piece of wood. Not only is the screw a means for getting the pile into the ocean bottom, but its three-foot blade provides additional bearing surface.

The inventor of the screw-pile lighthouse was

Approaching the present Minots Ledge lighthouse on a foul day around 1900. Waves have overtopped this tower many times since its construction, and still it has held. *U. S. Coast Guard official photo.*

Absecon light tower in 1891, and *(below)* as drawn for the Historical American Buildings Survey, National Park Service, in 1964. Constructed under the supervision of Lt. George G. Meade and lighted in 1857, the tower displayed a first-order light 167 feet above the sea. The light was discontinued in 1933. *U. S. Coast Guard photo 26-LG-10-1 in the National Archives.*

Alexander Mitchell, an Englishman, and he built the first such structure on Maplin Sound at the mouth of the Thames River in 1838.

Congress heard about this new method of constructing lighthouses, and in the mid-1840's the Committee on Commerce announced it believed the screw-pile lighthouse would replace light vessels, and they proposed that the first such structure in the United States be erected at Flynn's Knoll in New York Harbor. But there weren't many people outside Congress who felt that anything more than a buoy was needed at Flynn's Knoll, and the project died.

The first screw-pile lighthouse in the United States was erected on Brandywine Shoal in Delaware Bay. Brandywine Shoal had been a light-vessel station since 1823, except for a brief period in 1828 when an ordinary pile lighthouse stood there until it was "demolished by action of the sea." Major Hartman Bache, who had a distinguished career as an army engineer and spent much of his time in the lighthouse service, designed and built the Brandywine Shoal screw-pile lighthouse. Construction began in 1848 and on October 28, 1850, the keeper lighted the new third-order lens. The light was forty-six feet above sea level.

A threat to any lighthouse in Delaware Bay is floating ice during the winter months. To fend off the ice, Bache installed a fence, consisting of screw piles five inches in diameter, around the lighthouse. In 1857, an outer fence was added, and the space between the two fences was platformed over. To help further in fending off the ice, the Lighthouse Board had tons of stone riprap dumped around the lighthouse.

An examination of the screw piles of the lighthouse twenty-three years after building showed that

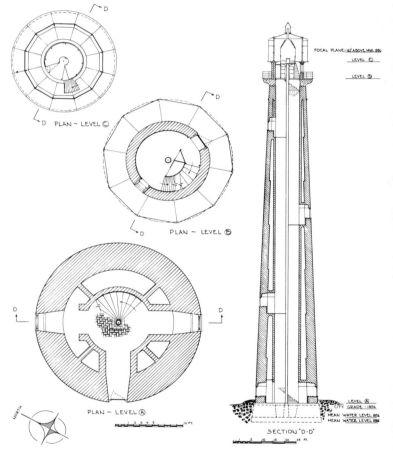

they were in remarkably good condition. There was some corrosion and a few of the braces had been bent out of position, but damage was minor. The lighthouse was looked at closely in 1910—when it was sixty years old—and a diver found the metal badly rusted and many of the braces broken. The inspecting party concluded the lighthouse sorely needed rebuilding. In 1913, a contractor began building a reinforced-concrete, cylindrical lighthouse adjacent to the old lighthouse. The new tower displayed its light on October 20, 1914.

The success of the Brandywine Shoal lighthouse encouraged the board to attempt other screw-pile lighthouses in Delaware Bay. In 1855, the board began erecting such a light structure at Cross Ledge, not too far from Brandywine. But the ice floe of 1856 destroyed the foundation work. The board began having second thoughts about the efficacy of a screw-pile lighthouse in that location, and decided to depend upon the lightship which had been there since 1823. A lighthouse was finally lighted at Brandywine Shoal in 1878.

*Absecon Light (1857)*

One of the most frequently visited light stations during its active days was the lighthouse at Absecon in Atlantic City, New Jersey. Although first authorized in 1837, the Absecon light was not completed and lighted until January 15, 1857. Built under the supervision of Lt. George G. Meade, the brick tower, which was erected on a stone foundation resting on a wood platform, rose 150 feet into the air. In keeping with its role as a primary seacoast light, the board installed a first-order lens on the tower. Its purpose was to guide ships past Absecon and Brigantine Shoals. The wrecks along that section of the coast had been "frequent and appalling," but in the first ten months of the light's service not a single wreck was reported. To increase its effectiveness as a daymark, the board in 1872 had the tower painted white with a wide red band about its middle. The board changed this marking in 1898 to an orange tower with a black middle band.

The Lighthouse Bureau discontinued the light in July, 1933; an electric beacon on the Steel Pier had replaced it. Although the station's other buildings disappeared in subsequent years, the tower remained standing. In 1948, the U. S. Coast Guard gave the tower to the city, which in time restored it as a historic structure. Today the old tower is the centerpiece of a city park.

*The Caisson Lighthouse: Ship John Shoal (1877) and Fourteen Foot Bank (1886)*

The board had planned to put a screw-pile structure at Ship John Shoal (named for the ship *John* that

sank there in 1797), but when it heard of the disaster at Cross Ledge, it called off construction work at Ship John Shoal. A lighthouse was finally put there in 1877 with the building of a caisson-base structure.

One of the more prominent caisson structures was the Fourteen Foot Bank lighthouse in Delaware Bay. The cast-iron cylinder was floated out to the site in 1886 and put into position. Rock was piled around the exterior of the seventy-three-foot-high cylinder to keep the sand from scouring away. The workmen then filled the cylinder with concrete. On top of that they built a dwelling surmounted by a lantern. It was completed and lighted in 1887.

In the 1850's, two smaller but interesting lighthouses erected were Bass Harbor Head light and St. Croix River light. Built in 1858 on Mount Desert Island, the site today of Acadia National Park, Bass Harbor Head light served to assist vessels in getting into the harbor. Consisting of a white tower attached to a dwelling, the original structure has lasted to the present.

The St. Croix River light was erected in 1856 on Dochet Island, the place where Samuel de Champlain established a short-lived French colony in 1604. In the middle of the river separating Canada and the United States, Dochet Island was difficult for the increased shipping to Calais, Maine, to pass at night without the aid of a light. Fire recently destroyed the lighthouse and several other structures. The present light rests on a slender steel skeleton tower.

The Statue of Liberty, perhaps the most famous national monument in the country, once served as a lighthouse. In 1877, Congress authorized the president to accept the statue from France and maintain it as a beacon. It was dedicated on October 28, 1886, and President Grover Cleveland turned the statue over to the Lighthouse Board a little over two weeks later. On November 22, 1886, the statue, then known as *Liberty Enlightening the World,* was lighted. The flame of the torch Liberty holds had been cut away at the sides and glass inserted. The electricity for the light that beamed from the torch came from an electric plant specifically placed on Bedloe Island (now Liberty Island) for that purpose. The light remained active for over fifteen years, and on March 1, 1902, the board extinguished it and turned the station over to the War Depart-

St. Croix River lighthouse on Dochet Island, Maine, before the fire. During its active years this light station occupied the number-one position in the *Light List* since its lighting in 1856, because of its proximity to the U.S.–Canada border. The metronome-shaped structure held the fog bell. Dochet Island is now part of St. Croix National Monument. *U. S. Coast Guard official photo.*

ment. Under local pressure, the War Department maintained a light in Liberty's torch for several years more. The statue and the island came into the National Park System in 1937.

A much smaller light is located at Salem Maritime National Historic Site in Massachusetts. On the end of Derby Wharf, not far from the custom house where Nathaniel Hawthorne worked, the Lighthouse Board placed a light on an old building in 1871. Neither a large nor powerful light was required, and from 1886 to 1906 a ship's side light was used. In 1906, a fourth-order lens was installed. To-day a small square white tower holds the light, which serves primarily to guide pleasure boats into the harbor.

By the end of the nineteenth century the country's coast north of Delaware Bay had been well marked, and most of its harbors, bays, sounds, and rivers were adequately equipped with aids to navigation to make the seaman's occupation safer. Although during the next half century or so there was an increase in the number of aids to navigation, these were minor aids, such as buoys and post lights, for marking channels and obstructions.

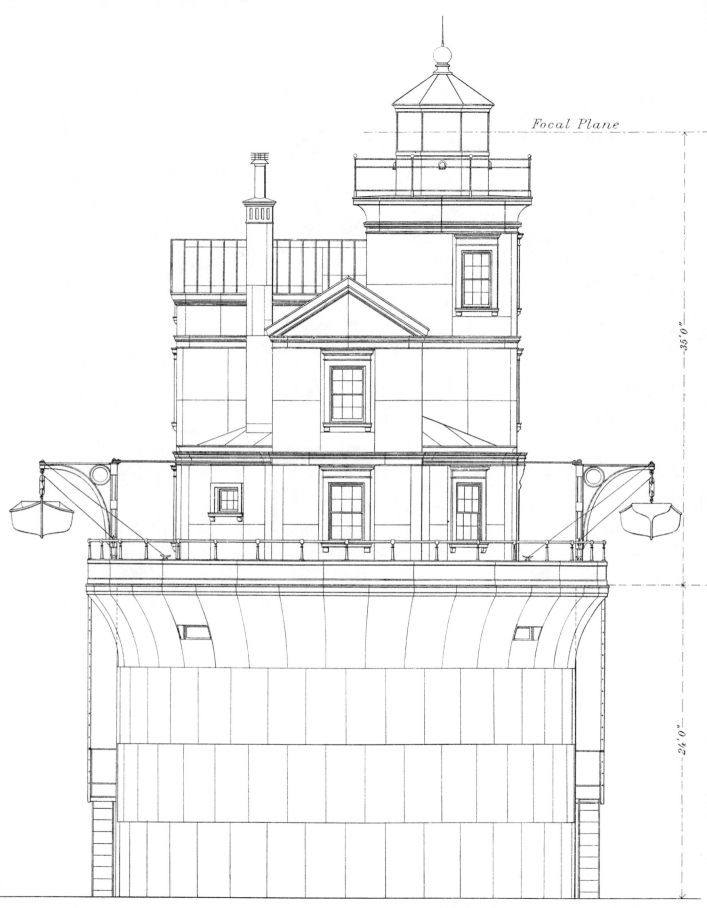

*Focal Plane*

35'0"

24'0"

South and sectional elevations (1886) of the caisson lighthouse established in 1887 at Fourteen Foot Bank in Delaware Bay. The cast-iron caisson was floated into position and filled with concrete. Compare this elevation with the exterior photograph of Sandy Point (Maryland) light, on page 117. *Drawing in the author's collection.*

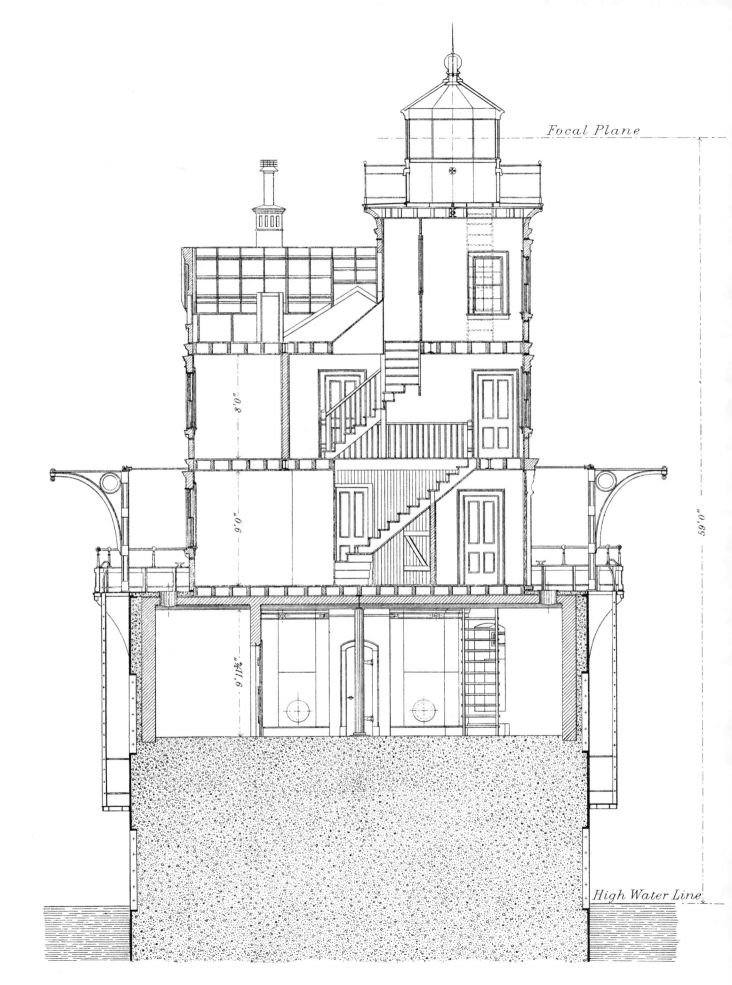

*Focal Plane*

59' 0"

8' 0"

9' 0"

9' 11¾"

*High Water Line*

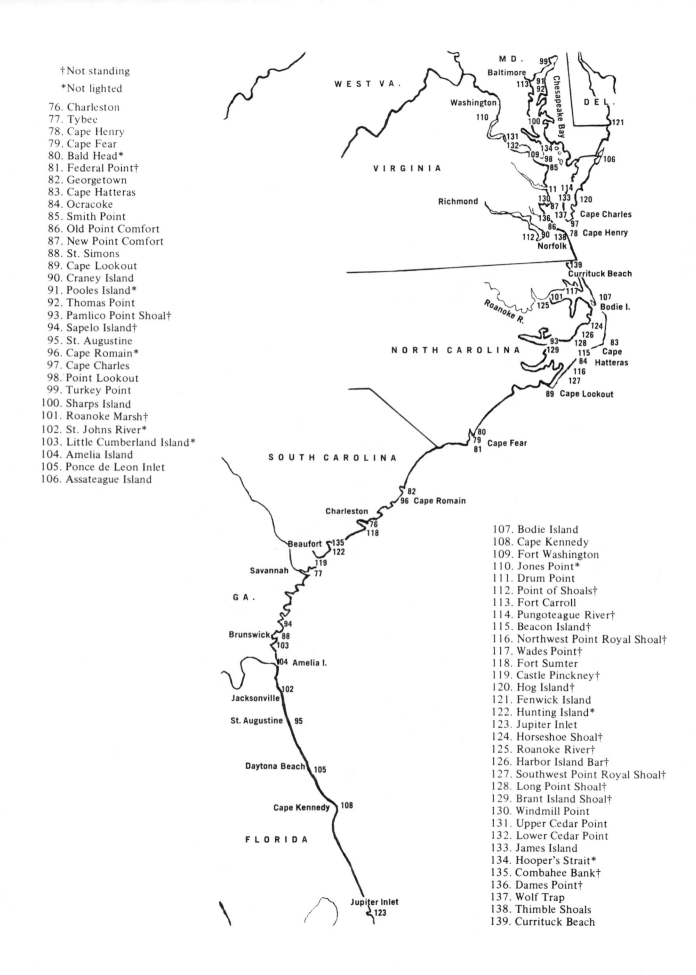

†Not standing

*Not lighted

76. Charleston
77. Tybee
78. Cape Henry
79. Cape Fear
80. Bald Head*
81. Federal Point†
82. Georgetown
83. Cape Hatteras
84. Ocracoke
85. Smith Point
86. Old Point Comfort
87. New Point Comfort
88. St. Simons
89. Cape Lookout
90. Craney Island
91. Pooles Island*
92. Thomas Point
93. Pamlico Point Shoal†
94. Sapelo Island†
95. St. Augustine
96. Cape Romain*
97. Cape Charles
98. Point Lookout
99. Turkey Point
100. Sharps Island
101. Roanoke Marsh†
102. St. Johns River*
103. Little Cumberland Island*
104. Amelia Island
105. Ponce de Leon Inlet
106. Assateague Island

107. Bodie Island
108. Cape Kennedy
109. Fort Washington
110. Jones Point*
111. Drum Point
112. Point of Shoals†
113. Fort Carroll
114. Pungoteague River†
115. Beacon Island†
116. Northwest Point Royal Shoal†
117. Wades Point†
118. Fort Sumter
119. Castle Pinckney†
120. Hog Island†
121. Fenwick Island
122. Hunting Island*
123. Jupiter Inlet
124. Horseshoe Shoal†
125. Roanoke River†
126. Harbor Island Bar†
127. Southwest Point Royal Shoal†
128. Long Point Shoal†
129. Brant Island Shoal†
130. Windmill Point
131. Upper Cedar Point
132. Lower Cedar Point
133. James Island
134. Hooper's Strait*
135. Combahee Bank†
136. Dames Point†
137. Wolf Trap
138. Thimble Shoals
139. Currituck Beach

# VIII

# Lighthouses of the South Atlantic Coast:

## *Maryland to the Florida Keys*

NOT ONLY did a system of aids to navigation develop more slowly on the coast south of Delaware Bay than north of it, but the coast itself presented a different, and in many ways simpler, lighting problem. The rugged coast of New England, with its numerous islands, ledges, shoals, and precipitous shoreline, presented innumerable obstacles to shipping that required a variety of types of aids. It was a hazardous coast to navigate, and often it was made more so by the gales and storms that lashed the sea in its vicinity.

The southern shore, although longer, was a cleaner coast without the cragginess of New England. For the most part it was a low, sandy coast. It, therefore, required tall light towers to put the light at such a height that the mariner could see it sufficiently far at sea.

One cannot but wonder at the failure of the southern colonies to develop many aids to navigation prior to the Revolution. Although not as important nor as large as New England's, considerable maritime activity revolved around many southern ports.

Of course, there were more aids to navigation along the southern shore than has heretofore been realized. For example, historians in the past have accepted the statement that the Tybee light at the mouth of the Savannah River was lighted in 1791 and was the first aid to navigation at that point. But in 1965, an article based on the records of colonial Georgia appeared in the *Georgia Historical*

*Quarterly* and established that a daymark dating to the earliest days of the colony existed on Tybee Island and that it became a lighted beacon in the years prior to the Revolution. In North Carolina, one of the most important entrances to the sounds of that state was Ocracoke Inlet. One of the islands just inside the inlet is called Beacon Island, and had been known by that name for many years prior to 1800, when the United States government acquired it for a fort. There is no evidence presently available that a light, beacon, daymark, or other navigational aid existed there, but the name implies that one may have been there at some time. Some day, perhaps, a historian searching the colonial records of North Carolina will run across a reference to a lighthouse on Beacon Island.

The point is, simply, that there were probably more aids to navigation on the southern coast than historical writings presently indicate. By no stretch of the imagination, however, was there a great quantity of these aids nor were they apparently permanently built.

If the southern colonies had a reasonably brisk maritime trade, why didn't aids to navigation develop more rapidly on that coast? One can only speculate at this stage of research, but the reason may have something to do with the home ports of ships. Probably ship ownership was rare in southern ports, and those who did own ships, being few, were not an influential segment, nor were their closest allies, the merchants. After all, these two

Charleston Light Station on Morris Island, South Carolina, in 1885. This tower, because of erosion and earthquakes, today stands a quarter of a mile off shore and is no longer in operation. *U. S. Coast Guard photo 26-LG-27-5 in the National Archives.*

groups in the north were the ones responsible for the lighthouses that existed there. They agitated for these lighthouses out of economic necessity rather than humanitarian considerations. In the south the government was dominated by the agrarian class who probably had difficulty understanding the subtleties of so esoteric a subject as aids to navigation.

### Charleston (Morris Island) Light (1767)

But whatever the reasons, actuality boils down to the fact that in 1825, only one-fourth of the nation's lighthouses could be found south of Delaware Bay. Indeed, at the end of the Revolution there were only two lighthouses south of Delaware Bay: the Charleston light and the Tybee light. The Charleston lighthouse, located on Morris Island at the entrance to Charleston Harbor, South Carolina, survived the war and around 1790, as a result of the act of 1789, became the responsibility of the federal government. The tower was 102 feet tall, from base to lantern, and, according to a light list in 1832, the light, a revolving one, was 125 feet above sea level. In 1857 the Lighthouse Board equipped the tower with a first-order lens and lighted it on January 1, 1858. At the beginning of the Civil War, the Confederates seized all aids to navigation in their states, and the Charleston light was no exception. The Confederates destroyed the lantern and lens, and at some time during the conflict someone destroyed the tower. The Lighthouse Board accused the Confederates, and certainly the southern forces were not above destroying a lighthouse. The Confederates did what their forefathers to the north had done during the Revolutionary War. On the other hand, the tower could have been a victim of battle. Battery Wagner was on Morris Island and there had been a hotly contested struggle for that fortification.

After the federal forces took Charleston in 1865, the Lighthouse Board found that the harbor had changed radically. There were no channels as they

New Charleston Light Station today. Built on Sullivan's Island in 1962, this will probably be the last traditional light tower built by the United States. This tower, the only one in the United States equipped with an elevator, is surmounted by the most powerful light—28 million candlepower—in the Western Hemisphere. *U. S. Coast Guard official photo.*

were in 1860, and many new ones had opened. The board went about establishing temporary lights, and in 1873 began taking steps to rebuild the light tower. In 1874, work began. Situated near the old tower, the new one had a substantial base and foundation. The base consisted of piles, some driven as deep as fifty feet into the ground, on which the workmen laid two courses of 12″ x 12″ timbers, the top course at right angles to the bottom. They encased this grillage in concrete. On this base the workmen formed a concrete foundation eight feet thick. They then erected the brick tower on this foundation. The new tower, 161 feet high, received a first-order lens that the keeper lighted for the first time on October 1, 1876. Despite damage from a hurricane in 1885 and an earthquake the following year, the tower has survived. Sometime prior to 1892 the tower was painted with black and white bands that enhanced it as a daymark. It was replaced in 1962 by the new tower on Sullivan's Island. Today the Morris Island tower rises from

the water like a lighthouse cast adrift, for its former island has eroded completely from around the tower's foundation.

### Tybee Island Light (1748?)

The Tybee light, Georgia, especially in its early years, is enshrouded in more mystery. Although active at least as a daymark prior to the Revolution, the tower that eventually showed the light has generally been regarded as still in the building process after the war. Perhaps it had been damaged during the war and received repairs after the conflict, giving the impression that workmen were completing the tower. The exact status of the lighthouse between 1775 and 1791 is not known, but there is no question that the light was in use when the federal government received the light station in 1791,[1] at

---

[1] As pointed out previously, Tybee may have been first lighted before the Revolution. See also p. 10.

Tybee Island Light Station, Georgia, in 1885. Construction and lighting of this tower took place sometime prior to 1791. The tower was badly damaged by an earth- quake in 1886. *U. S. Coast Guard photo 26-LG-30-21 in the National Archives.*

which time, according to tradition, the tower's light consisted of spermaceti candles. Later, of course, the lantern was fitted with Winslow Lewis's lamps and reflectors. In 1857, this lighting apparatus gave way to a second-order Fresnel lens. Shortly after the Civil War began, the Confederates removed the lens and set fire to the interior of the tower and

lantern, causing considerable damage.

At the end of the war the Lighthouse Board found that the damage to the 100-foot tower was extensive and repairs would take some time. The board put back into operation as a temporary light the beacon that had been built near the tower in 1822. In 1866, repairmen began the work of restoring the old tower. Fire damage had greatly weakened the structure, so much so that it became necessary to tear away the upper portion of the structure and rebuild the octagonal tower. Work was progressing well when in July, 1866, federal troops arrived on the island, and in their midst they carried the dreaded cholera. The workmen panicked and all work ceased when the foreman and four "mechanics" died of the disease. After the soldiers left, the workmen returned to find that the soldiers had extensively vandalized their work up to that time, and additional funds had to be secured to complete the repairs. The workmen increased the height of the tower so that the focal plane of the new first-order lens would be 144 feet above sea level. Tybee tower was re-lighted October 1, 1867.

In 1871, heavy gales struck Tybee Island and so vibrated the lighthouse that cracks appeared in the tower. The Lighthouse Board condemned the tower and recommended building a new one. The board repeated this recommendation for the next eight years, but Congress did nothing, and the board had to settle for repairs to the tower. In 1878, gales further shook the tower, and in 1886, an earthquake broke the lens and lengthened the cracks already in the tower, but neither calamity spurred Congress to pass necessary appropriations to rebuild the lighthouse and dwelling. Consequently, the old tower stands today at the mouth of the Savannah River, a memorial to its fine workmanship and to the wisdom, or parsimony, of Congress in not providing reconstruction funds in the late nineteenth century. It is painted black with a wide, white, middle band.

## Cape Henry Light (1792)

Shortly after the central government took over responsibility for aids to navigation, work began in earnest on the Cape Henry and Cape Fear lighthouses. Located in Virginia on the southern cape at the entrance to Chesapeake Bay, the Cape Henry lighthouse had been in the building process for a long time. As early as 1721, Governor Alexander Spotswood had urged construction of the lighthouse, and through the years the proposal recurred, but no one could get all parties—Virginia, Maryland, merchants, and the British Board of Trade—to agree all at one time on the proposition. Finally, as the break with England approached, the various

groups reached an agreement, and in 1774, work began on the light tower with the laying of a stone foundation and the gathering of thousands of tons of stone at the site for use in the tower. Work ceased in 1775 for lack of money, and before the parties could get this problem resolved, the Revolution broke out. After the war no one exerted any real effort to resume construction, and in 1789, Virginia gave two acres of ground at Cape Henry to the federal government with the understanding that it would build a lighthouse there within seven years.

In 1790, Congress authorized and appropriated money for a lighthouse at Cape Henry, and the following spring Secretary of the Treasury Alexander Hamilton entered into a contract with John McComb, Jr., to build an octagonal structure that would rise seventy-two feet above sea level and would be crowned with a lantern "ten feet high, and have a semicircular roof of five feet or more. . . ." In addition, the light station was to consist of a keeper's quarters and an oil house.

McComb began work on the light tower, and in August of 1791, he completed the foundation, which he laid twenty feet below the water table. McComb was able to salvage some of the stone the colonial officials had collected for the first proposed light tower. Most of the stockpiled stone had become buried so deep beneath the sand that it was not economically feasible to dig the blocks out. Additional sandstone was obtained, and McComb completed the tower in October, 1792, at which time the new keeper touched the flame to the wicks of the lamps in the lantern.

The necessity of having to place the foundation much lower than anticipated caused further adjustments in the size of the tower, and when Benjamin Latrobe examined the tower in 1798, he reported that it rose ninety feet to the light.

Later equipped with lamps and reflectors, the tower served through the years. In 1857, it received a Fresnel lens, and at the same time it was lined with brick.

Damaged by the rebels at the beginning of the Civil War, the tower received repair work and went back into service in 1863 to facilitate use of Chesapeake Bay by Union forces.

In the 1870's large cracks began to streak the tower, and the Lighthouse Board, fearing for the stability of the structure, proposed erecting a new one. A new tower was finished and lighted Decem-

Office of the Light House Board, May. 1879.

Engineer Secretary

Elevation and vertical section (1879) of Cape Henry first-order light tower, Virginia. The tower was finally lighted in 1792 after 71 years of administrative, finan-cial, and practical difficulties; it served for 89 years, being replaced for safety reasons in 1881. *Drawing in the author's collection.*

Bald Head (Cape Fear) Light Station, North Carolina, in 1893. Though no longer in service, the tower still stands, and in time perhaps will become the centerpiece of the now-proposed park at Cape Fear. *U. S. Coast Guard photo 26-LG-26-9 in the National Archives.*

ber 15, 1881; it was situated about 350 feet southeast of the old tower. The light stood 165 feet high and had a first-order lens. The old tower was left standing, and despite its weakened condition, it has remained standing. The old tower today is the centerpiece of a plot of ground set aside by the Association of Virginia Antiquities to commemorate the first landing of English settlers on Virginia soil.

### Cape Fear (Bald Head) Light (1795)

Not long after construction began on the Cape Henry light, the government began tangible action toward getting a lighthouse in North Carolina at Cape Fear. In April, 1792, Congress appropriated $4,000 to complete a lighthouse that the state of North Carolina had begun in 1791 at Bald Head at the mouth of the Cape Fear River. Work proceeded fitfully on the structure and four years and two additional appropriations later, the Cape Fear lighthouse, or Bald Head as it was then better known, was lighted. From 1796 until 1818, when a new tower was built and illuminated nearby, the light guided shipping into the Cape Fear River. Whether the light was effective enough to guide vessels safely past Frying Pan Shoals, which extended out from Cape Fear, is questionable. The second tower, whose light was about 110 feet above sea level, was, according to the Lighthouse Board in 1851, useless as a seacoast light and its effective range did not extend to the end of the shoals. One of its main

111

problems was the tower's location—some four miles from the pitch, or end, of the cape. The board proposed raising the tower to 150 feet and equipping it with a first-order lens so that it could be seen outside Frying Pan Shoals. But all the board wound up doing was installing a third-order lens on the tower.

Like virtually all the southern lighthouses, Cape Fear was closed down by the Confederates in 1861. And five years later, the board officially discontinued the light at this station because of the building of a new screw-pile lighthouse at Federal Point some eight miles away.

With the closing of New Inlet in 1879, the board discontinued the Federal Point light and a year later reactivated the Bald Head Light Station, placing a fourth-order lens on the structure so that it still was not a coast light. The board proposed building a new tower 150 feet tall and installing a first-order lens on it, but Congress failed to respond with the necessary funds. In 1893, the board revised its estimates downward when it proposed building a skeleton tower on Smith Island. After a time, Congress went along with this proposal and in 1898 made the first appropriation for the new tower. In 1903, the new tower, whose light was 159 feet above the sea, was activated. At that time the new station became officially known as Cape Fear and the old station was called Bald Head. Bald Head remained active until 1935, when the Lighthouse Bureau deactivated it. Still standing, the old tower will be a centerpiece of a national seashore, if conservationists have their way.

Thus, with the advent of the nineteenth century, the southern coast from Delaware Bay to the Florida border had only four lights, and in the first decade of the century the coast was to see but three additional lighthouses. One was in the building stage in 1799, and was completed and lighted in 1801. Located on North Island at the entrance to Winyah Bay in South Carolina, it became known as the Georgetown light. It was, however, never more than a harbor light. Rebuilt in 1812 and again in 1867, the eighty-five-foot tower has never had a more powerful light than a fourth-order lens. The light is still active.

### Cape Hatteras Light (1803)

The southern coast, especially from Cape Hatteras southward, had a navigational problem peculiar to it: namely, the Gulf Stream. Coming out of the Caribbean, the stream rounds the end of Florida and courses northward to the vicinity of Cape Hatteras in North Carolina. Here the stream apparently goes beneath the water and surfaces occasionally in unpredictable places. That it remains an entity north of Hatteras there is no doubt, for several northern ports that one would normally expect to be closed during the winter in view of their latitude remain open year around because of the warmth brought by the Gulf Stream. Murmansk in Russia is an example of an ice-free port, thanks to the Gulf Stream.

As the Gulf Stream passes along the coast of the southern United States it is well defined in its width, a fact known to Benjamin Franklin; indeed, a 1770 chart of the stream is attributed to Franklin. This "river in the sea," as it has been termed, is almost as sharply defined as any river whose width is controlled by banks of earth. Spaniards soon found that the stream could speed their treasure-laden ships bound from the Caribbean to Spain. Their ships followed the Gulf Stream out of the "Spanish lake" and continued northward along the coast of Florida, as they called the mass of land north of Cuba, to about Cape Hatteras where they jumped off for Spain.

The stream does not hug the shore of the southern states but rather is kept off-shore by a south-flowing cold stream called the Labrador Current. American seamen engaged in the coastal trade followed the Labrador Current when south-bound and the Gulf Stream when headed north. A vessel pointed southward could lose much time attempting to buck the swift Gulf Stream, which at times flows as rapidly as four knots. Moreover, getting into the Gulf Stream under certain conditions could be unnerving. One nineteenth-century skipper of a coasting schooner described his experience:

Had a good run to Cape Hatteras. Here a heavy northwester hit me and blowed my spanker away. It blew a heavy gale and began to freeze the ropes hard. And for the want of after sail I could not hold the beach and I drifted ever so far off-shore into the Gulf Stream. This cold air on this warm water made the ghostliest sight I ever laid my eyes on before. For miles, before getting into the warm water of the Stream, it would seem I saw thousands of water spouts. Then it would look like forestry. This would pass off for a minute. Then next I would see some great city and to

5th Dist

Brick Color
Top of old granite Tower

Top of Whitewashing

OLD TOWER . CAPE HATTERAS N.C , OCT. 24 '70

View from the West

Height of Sand Hill above the general level of the Beach. 20 feet
From base to top of whitewashing = 70 feet
"     "     focal plane = 140. "

5th Dist,
2 C.

Eng' Office 5th L.H. District
Nov. 24th 1870

J. H. Simpson

Sketched by Geo. B. Nicholson.
Cast. Eng' 5th L.H.District.     filed 10 Nov.'70.

Col. Eng' and Brv't Brig. Gen'l.
Eng' 5th L.H.District.

The first Cape Hatteras light tower, originally lighted in 1803. This 1870 sketch by George B. Nicholson, assistant engineer of the Fifth Lighthouse District, shows the height of the original tower and the 1854 addition. *U. S. Coast Guard photo from the National Archives.*

be honest I felt scared. After a while I drifted out of the cold water into the warm water and then I was enclosed into this vapor and I could see nothing but cities, towns, forestry, and ships of all kind of rigs. And this was all vapor rising off of this warm water. Sometimes the sailors would squeal out, "There is a ship on the port." I would jump forward to get the bearing of her and about that time she would disapear [sic] and roll away as nothing but mist. Now I was lying right in the track of ships from New York or Philadelphia bound south. All that night I never shut my eyes in sleep and none of the crew got much. I expected every moment to be runed [sic] over. All day the next day, the wind continuing to blow a gale from the northwest, we continued to see these phantom ships, cities, forestry and water spouts. I was hove to all this time drifting to north and east.[2]

The most dangerous place along the southern coast was Cape Hatteras. Here, a rocky, shallow finger known as Diamond Shoals extended out from the cape about eight miles, thus leaving only a narrow path a few miles wide that southbound vessels could follow in getting past Cape Hatteras. A course too much to port put the vessel into the counter-running Gulf Stream; too much to starboard piled the ship on the shoals. Consequently, from the beginning the desire was to put a lighthouse on the end of Diamond Shoals where it could more effectively aid the mariner. But in reality by the late eighteenth and early nineteenth centuries, when the subject was first discussed, technology simply had not progressed to an extent where man could successfully put a lighthouse on such a wild and tempestuous spot. Therefore, Congress had no choice but to put the lighthouse they proposed in the 1790's on land at Cape Hatteras.

The date of the establishment of the Cape Hatteras lighthouse is given by most sources, including the usually reliable Coast Guard *Light List*, as 1798. But the lighthouse was not established until 1803.

Congress authorized the lighthouse at Cape Hatteras in 1794, but difficulties over obtaining the land and securing a contractor to build the structure resulted in construction not starting until late 1799.

The contractor was Henry Dearborn, former congressman later to become secretary of war, collector of customs in Boston, senior major general of the army, minister to Portugal, and the one for whom the well-known Michigan city was named. In addition to the Cape Hatteras light, Dearborn's contract called for him to build the Ocracoke beacon about forty miles to the southward.

Construction was slow, due primarily to Dearborn's workmen being hard hit by sickness during the summers. Illness, probably malaria, was to be a factor in the building of many of the southern lighthouses. Finally, however, Dearborn completed his contract in August, 1802, but for some reason the lighting of the tower did not take place until some time between June 28 and October 29, 1803.

This tower, with its light ninety-five feet above the sea, suffered the usual vicissitudes of weather and had the normal upkeep and repair. It experienced at least one fire in the lantern, and the fifth auditor received a number of complaints through the years about the quality of the light. When the Lighthouse Board investigated the country's lighthouses in 1851, the members found the reputation of the Cape Hatteras light among navigators to be poor. The board concluded that "no single light on the coast" required improvement more than Cape Hatteras. The board felt the tower should be raised and a first-class illuminating apparatus put on it, since "there is perhaps no light on the entire coast of the United States of greater value to the commerce and navigation of the country. . . ."

In 1854, the Lighthouse Board raised the tower so that the focal plane of the light from the new first-order lens was 150 feet above sea level. The light could now be seen twenty miles at sea, well beyond the end of Diamond Shoals.

At the beginning of the Civil War, the rebels removed the lens from the tower, but they did no damage to the structure. Playing a role as a rendezvous point during the struggle for military control of the Outer Banks of North Carolina, the tower remained unlighted until the federal troops had driven the Confederates from the banks. The Lighthouse Board used a second-order lens when it relighted the tower in June, 1862, but in 1863 it installed one of the improved first-order lenses on the tower.

By the end of the war the Lighthouse Board, upon recommendation of the district engineer, decided that Cape Hatteras needed a new tower, since the old one was beyond repair. In 1867, Con-

[2] Robert H. Burgess, ed., *Coasting Captain: Journals of Captain Leonard S. Tawes Relating His Career in Atlantic Coastwise Sailing Craft from 1868–1922* (Newport News, Va.: The Mariners Museum, 1967), p. 83.

The present Cape Hatteras tower (lighted 1870) in 1893. At 190 feet, this is probably the tallest brick light tower in the United States. *Right rear,* the site of the original tower, dynamited for safety reasons on completion of the new tower. *U. S. Coast Guard photo from the National Archives.*

gress appropriated the necessary funds, and in 1868, construction began on a new brick tower to be thirty feet taller than its predecessor and situated 600 feet northeast of the old tower. Various problems plagued the builders, including the sickness that had caused the workers on the original tower so much trouble. An army doctor sent to find a solution recommended giving each man a daily issue of one and a half ounces of whiskey and five grains of quinine as a preventative.

Despite these problems construction proceeded well, and on September 17, 1870, the keeper lighted the lamp in the new first-order lens. The light was 190 feet above mean low water. The district lampist removed the lens and lantern from the old tower, and, since there was danger it might topple in a storm, the district engineer set off in the tower three charges of explosives, "blowing out," he reported, "a large wedge on the side toward the beach & this old land mark was spread out on the beach a mass of ruins."

The new tower functioned well. To make it a better daymark the Lighthouse Board in 1873 had the tower painted with black and white spiral stripes.

At about the end of World War I erosion began to threaten the tower. Efforts through the 1920's and into the 1930's to halt the incursion of the sea were of little avail, and in 1936 the Lighthouse Bureau erected a new skeleton tower safely away from the marauding sea and moved the Cape Hatteras light to that point. The bureau then turned over the light station to the National Park Service to be included in Cape Hatteras National Seashore. In time the erosion threat eased, and in 1950 the Coast Guard made arrangements with the Park Service to re-exhibit the light in the old brick tower. Today visitors to the national seashore can visit the old station, view the maritime museum the National Park Service has created in the large keeper's dwelling, and, if in good physical shape, climb what was, and still may be, the tallest brick light tower in the world for a fine panorama of the Outer Banks, the sounds, and the Atlantic Ocean. The visitor, however, cannot go into the lantern where the lens, now automatic, is located.

Fittingly, this old tower, considered by the Lighthouse Board and others during the nineteenth century to be the most important light on the Atlantic Coast, is the national seashore's symbol.

## Ocracoke Light (1803)

As mentioned earlier, Dearborn built the Cape Hatteras tower and the lighthouse at Ocracoke Inlet at the same time. The one at Ocracoke was erected on a small plot of land on Shell Castle Island inside the inlet. This beacon was there to help vessels cross the Ocracoke bar at night. Completed and lighted in 1803 about the same time as the Cape Hatteras light, this beacon remained in use until August 16, 1818, when lightning destroyed both the tower and the keeper's dwelling. The lighthouse was rebuilt in 1823 on the banks near the village of Ocracoke. Primarily an inlet light, the tower received a fourth-order lens in 1854. The Confederates removed the lens in 1861, and in 1864 the Lighthouse Board installed and lighted another one. The still active old tower, with its light seventy-five feet above the water, has never been rebuilt and is one of the most ancient lighthouses on the Outer Banks and one of the oldest active lights on the South Atlantic Coast.

## Smith Point Light (1802)

In the first decade of the nineteenth century the Chesapeake Bay began to get attention. The government established a light at Smith Point in 1802 to mark the entrance to the Potomac River; the nation's capital had been moved to Washington two years previously. This lighthouse lasted until 1828 when it had to be rebuilt. Twenty-five years later it was reported to be in a dilapidated condition, and the board made a fitful effort to reconstruct the iron frame tower, but Congress failed to appropriate adequate funds. In 1859, the board replaced the Smith Point lightship (established in 1821) with a new and larger one that made the lighthouse seem superfluous, so it was discontinued. Following its policy of replacing lightships with screw-pile lighthouses, the board in 1868 built a screw-pile lighthouse at Smith Point, and removed the light vessel.

In 1893, floating ice damaged the lighthouse. The keepers became so alarmed that they abandoned their duty station. Although the lighthouse survived this onslaught, it was in for another attack two years later. This time the ice pushed the screw-pile structure over. The lighting apparatus as well as some of the other equipment and supplies were later salvaged.

116

Sandy Point lighthouse, Maryland, in 1885. This typical caisson-based structure is located in Chesapeake Bay. *U. S. Coast Guard photo 26-LG-24-56 in the National Archives.*

Immediately replacing the lost lighthouse with a lightship, the board went about getting funding for a new structure. This time it built a caisson-type foundation—a concrete-filled, cast-iron cylinder—topped by an octagonal brick dwelling with a square tower. The new fourth order-lens was lighted in 1897.

## Old Point Comfort Light (1802); New Point Comfort Light (1805)

In 1802, the secretary of the treasury had a lighthouse built at Old Point Comfort at the entrance to Hampton Roads near Fortress Monroe. Three years later the contractor completed building a light tower at New Point Comfort at the entrance to Mobjack Bay. In 1852, the Lighthouse Board found this light manned by a retired sea captain and his assistant—a female Negro slave. Badly battered during the Civil War, the tower was repaired and relighted in 1865. Both the Old Point Comfort and the New Point Comfort light towers have survived through the years essentially as they had been built.

## St. Simons Light (ca. 1815)

The second decade of the nineteenth century saw the erection of two additional coastal lights and one beacon light. The first one may have been at first primarily a harbor light but in subsequent years it evolved into a coast light. Located on the southern extremity of St. Simons Island east of Brunswick, Georgia, this light served to mark the entrance to St. Simons Sound. The Lighthouse Board raised the lighthouse to the status of a coastal light in 1857 by installing a third-order lens.

During the Civil War the Confederates destroyed the tower and other buildings at the station. In 1869, the board laid plans and let a contract to rebuild the station. This time, however, the board ordered construction of a tower 100 feet tall. As in the building of many southern lighthouses in the nineteenth century, sickness, apparently malaria, plagued the work crew. One victim was the contractor, who died on the job in 1870. One of the bondsmen, to protect his investment, came down to take charge, but shortly after his arrival, he, too, fell victim to the sickness. A second bondsman took charge and completed the work in 1872. A third-order lens, 104 feet above sea level, surmounted the tower, and the keeper lighted it September 1, 1872.

Even after construction the sickness continued to plague the keepers, and the Lighthouse Board concluded that nearby stagnant ponds were the cause and had them drained in 1875 and again in 1884. The white tower adjoining the two-story brick dwelling still functions; its light is visible sixteen miles.

## Cape Lookout Light (1812)

In North Carolina two lights came into being: the previously mentioned Federal Point light at the Cape Fear River and a lighthouse at Cape Lookout. Cape Lookout has long been regarded as a hazard to navigation; indeed, one early map maker labelled it "Promontorium tremendum" which means roughly "horrible headland." Shoals that extend out some ten miles are the principal cause of danger. Mitigating this danger is the fact that Cape Lookout has long been known as a harbor of refuge. The point of the cape curves around, forming a bight, and provides a quiet harbor for passing ships caught in a storm. It was also a rendezvous used by pirates such as Blackbeard, as well as by Spanish privateers, British warships during the Revolution, and Europe-bound convoys in World Wars I and II. One colonial official considered Cape Lookout Bight as the "best and safest [harbor] from Boston to the Capes of Florida," which, of course, was an exaggeration; but the statement, nevertheless, indicates that this place was not just an ordinary fair weather anchorage.

First authorized by Congress in 1804, the Cape Lookout lighthouse was completed and lighted in 1812. It was reported to consist of two towers, "the inside one is of brick—the outside one is a wooden framed building, boarded and shingled, and painted in red and white stripes horizontally."

Ninety-six feet above the ground, and about 104 feet above the sea, the light left something to be desired. In the 1830's it was reported as being fine at night, but as day approached, the light grew dim. Some years later Lt. David D. Porter, commanding a mail steamer, reported he found himself "two or three times inside the shoal, looking for the light, and have been obliged to haul out without seeing it." Lt. H. J. Harstene, skipper of another mail steamer, was more blunt; he said, "The lights on Hatteras, Lookout, and Cape Florida, if not improved had better be dispensed with as the navigator is apt to run shore looking for them."

118

The second (and present) Cape Lookout lighthouse, North Carolina. The diamond pattern on the tower resulted in a community on nearby Shackleford Banks being named Diamond City. Now an unmanned, first-order lighthouse, it is surrounded by Cape Lookout National Seashore. *U. S. Coast Guard official photo.*

In 1856, the Lighthouse Board fitted a first-order Fresnel lens on the tower. The following year the board began constructing a new and taller tower. Exhibited on November 1, 1859, the new light was 150 feet above the ground and 156 feet above sea level; it was visible nineteen miles. The old tower remained standing and was not taken down until well after the Civil War.

The Confederates, after the surrender of the nearby Fort Macon on the mainland, vandalized the lens, making it inoperable. The board relighted the tower in 1863 with a third-order lens. Four years later the original first-order lens was repaired and reinstalled in the tower. At the same time, a metal stairway was substituted for the original wooden spiral stairway, which had been a potential fire hazard.

In 1873, to increase the tower's effectiveness as a daymark, the board ordered it painted its distinctive black and white diamond pattern, a design, incidentally, that gave the name Diamond City to the settlement on the adjacent Shackleford Banks.

Ice threatens the Love Point, Maryland, screw-pile lighthouse on Chesapeake Bay in this rare photograph from 1902. A side-wheel lighthouse tender stands by. Several lighthouses of this design were destroyed by ice, and some were replaced by caisson lighthouses. *U. S. Coast Guard photo 26-LG-23-21B, National Archives.*

There is no foundation to the local tale that the painter made a mistake and put the diamond pattern on the wrong light tower; that really the diamonds were supposed to have been painted on the Cape Hatteras tower because of its proximity to Diamond Shoals. This writer has seen in the National Archives the letters from the Lighthouse Board to the district engineer specifically instructing him to have the Cape Hatteras tower painted with spiral stripes and the Cape Lookout tower with "diagonal checkers."

In 1950, the Coast Guard converted the light to an unmanned, automatic one. Still in operation, the light tower today is one of the principal historic structures in Cape Lookout National Seashore.

### Lights in Chesapeake Bay (1820–1825)

In the 1820's additional lights were exhibited in Chesapeake Bay. Craney Island light (1820) was placed to mark the entrance to the Elizabeth River, the pathway to Norfolk and Portsmouth, Virginia. Pooles Island and Thomas Point lights were both established in 1825 in the upper Chesapeake Bay.

### Pamlico Point Shoal Light (1828)

Even the sounds of North Carolina received some attention with the placing of a light at Pamlico Point Shoal at the entrance to the Pamlico River in 1828. This light had an unusual history in that during the Civil War federal troops set fire to the structure in an attempt to destroy it, but the Confederates arrived in time and put out the fire. Usually just the opposite happened.

### Sapelo Island Light (1820)

Farther south, the Sapelo Island light, just north of the one at St. Simons Island, came into being in 1820. Principally a harbor light marking the entrance to the sound that led to Darien, Georgia, the tower was in the next century to wage a six-year losing battle with the sea which eroded the south end of the island where the tower was located.

The three most significant lights erected in the 1820's were at St. Augustine, Florida; Cape Romain, South Carolina; and Cape Charles, Maryland.

### St. Augustine Light (1821)

Shortly after the United States took possession of the territory of Florida in 1821, it turned its attention toward navigational aids. The first concern, of course, was St. Augustine, since it was the leading port of the territory. Someone told Congress that the Spaniards had had a lighthouse there and that the tower still stood and could be used for similar purposes by the United States. Stephen Pleasonton had the collector of customs in St. Augustine examine the tower to determine what funds and work would be necessary to restore the tower as a lighthouse. The collector, John Rodman, in the company

## Black and white spiral bands

of a carpenter and a mason found the three-story stone structure, some forty-four feet tall, near "a valuable quarry of calcareous stone, which has, for a long time, furnished materials for the public and private buildings at St. Augustine." Rodman went on to note that the tower compound, which also included a small building, comprised less than a quarter of an acre within a stone wall ten feet high and sixteen inches thick.

After examining the structure more closely, Rodman concluded that the Spaniards had not used it as a lighthouse, but rather as a lookout tower. The cost to repair the tower, he said, would be $5,000, but even with that work the tower would not be strong enough to build upon. The fifth auditor, consequently, felt that a new tower was called for, and, accordingly, had one constructed that put the light seventy-three feet above sea level. At best, this light was only a harbor light marking the entrance to St. Augustine Harbor, and the Lighthouse Board further confirmed the status of the light when it installed only a fourth-order lens on the tower in 1855.

The Confederates eliminated the light at the beginning of the war, and the Lighthouse Board did not re-light the tower until 1867. Soon thereafter, the board received word that erosion threatened the tower. In 1870, the board urged that the light be relocated and converted to a seacoast light. By the end of the year, the ocean was but forty-eight feet from the tower. Erosion ceased for a time, and this was fortunate, because the board had difficulty obtaining a site for the new tower. Finally the board secured five acres about one-half mile from the old tower.

In 1872, construction began on the new tower, and by the middle of summer the foundation had been laid and the brickwork carried up a few feet. At this point construction funds ran out. About the same time the ocean took another bite out of the beach, and water lapped within thirty-five feet of the emerging tower. The sea continued eating away and at high tide the water reached a point but ten feet from the tower. The workers at the new tower turned their attention to this problem and began laying a jetty of brush and coquina from the nearby quarry to halt erosion. Coquina is a soft limestone composed of shells and coral and had been used in building Castillo de San Marcos across the harbor. The main part of the Castillo had been completed

in 1686, and the coquina fort, today a national monument, is in a remarkably fine state of preservation. Coquina is a fine building stone out of water, because it hardens when dried, but it is quite light and not permanent material for a jetty, since the water easily washes it out of place. Nevertheless, the jetty was adequate to hold back erosion temporarily, and work resumed on the tower. The keeper lighted the new first-order lens on October 15, 1874. The light, whose focal plane was 161 feet above the sea, could be seen nineteen miles. The tower was typical of those being built on the southern coast at that time. Cape Hatteras, Bodie Island, and Currituck Beach light towers, all built in the 1870's, are nearly exact duplicates of the St. Augustine tower. To make the tower a better daymark the board ordered it painted with black and white spiral bands, as had been done at Cape Hatteras. Possessing an automatic light today, the tower stands as one of St. Augustine's most prominent landmarks.

### Cape Romain Light (1827)

The light at Cape Romain was built on Raccoon Key about ten miles southwest of the entrance to the Santee River in South Carolina. Lighted in 1827, the sixty-five-foot tower, whose light was eighty-seven feet above sea level, served, like the Cape Hatteras and Cape Lookout lights, to guide ships past the dangerous shoals in that vicinity. This light was particularly important to those southbound vessels trying to stay out of the Gulf Stream. In 1851 the Lighthouse Board reported that the lamps and reflectors then in the tower's lantern were no better than a fourth-order lens; to be of most effective use, Cape Romain, the board felt, should have "a first-class seacoast light, including a new tower." Congress agreed, and on January 1, 1858, the keeper lighted the lens in a new 150 foot tower, erected near the old tower.

In 1861, the rebels destroyed the lantern and lens, but the board repaired and relighted the tower in 1866. Three years later a few cracks began to appear in the tower. In 1873, more cracks appeared, and the district engineer noticed that the concrete foundation of the tower had settled on the west side, throwing it "23½ inches from the vertical," and necessitating an adjustment of the lens to bring it back to level. A year later, the tower leaned nearly four more inches from the perpendicular. Settling stopped until 1891, when the tower leaned over enough to throw the lens out of level again. Further adjustments were made and the light continued to serve until 1947, when the Coast Guard reduced the lighthouse to just a daymark. Today, lighted buoys visible eight and nine miles assist mariners along this section of the coast.

### Cape Charles Light (1828)

Established on Smith Island in 1828, the Cape Charles light, whose tower was only fifty-five feet tall, marked the north side of the entrance to Chesapeake Bay. Under the best conditions the light could be seen only twelve miles, hardly adequate for a seacoast light or for the important duty of aiding ships into the bay. The Lighthouse Board in 1851 reported that Cape Charles was "one of the lights requiring the earliest attention of the lighthouse department," and it "should be increased to a first order one."

In 1858, the board began construction of a new tower 150 feet tall. Work progressed slowly, and in 1862 the new tower had been raised to only eighty-three feet. A group of Confederates destroyed the old light and pilfered materials at the construction site. Work soon resumed on the tower, however, and on May 17, 1864, the keeper lighted the new first-order lens. For the remainder of the war a military guard protected the tower.

In 1883, district officials suddenly realized that the sea had been encroaching on the light station at the rate of about thirty feet per year, and now the sea was but 300 feet from the tower. Two years passed and seventy-five feet more disappeared. In 1886, the board had jetties built, but at best they only temporarily halted erosion. By 1889, the board realized that a new location was needed, and in time approved a site three-quarters of a mile from the old tower. Construction began in 1893 and the first-order lens in the new tower blinked on August 15, 1895. The light, 180 feet above water, was visible twenty miles. Today the station is unmanned and the light is automatic.

### More Lights in Chesapeake Bay (1830–1838)

The 1830's saw additional lights flash on in Chesapeake Bay at such places as Point Lookout (1830)

at the entrance to the Potomac River, Turkey Point (1833) at the head of Chesapeake Bay, and Sharps Island (1838) near the entrance to the Choptank River. The keeper of the Sharps Island light had a wild experience in February, 1881, when ice ripped the screw-pile structure from its foundations and floated it down the Chesapeake. The keeper rode the lighthouse for some miles before it grounded. Needless to say, the Lighthouse Board concluded that a screw-pile building was not sturdy enough for the site, and rebuilt the lighthouse using a caisson design.

### Roanoke Marshes Light (1831)

Several lighthouses went into service in the sounds of North Carolina during this decade. In 1831, the Roanoke Marshes lighthouse blinked on. Not long afterwards, a man named Van Pelt claimed the land the lighthouse was on and eventually went to court and proved his claim, after which he had the keeper ejected. Apparently, the government offered no resistance to the lawsuit due to the failure of the local collector of customs to notify Pleasonton of the claim. Pleasonton abandoned the lighthouse in 1839, and despite the petitions of local mariners refused to re-establish it. The Lighthouse Board in 1857 finally re-established a light at Roanoke Marshes with the erection of a screw-pile structure.

Farther south other lights came into use. In 1830, a lighthouse was established at the mouth of the St. Johns River at Jacksonville; in 1929 a lightship replaced this third-order light. In 1838 Little Cumberland Island at the entrance to St. Andrew Sound just south of Brunswick, Georgia, received a lighthouse. Today the white conical tower is inactive, but it serves as a day beacon. And just to the south, Amelia Island, Florida, obtained a lighthouse in 1839. Near the entrance to St. Marys River (the Georgia-Florida border), the original brick tower with its third-order lens has survived to the present as an active lighthouse.

### Ponce de Leon (Mosquito) Inlet Light (1887)

The first attempt to erect a lighthouse at Ponce de Leon Inlet, or Mosquito Inlet as it was then called, occurred in the 1830's. Located just south of Daytona Beach, Florida, the inlet received its first tower in 1835. Because oil for the tower's lamps did not arrive, the light was never exhibited. A strong gale that year swirled sand away from the foundation of the tower. Workmen could not get back to the area to prevent further damage, due to fear of the Indians then waging the Seminole War. A little later the undermined tower toppled over. The war prevented further efforts down there, and, in time, the project was either forgotten or ignored.

In the 1870's the Lighthouse Board noted the ninety-five miles between the St. Augustine and Cape Canaveral lights and realized that sixty miles of that space had no light. The board recommended a tower at Mosquito Inlet (the name Ponce de Leon did not come into use until 1927), and in 1882, Congress appropriated funds. Work on the tower started in June, 1884, with the landing of materials at the inlet. While participating in the landing, Major O. E. Babcock, engineer of the Fifth and Sixth Lighthouse Districts, drowned.

Work on the tower moved slowly forward and the tower was finally completed and lighted in the autumn of 1887. Today the tower's third-order lens, 150 feet above sea level, can be seen nineteen miles.

### Assateague Island Light (1833)

In 1830, there was no light between Delaware and Chesapeake bays. In 1831, Congress appropriated money for one in the general area of the Chincoteague Islands. The following year the collector of customs in Norfolk selected a site on Assateague Island on the Atlantic Coast a few miles south of the Virginia-Maryland border.

Lighted in January, 1833, the tower was too low and too poorly illuminated to perform effectively its job of warning ships of the shoals that protrude out from that section of the coast. In 1852, the Lighthouse Board said, "The very dangerous Shoals extending along this entire coast at a considerable distance from the low coast . . . make it the duty of the government to cause this light to be increased in power and range to the rank of the first-class sea-coast light, without delay."

Congress appropriated funds in 1859 and work began the following year. Construction soon ceased because of the advent of the Civil War. In 1865 work resumed, and on October 1, 1867, the light shone from the new first-order lens for the first time. The light was high enough to be visible nineteen miles.

This tower has served well through the years and today Chincoteague National Wildlife Refuge, adjacent to Assateague Island National Seashore, surrounds the station which is now unmanned but still active.

The year 1848 saw the erection of two very important towers: Bodie Island, North Carolina, and Cape Canaveral, Florida.

### Bodie Island Light (1848)

In 1837, a naval officer, in response to a request from Congress, investigated a site for the proposed Bodie Island lighthouse. He said that "more vessels are lost [on Bodie Island] than on any other part of our coast." There was no light between Cape Henry and Cape Hatteras. Southbound vessels, following the inshore current, needed a mark to shape a course to round Cape Hatteras without getting into the Gulf Stream.

Difficulty in obtaining land on the Outer Banks and the failure of Congress to appropriate adequate funds delayed construction of the lighthouse for ten years, but finally, in 1847, the fifth auditor let a contract for the station to Francis A. Gibbons of Baltimore. In five years Gibbons was to figure prominently in the building of the first lighthouses on the Pacific Coast. The fifth auditor employed an ex-collector of customs to oversee the work of the contractor. That the overseer had little knowledge of construction was manifested in an inauspicious decision. Pleasonton had told the ex-collector to have piles driven if the foundation of the site proved to be mud. The contractor dug down and indeed found the viscous substance. But the ex-collector ignored Pleasonton's advice, and, as construction supervisor, instructed the contractor to lay a foundation consisting of two layers of bricks; on this foundation the contractor raised the walls of the fifty-four-foot-tall brick tower. Pleasonton did not find out about this foundation until after the tower had been finished and the contractor entered a $200 claim for the extra work.

Gibbons finished the tower in September, 1847, but Winslow Lewis was slow in getting the lighting apparatus installed and the keeper did not exhibit the light for the first time until after January 22, 1848. The lighthouse was functioning before June 29, 1848.

Within two years of construction the tower was

123

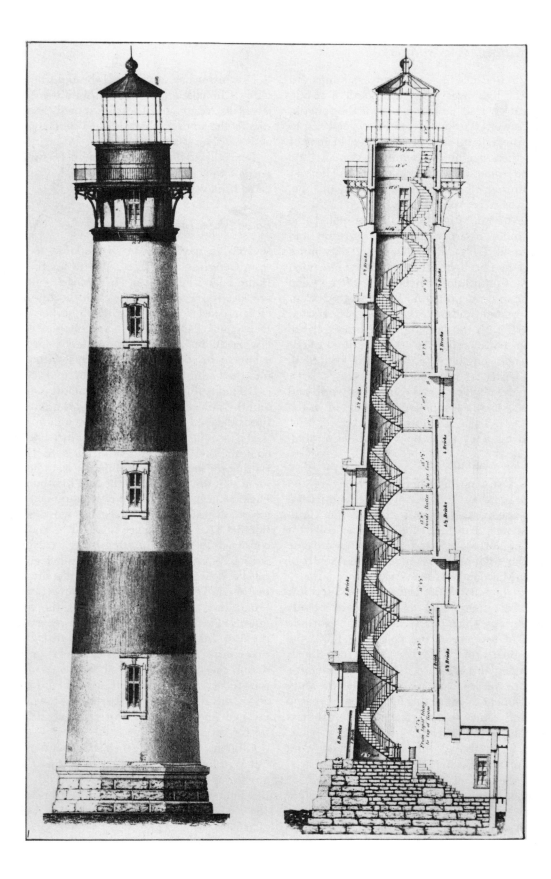

Bodie Island Light Station, North Carolina. This tower, the third at this location, was lighted in 1872. Unmanned today, it displays a first-order light, visible for nineteen miles, that is instrumental in helping southbound vessels to round Cape Hatteras without encountering the Gulf Stream. *Opposite:* elevation and vertical section, probably from engineering drawings of the early 1870's. *Above:* the station in 1893. The double keepers' dwelling to the left has today been converted to a small museum and visitor contact station for Cape Hatteras National Seashore. *From Record Group 26, National Archives.*

"canted to eastward," one foot out of plumb. Pleasonton had to spend $1,400 straightening the tower. In 1854 the Lighthouse Board installed a fourth-order lens in the tower's lantern; the lantern was too small to hold a larger lens.

By 1859, the tower was beyond repair, and the Lighthouse Board received $25,000 to build a new one. The new tower, this time built on piles, rose eighty feet into the air and held a third-order lantern whose light was ninety feet above sea level. Lighted July 1, 1859, the tower had a short life. In November, 1861, the Confederates set off explosives that left the structure in ruins.

After the war the Lighthouse Board began thinking of places other than Bodie Island for the light, but it soon received petitions from ships' masters and insurance executives urging the rebuilding of the light at Bodie Island. The board thought that it would be better to position the light more nearly halfway between the Cape Henry and the Cape Hatteras lights, but it changed its mind and decided to erect a light at Bodie Island and another further northward at Currituck Beach. In its old position the Bodie Island light would be more effective in performing its task of helping southbound vessels shape a course to round the tricky Cape Hatteras.

Upon completion of the new Cape Hatteras tower in 1871, the district engineer moved storage buildings, excess materials, and the tramway used for getting materials from the shore to the site to Bodie Island. Work on the station proceeded well, and on October 1, 1872, the keeper displayed the light of the first-order lens for the first time. It was 156 feet above sea level and visible nineteen miles. About the same time the tower was painted with wide black and white horizontal bands to make it a more distinctive daymark.

The new light had been in operation less than thirty days when a flock of geese smashed into the lantern, breaking much of the glass and seriously damaging the lens. The district engineer rigged a heavy wire netting around the outside of the lantern to prevent another such incident.

The light in the tower today is automatic and is checked once a week by Coast Guard personnel. All the land and buildings of the station, except for the tower and a small plot of ground it rests on, have since 1953 been a part of Cape Hatteras National Seashore. The National Park Service maintains a small visitor center in the brick keeper's dwelling in front of the tower. The tower, however, is closed to visitation.

## Cape Kennedy (Canaveral) Light (1848)

At about the time the first Bodie Island lighthouse was being built, workmen were busily at work in Florida erecting a sixty-five-foot tower at Cape Canaveral. Placed primarily to warn ships of the shoals that extended out from there, the tower had too inadequate a light to be effective; ships had to come in too close to see it and thereby placed themselves in danger of wrecking on the very shoals the light was supposed to guard them against. The board recommended erecting a new tower 150 feet tall. Just before the Civil War began, workmen started putting up an iron tower; hostilities soon called a halt to the endeavor. In 1865, the board resumed work on the tower, completing and lighting it May 10, 1868. The light from the first-order lens was 139 feet above sea level and visible eighteen miles. The conical tower was built of cast iron and lined with bricks. In 1873, the board had it painted with black and white horizontal bands, similar to the Bodie Island tower.

Sea erosion threatened the tower, and by 1883,

only 192 feet of beach separated the structure from the Atlantic Ocean. After futile attempts to halt the erosion with jetties, the Lighthouse Board tore down the tower and re-erected it in 1893–94 one and one-quarter miles west of the old site. The keeper lighted the lens at its new location on July 25, 1894. Still active, the lighthouse is known today as the Cape Kennedy light.

## Still More Lights in Chesapeake Bay (1853–1857)

The decade prior to the Civil War saw additional lights established in Chesapeake Bay and in navigable rivers emptying into the bay. Fort Washington light (1857) in the Potomac River, Drum Point light (1853) in the Patuxent River, Point of Shoals screw-pile lighthouse (1855) in the James River, and the light at Fort Carroll (1854) in Baltimore Harbor are examples of the spread of navigational aids in the bay and its tributaries. These were small lights, all equipped with fifth-order or lesser lenses.

Another Chesapeake Bay light established at this time was the one at the mouth of Pungoteague River. Lighted in November, 1854, the structure was in service less than eighteen months when a large mass of floating ice overturned it. Many years passed before another aid was established at this point.

The sounds of North Carolina also received a number of lights during this decade. A screw-pile structure replaced the Wades Point light vessel in 1856; Beacon Island obtained a light in 1853 to range with the nearby lightship and thus help vessels in crossing the Ocracoke Inlet bar; and a new light went into service at Northwest Point Royal Shoal in 1857.

In Charleston Harbor, South Carolina, Fort Sumter received its first light—a sixth-order lens—in 1855. At the same time, the board placed a small light on Castle Pinckney.

## Hog Island Light (1854)

The Lighthouse Board established three important coastal lights in the 1850's at Hog Island, Virginia; Fenwick Island, Delaware; and Hunting Island, South Carolina. Hog Island actually was authorized in the latter days of the fifth auditor's reign, but the

Point of Shoals light, Virginia, in 1885. This typical screw-pile lighthouse was established in the James River in 1855. *U. S. Coast Guard photo 26-LG-24-26 in the National Archives.*

light was not completed until 1854. This light was to serve both as a coastal light and as a guide to the Great Matchipungo Inlet. As a coast light it helped fill the darkened area between the Assateague and Cape Charles lights. It had only a fourth-order lens and the Lighthouse Board by 1888 felt that the light was inadequate as a coastal light, and recommended that a new tower, 150 feet tall

and equipped with the first-order lens, be erected. Several years later, Congress made the necessary appropriation and work on the new tower began; and in November, 1895, the keepers moved to the new site. The new tower was an iron skeleton type, and the keepers lighted the first-order lens on January 31, 1896.

Four years later, the tower was literally attacked

by birds. On Washington's birthday in 1900, between 7:00 and 8:30 P.M., a great flock of birds, apparently attracted or confused by the light of the tower, began pelting the lantern, breaking the panes of glass. The watch quickly called the other keeper who arrived on the double, clutching shotguns. The keepers fired on the frightened birds, hoping to drive them away from the lantern so that they would not damage the lens. The battle raged for an hour and a half, and the weapons became almost too hot to hold. The keepers' shoulders ached from the constant recoil of the shotguns. The birds kept coming, and in time the keepers had to give up because their ammunition ran out. In the morning, they counted sixty-eight wild geese, brandts, and ducks at the foot of the tower.

The keepers had still not recovered when the birds assaulted the tower two days later. The men had no ammunition, so they used sticks and began clubbing the birds. They had knocked down 150 birds when a huge flock of the winged creatures drove the keepers inside. Wave after wave of birds pelted the tower, many penetrating the heavy protective screen surrounding the lantern. When the honking, screeching horde had passed, the keepers found a number of panes broken and the light out.

The tower was repaired and the light continued to function until 1948 when, after ten years as an unwatched station, the Coast Guard discontinued it and tore down the lighthouse.

### Fenwick Island Light (1858)

To the north of Assateague there was a darkened space between it and Cape Henlopen. To lighten the coast and to help vessels from the south enter Delaware Bay, especially when the Cape Henlopen light was obscured, the board established a lighthouse on Fenwick Island that was virtually on the Mason-Dixon line separating Delaware and Maryland. Lighted in 1858, the third-order lens, eighty-three feet above the sea, was visible fifteen miles. The original white tower still functions as a lighthouse.

### Hunting Island Light (1859)

Down the coast about halfway between Charleston and Savannah, the Lighthouse Board erected a light tower in 1859 on Hunting Island. Either blown up

by the Confederates or undermined and toppled by sea erosion, the light tower no longer stood at the end of the Civil War.

Selecting a new site one mile from the end of Hunting Island, the Lighthouse Board built a new tower and lighted it July 1, 1875. Within three years, the effects of sea erosion were evident, and waves curled up on the beach just 440 feet from the light station's dwelling. A series of jetties and revetments was of little help and in 1887 the water was 60 feet from the dwelling and 152 feet from the tower. When the water reached 133 feet from the tower, the board decided to move it. In 1889, workmen dismantled the cast-iron tower and rebuilt it one and one-quarter miles from the old site. The keeper lighted the rebuilt tower on October 3, 1889. Moving the tower cost about half the original construction price. The tower is no longer active.

### Jupiter Inlet Light (1860)

In the late 1850's the Jupiter Inlet light, about fifteen miles north of Palm Beach in Florida, was under construction. Although scheduled for lighting earlier, the tower did not exhibit its light until July 10, 1860, four years after construction began. Indian hostilities, heat, and stinging insects all combined to hamper the progress of work. About a year after its lighting the Confederates put it out. Relighted in 1866, the first-order lens with its focal plane 146 feet above the sea has continued to serve a dual function of warning vessels of the shoals just off the coast and as a seacoast light guiding coasting vessels. The brick tower, now painted red, is still active. There was a one-room schoolhouse in Jupiter and according to local tradition teachers tended to marry Jupiter Inlet light keepers and the newlyweds settled in the vicinity, thus contributing substantially to populating the area.

## THE SPREAD OF THE SCREW-PILE LIGHTHOUSE

The Civil War gave impetus, at least in the South, to the Lighthouse Board's stated policy of replacing, where possible, light vessels with screw-pile lighthouses. Virtually all the light stations in the Chesapeake Bay and the sounds of North Carolina that had lightships before the war were reestablished after 1865 with screw-pile lighthouses. In

128

Currituck Beach lighthouse on the Outer Banks of North Carolina in 1893. Lighted in 1875, this is a first-order light that, like Bodie Island, is visible nineteen miles and is essential in helping southbound coasting traffic to avoid the Gulf Stream. *U. S. Coast Guard photo from the National Archives.*

North Carolina the screw-pile lighthouses at Horse-shoe Shoal (1868), Roanoke River (1867), Harbor Island Bar (1867), Southwest Point Royal Shoal (1867), Long Point Shoal (1867), and Brant Island Shoal (1864) were all stations that had light vessels before the war.

To the north, the screw-pile lighthouses at Windmill Point (1869), Upper Cedar Point (1867), Lower Cedar Point (1867), and James Island (1867), were all stations in Chesapeake Bay or its tributaries that before the war had light vessels assigned to them.

### Hooper's Strait Light (1867)

Another screw-pile lighthouse that replaced a lightship in Chesapeake Bay was the one at Hooper's Strait. Built in 1867 and lighted on September 14 of that year, the structure was but ten years old when ice carried it away. The district tender, dispatched to see what could be salvaged, found the wreckage five miles south of its station. Some property, including the lens and lantern, were rescued. The Lighthouse Board built a new screw-pile lighthouse at Hoopers Strait and lighted it October 15, 1879. It had a fifth-order lens.

In 1954, the Coast Guard made the light automatic. Later the lighthouse was declared surplus. The Chesapeake Bay Maritime Museum acquired the structure and moved it to St. Michaels, completing the restoration of the lighthouse on its new site in 1967. Today it is viewed by the many visitors to the nearby maritime museum.

Other southern stations, too, such as the Combahee Bank lighthouse (1868) in St. Helena Sound, South Carolina, and Dames Point (1872) in the St. Johns River, Florida, were changed from light vessels to screw-pile lighthouses.

### Wolf Trap Light (1870)

In the 1870's, in Chesapeake Bay, screw-pile lighthouses replaced lightships at Wolf Trap and Thimble Shoals. The Wolf Trap structure was lighted October, 1870, and served well until January 22, 1893, when floating ice ripped it from its foundations. About the same time floating ice tipped over the screw-pile lighthouse at Solomon's Lump further up the bay. A revenue cutter found the Wolf Trap lighthouse, submerged to the roof, drifting toward the capes. The captain of the vessel had a hawser tied to the lantern of the lighthouse and towed the peripatetic structure toward the beach, where it was allowed to drift ashore. Floating about at night, the lighthouse could have been a terrible hazard to navigation. The Lighthouse Board replaced the screw-pile structure with a sturdier caisson lighthouse in 1894.

### Thimble Shoals Light (1870)

One of the most accident-prone lighthouses was the screw-pile building at Thimble Shoals at the entrance to Hampton Roads. Lighted in 1870, it replaced the last lightship in the Fifth Lighthouse District. In 1880, fire destroyed the lighthouse, but so important was this station that another lighthouse was erected on the spot in fifty-five days—unquestionably a record. In 1891, an unknown steamer ran into the lighthouse, damaging it considerably. Later a coal barge inflicted severe damage, and in 1909 the schooner *Malcolm Baxter, Jr.,* under tow, rammed the lighthouse and set it on fire, completely destroying the structure. This time the Bureau of Lighthouses built a caisson lighthouse, and it has survived much better, perhaps because it presents a more formidable obstacle to accident-inclined vessels.

### Currituck Beach Light (1875)

The last major new coastal light station to be established on the South Atlantic Coast was at Currituck Beach, North Carolina. A distance of eighty miles separated the stations at Cape Henry and Bodie Island. After deciding to rebuild the Bodie Island light near its pre-Civil War site, the board realized that there would be a forty-mile unlighted stretch between that station and Cape Henry to the north. The Lighthouse Board reported that many ships with their cargo and lives had been lost on this section because there had been no light. Moreover, the light was sorely needed by southbound coasting traffic trying to avoid the Gulf Stream.

In 1873, the Lighthouse Board determined that Whale's Head Hill on Currituck Beach was halfway between Cape Henry and Bodie Island, and in 1874 the work crew began driving piles and laying the wooden grillage that was to be the foundation of the lighthouse. Work continued well and evenly, and on December 1, 1875, the first-order lens in the brick tower was lighted. The light, 158 feet above sea level, could be seen nineteen miles, thus illuminating the last dark section on the southern coast.

# IX

# Lighthouses of the Gulf Coast:

## *The Florida Keys to the Mexican Border*

### LIGHTS IN FLORIDA

As indicated in the previous chapter, once Florida became a territory of the United States, the federal government rather rapidly began establishing navigational aids where it was felt the greatest dangers lay. Certainly the most treacherous area for the navigator was the keys off the tip of Florida. Here were shoals, reefs, low islands that were difficult to see until the ship was virtually on top of them, and here, too, were the wreckers. At this time the wreckers enjoyed a rather notorious reputation; they received the blame for many of the wrecks. In recent years, however, the wreckers have come in for kinder consideration. Some today contend that they rendered a distinct and useful service, often being the first on the scene to aid survivors and salvage property.

Florida's best known set of keys begins at Biscayne Bay on the east side of the state near its tip. The series of small, low islands forms a gently curving line that trends toward the southwest and then swings westward to its termination at Key West. Spaced along the islands, and out from them a few miles, is a series of reefs. The reefs and the keys combine to form a hazard dreaded by mariners, and when near this area the sailor needs some sort of navigational aid to tell him where he is at all times.

### *Carysfort Reef Light (1825)*

To help the mariner get past the keys, Congress quickly appropriated money for lights at Carysfort near the north end of the keys, at Key West, and at Dry Tortugas some seventy miles in the ocean west of Key West. The fifth auditor let contracts, and in 1825 lights beamed from these three sites—one from a lightship. A lightship had been deemed best for Carysfort, probably because of the expense of building a lighthouse on a submerged reef. The first lightship remained less than five years when it was found that the vessel was so infested with dry rot as to be unrepairable. A second lightship replaced the first. In 1848, construction began on an iron-pile lighthouse for Carysfort, and four years later the light blinked on. Engineers had determined that the reef and underlying sand were an inadequate foundation for the then popular screw-pile construction. Iron piles were driven ten feet into the bottom up to large, square, iron foot-plates—much like a sword pushed into the sand up to its hilt. Cross members connected these eight iron piles with each other and gave the tower its strength and sturdiness. Keepers reached the light, whose focal plane was 106 feet above sea level, through a center column that gave additional strength to the structure. Still standing after well over 100 years, this lighthouse

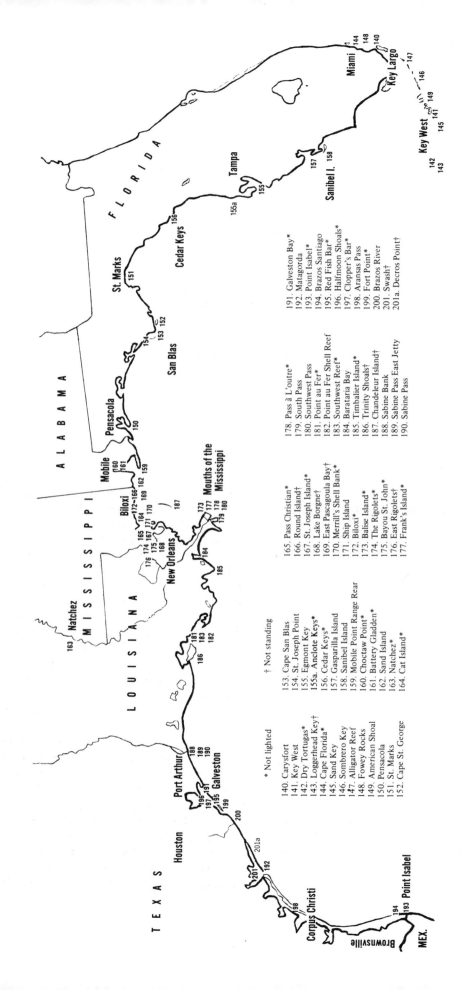

FLORIDA

Miami 144 148
140

Key Largo 147

Key West 149
146
141
145
142
143

Tampa

Sanibel I. 158

157

155

155a

Cedar Keys 156

St. Marks

151

San Blas

152
153
154

Pensacola

150

ALABAMA

Mobile 160
161

159

162

Biloxi 172-166 169
164 170
165 167 171
175 168
176 174

187

Mouths of the
Mississippi

173 177
178
179 180

184

185

New Orleans

Natchez

MISSISSIPPI

163

LOUISIANA

181
183
182

186

Port Arthur 188
189
190

Galveston

196 191
197 195 199
200

201a

201 192
198

TEXAS

Houston

Corpus Christi

Point Isabel

194
193

Brownsville

MEX.

* Not lighted

140. Carysfort
141. Key West
142. Dry Tortugas*
143. Loggerhead Key†
144. Cape Florida*
145. Sand Key
146. Sombrero Key
147. Alligator Reef
148. Fowey Rocks
149. American Shoal
150. Pensacola
151. St. Marks
152. Cape St. George

† Not standing

153. Cape San Blas
154. St. Joseph Point
155. Egmont Key
155a. Anclote Keys*
156. Cedar Keys*
157. Gasparilla Island
158. Sanibel Island
159. Mobile Point Range Rear
160. Choctaw Point*
161. Battery Gladden*
162. Sand Island
163. Natchez*
164. Cat Island*

165. Pass Christian*
166. Round Island†
167. St. Joseph Island*
168. Lake Borgne†
169. East Pascagoula Bay†
170. Merrill's Shell Bank*
171. Ship Island
172. Biloxi*
173. Balise Island*
174. The Rigolets*
175. Bayou St. John*
176. East Rigolets†
177. Frank's Island*

178. Pass à L'outre*
179. South Pass
180. Southwest Pass
181. Point au Fer*
182. Point au Fer Shell Reef
183. Southwest Reef*
184. Barataria Bay
185. Timbalier Island*
186. Trinity Shoals†
187. Chandeleur Island†
188. Sabine Bank
189. Sabine Pass East Jetty
190. Sabine Pass

191. Galveston Bay*
192. Matagorda
193. Point Isabel*
194. Brazos Santiago
195. Red Fish Bar*
196. Halfmoon Shoals*
197. Clopper's Bar*
198. Aransas Pass
199. Fort Point*
200. Brazos River
201. Swash†
201a. Decros Point†

## A dreaded hazard

Key West Light Station, Florida, before 1887. *U. S. Coast Guard photo from the National Archives.*

has served well—better, certainly, than its predecessor, which Lt. David D. Porter, U.S.N., had considered so unreliable that he avoided it and used the Moro lighthouse in Havana to establish his course. Incidentally, Porter generally had high regard for Spanish-kept lighthouses.

### Key West Light (1825)

Like the Carysfort Reef lightship, whose captain and mate at one stage in its career had been killed by Seminoles while ashore on one of the nearby islands, the Key West lighthouse also saw tragedy. Built on Whiteheads Point in 1825, the sixty-five-foot tower was destroyed in 1846 by a hurricane that killed the keeper and his family. A sixty-foot tower immediately replaced the wrecked one. Raised

twenty feet fifty years later by the Lighthouse Board, this light tower survives to the present.

### Dry Tortugas Light (1825)

The Dry Tortugas light had a different career. Originally erected on Bush Key—known today as Garden Key—the tower, its light seventy-five feet above sea level, stood proud and lonely for some years until the army began building Fort Jefferson, a part of the chain of fortifications the country erected in the first half of the nineteenth century to protect its coast. The fort was to become a prison during and after the Civil War; its most famous prisoner was Dr. Samuel Mudd, who had been unjustly convicted of involvement in the assassination of President Lincoln.

In 1858, the Lighthouse Board had a new brick tower built on Loggerhead Key and moved the Dry Tortugas light to this place. Its first-order light was 152 feet above sea level. The old tower, now on Fort Jefferson's parade, was reduced to a harbor light with a fourth-order lens. Moved ninety-three feet southeast in 1876 to a staircase on the fort after a storm severely damaged the tower, the light was of use as long as the fort remained active. Today, Fort Jefferson is a national monument, and it and the abandoned harbor light are available to the visitor who takes the three-hour boat trip from Key West.

The Loggerhead Key lighthouse was badly battered by a hurricane in 1873. Fearing that the tower would not survive another such storm, the Lighthouse Board asked Congress for money for a new light tower. Congress authorized the new tower, but before beginning construction, the board had the old tower repaired, which included rebuilding the upper nine feet of the tower below the lantern. Shortly after the repair work was completed, another hurricane swept the Keys. The repaired tower withstood the storm so well that the board reconsidered and abandoned plans to construct a new tower. The old tower is still in use, now holding a second-order lens.

### Cape Florida Light (ca. 1825)

About the same time these three lights were being established, a lighthouse was being constructed at the northern entrance to Biscayne Bay. Situated on Cape Florida, thirty some odd miles north of Carysfort Reef, the sixty-five-foot tower was to have had solid brick walls, five feet thick at the base and two feet thick at the top. Some years later the local collector of customs discovered that the contractor had defrauded the government; the walls were hollow from top to bottom!

The Cape Florida lighthouse went through one of the severest ordeals of any lighthouse in the country: an Indian siege. The threat of attack by Seminoles had apparently driven the keeper and his family to take refuge in Key West. He left the assistant keeper, John W. B. Thompson, and an old Negro man to maintain the light.

Late in the afternoon of July 23, 1836, the Seminoles came swooping in on the light station. They were barely sixty feet away when Thompson sighted

them. He and the old man beat a hasty path to the light tower and barely locked the door before the Indians piled up against it. The Seminoles, of course, attempted to get into the lighthouse, but Thompson drove them off with musket fire. He kept them away from the tower until dark when the Indians poured a withering hail of lead into the structure. Some of the musket balls penetrated the oil butts and little streams of whale oil doused the resolute keeper. The Seminoles set fire to the door. Thompson grabbed a musket, some balls, and a keg of powder and dashed to the top of the tower. He then tried to cut away the wooden stairway about midway of the tower, but flames drove him and his Negro companion to the lantern. Soon the fire burst into that haven, and the two men sought refuge outside the lantern, being careful not to expose themselves to the Indians below. The keeper's oil-soaked clothing caught fire, and the flames in the lantern heated the metal they lay against; the men were literally roasting alive. Notions of suicide flitted through the keeper's half-crazed mind, and he took up the barrel of powder and heaved it into the tower, hoping to blow it and himself to merciful death. But the explosion only shook the tower and dampened the flames briefly. About this time a ball struck the Negro, and with a cry of "I'm wounded," he fell unconscious and died. His friend dead and his own body racked with the pain of burns, heat, and musket ball wounds, Thompson once again thought of suicide to relieve his agony. He crawled to the railing of the lantern gallery and was about to plunge over it head first when something told him to return to his niche of safety. He had barely gotten settled when the flaming wood inside fell away to the bottom of the tower, and about this time a good breeze came to cool the tormented man. But his condition had improved little. Thompson later summed up his state at this point: "I was now almost as bad off as before, a burning fever on me, my feet shot to pieces, no clothes to cover me, nothing to eat or drink, a hot sun overhead, a dead man by my side, no friend near or any to expect, and placed between 70 and 80 feet from the earth with no chance of getting down."

Thompson remained this way until the afternoon, when he saw two ship's boats of the U. S. Navy, with his sloop in tow, headed for the light station's wharf.

Getting the keeper down caused problems to the

Abandoned Dry Tortugas light tower atop Fort Jefferson in the Florida Keys in 1962. Fort Jefferson is now a national monument.   *Photo by Jack Boucher for HABS.*

135

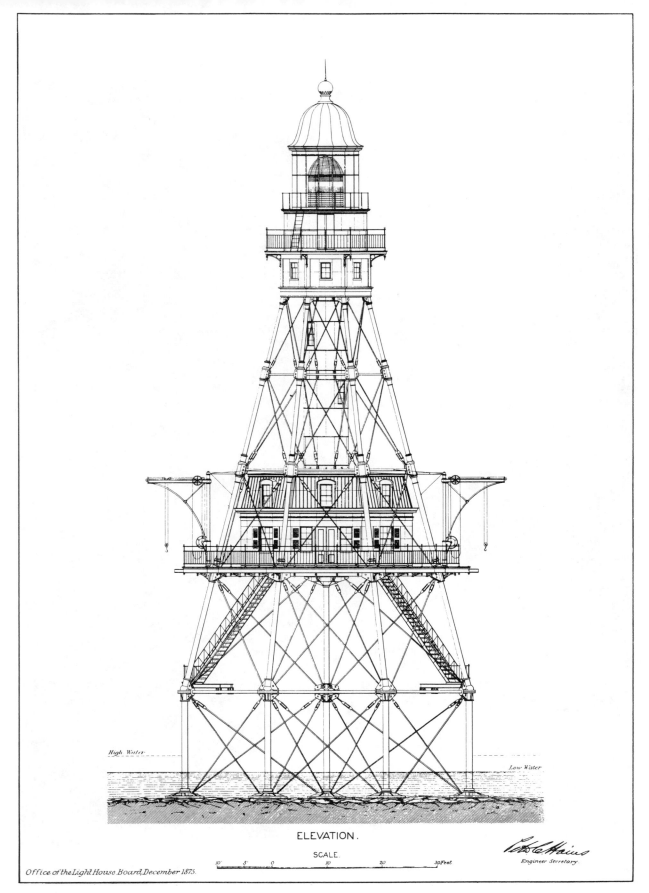

ELEVATION.

SCALE.

10'    5'    0          10          20          30 Feet

Office of the Light House Board, December 1875.

Engineer Secretary.

Elevation and vertical section (1875, apparently from different angles) of the first-order lighthouse at Fowey Rocks that replaced the Cape Florida light in 1878. Several lighthouses along the Florida Reefs were of this design. *Drawing in the author's collection.*

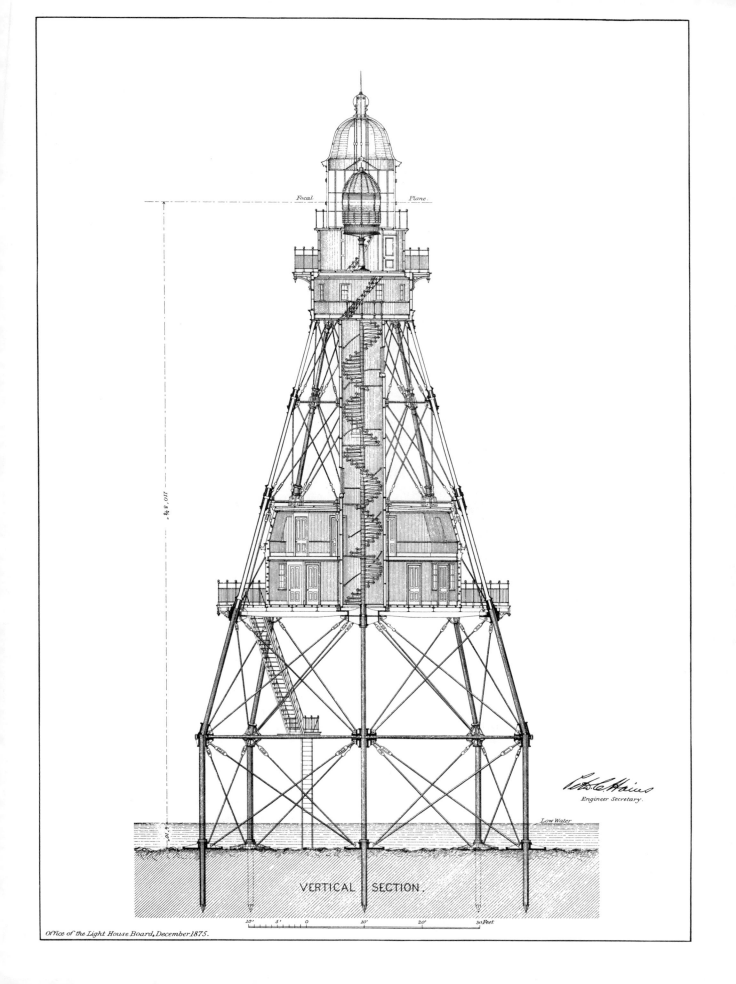

Focal          Plane.

110'.8.¾"

10'.4"

Low Water

*Engineer Secretary.*

VERTICAL SECTION.

10'    5'    0              10'              20'              30 Feet

*Office of the Light House Board, December 1875.*

The screw-pile tower at Sand Key Light Station, Florida, about 1890. The action of the sea has caused this island to disappear and reappear several times since the station was established. In 1846, the island was washed away in a hurricane and the original stone lighthouse destroyed. Its successor, shown here, has so far withstood the sea's onslaught. *U. S. Coast Guard photo in the National Archives.*

rescuers. An effort to fly a line to him by kite failed. Someone hit upon the idea of attaching a messenger (a small line) to a ramrod and firing it to the keeper. The idea worked, and Thompson pulled a block, with a heavier line attached, up to the lantern. He hooked the block to the railing, and the group below hauled two sailors up to him. They in turn lowered the wounded keeper to the ground

where he was taken to a military hospital for treatment.

Congress authorized rebuilding the Cape Florida lighthouse, but the continued threat of harassment from the Seminoles delayed construction. The light was not put back into service until 1846. Within a few years it had a reputation as a poor light. Several ship's captains reported in 1851 that wrecks often

138

occurred along that section that could have been avoided if Cape Florida had a decent light. To improve the light, the Lighthouse Board raised the tower in 1855 so that the focal plane of the light was 100 feet above sea level and installed a Fresnel lens to better mark "a prominent point on a most dangerous coast."

In 1861, "a band of lawless persons" destroyed the illuminating apparatus, and the light could not be restored until 1866. It remained in service until June 15, 1878, when the light was superseded by a new lighthouse at Fowey Rocks. Years later the abandoned tower became part of Cape Florida State Park, and in 1978 the Coast Guard re-established a light on it.

### Sand Key Light (1827)

The lighthouses erected at the Florida Keys in the 1820's were all built on the keys themselves, such as the already-mentioned Key West and Dry Tortugas towers and the Sand Key lighthouse that was completed in 1827. This latter lighthouse illustrates the danger of erecting ordinary towers on these sandy keys. Nineteen years after lighting, a hurricane blew through the keys churning up a foaming sea that swirled the sand from beneath the tower and the keeper's dwelling. Both structures became badly undermined and collapsed, burying their occupants beneath wood and stone. A screw-pile lighthouse, lighted in 1853, replaced the stone tower. A dozen years after lighting, another hurricane stirred up the ocean off the Keys, and this time the boiling sea washed away all of the island, leaving only the pile lighthouse to mark where the tiny island had been. Subsequently, the island has reappeared.

As time went on, engineering advances made it possible to erect strong pile lighthouses in the ocean on the reefs that were like an underwater barrier protecting the Florida Keys. The Carysfort Reef light was the model for the iron-pile lighthouses erected on the Florida Reefs, including the one on Sand Key. Five years after the lighting of the Sand Key pile lighthouse, Lt. George Meade finished a pile tower on Sombrero Key, or Dry Banks as it was then sometimes called. One historian of the lighthouse service termed Sombrero Key light "the most important light-house built by General Meade."

In subsequent years, the navigator was further assisted in steering clear of the Florida Reefs by the addition of lighthouses, similar in design, at Alligator Reef (1873) about midway between Carysfort Reef and Sombrero Key, at Fowey Rocks (1878) opposite the entrance to Biscayne Bay, and at American Shoal (1880) about halfway between Sombrero Key and Sand Key. When completed, these lighthouses, about thirty nautical miles apart, formed a curving line of lights that permitted the navigator to know where he was at all times in relation to the dangerous Florida Reefs.

### Pensacola Light (1825)

Meanwhile, the west coast of Florida received attention. The first site selected for a lighthouse on that coast was at Pensacola, for the government in 1824 designated that the town would be the site of a navy yard. The fifth auditor, upon authorization from Congress, had a tower erected at the south entrance to Pensacola Bay and lighted it in 1825; thus it became the first United States lighthouse in Florida. The focal plane of the light was eighty feet above sea level. The tower, however, proved not to be satisfactory. In 1837, an inspector of lighthouses recommended moving it to a place of greater height. But nothing was done, and in 1851, Congress's investigating board found the light "deficient in power, being fitted with only ten lamps and sixteen-inch reflectors"; it was little better than a harbor light. Moreover, the investigators found that the light was a revolving one, just like the Mobile light forty miles away. It was the changing of the Mobile light from stationary to revolving by Winslow Lewis, thus making it similar to the Pensacola light, that had caused such a furor among ship captains. The board felt that the characteristic of the Pensacola light should be changed and that the port, because it was an important naval station, rated "a first-class sea coast light." Two years later, the commandant of the naval station urged that the light be raised twenty to twenty-five feet. Finally, in 1858, the board had a new tower erected on the north side of the bay's entrance. Exhibited January 1, 1859, the first-order revolving light's beam was 160 feet above the ground and 210 feet above the sea.

During the Civil War the Confederates bombarded the tower with solid shot and put the light out of operation. In 1863, the installation of a fourth-order lens relighted the tower, and this lens continued in service until 1869, when a first-order lens was re-established in the tower. Many years after the fratricidal war the effects of the bombardment showed up when cracks on the side of the tower appeared. Repointing sufficed to render the tower strong again. No residual problems from that direction re-occurred, and the tower, the lower third white and the upper two-thirds black, has survived to the present.

### St. Marks Light (1831)

At St. Marks, which had been a principal Spanish town, the United States established a lighthouse in 1831. Winslow Lewis received the contract for the construction of the station's buildings and the installation of the lighting apparatus. Lewis kept the lighting contract, but sub-contracted the building of the station. The two sub-contractors built such a poor tower that the local collector of customs refused to accept it. The walls of the tower were hollow instead of solid as the contract called for. The tower was finally rebuilt by Calvin Knowlton in 1831.

Nine years later erosion threatened the tower, and Pleasonton had it moved to a safer location and rebuilt. Knowlton erected this tower also.

During the Seminole War the keeper became jittery and asked for a guard to protect the lighthouse, but Pleasonton denied this request. The keeper then asked that a boat be assigned to the station so he and his family could escape should the Seminoles approach the light station. Pleasonton was not sympathetic to this plea. Fortunately, the Seminoles did not come, either.

At the time of the Civil War the Confederates attempted to blow up the lighthouse, and they so badly damaged the base, blowing out a chunk of the wall about eight feet high and one third around the tower, that the tower had to be reconstructed. Relighted January 8, 1867, the tower has survived to the present and is today the rear St. Marks Range Light.

### Cape St. George Light (1833)

Other towers were added on the west coast of Florida as they were needed. In 1833, a new tower at Cape St. George near the entrance to Apalachicola Bay went into service. Rebuilt in 1847, the tower did not remain long, for a wind pushed it over in 1851. A new tower went up in 1852, and although damaged by the rebels during the war, this tower was repaired and is still in use today.

### Cape San Blas Light (1847)

A proposed lighthouse at Cape San Blas a few miles north of Cape St. George was regarded as a useless expenditure in 1837. Nevertheless, shoals extending out for four or five miles from that point caused reconsideration that resulted in a light being established there in 1847. A storm blew the tower over in 1851, and the following year Congress authorized a replacement. After some delay, workmen put final touches on the tower in 1856. The light was in operation only a few months when a storm "totally destroyed" the new tower.

Rebuilt three years later and lighted with a third-order lens, the Cape San Blas tower was extensively injured by the Confederates, and the board did not put it back into operation until July 1865.

Within a few years erosion became a problem. It was first noticed in 1869, when the beach in front of the tower began to wear away, and by 1875 the sea lapped only 150 feet from the tower. Two years later, Congress responded to an appeal for funds to halt the encroachment of the sea with a niggardly amount of money, and in 1878 the sea washed the base of the Cape San Blas light tower. But at this point the sea on its own relented, and the beach began to build, giving hope for the safety of the tower. With inadequate funds to build a proper jetty, the board took no action. In 1880, though, the sea once again splashed against the base of the tower, and the following year the board hastily laid a jetty of brush-work mattresses. It was a case of too little too late, and the sea quickly pounded the mattresses to pieces. The tower now stood in water; it was unquestionably doomed. Foregoing any further hope of saving the tower, the board asked Congress for funds to erect a skeleton tower to replace the stone one. But no appropriation was forthcoming. Meanwhile, workmen removed the lens from the tower's lantern. On July 3, 1882, the tower stood in eight feet of water with heavy seas pounding against her. The undermining action of the water caused her to begin tilting. As she leaned further cracks began to appear, and soon the tower fell over like a huge giant that had lost his balance.

Placing a sixth-order lens on a spar temporarily so that the mariner would be warned of the shoals that extended out from Cape San Blas, the Lighthouse Board once again asked Congress for funds to erect a skeleton tower. Receiving the appropriation, the board erected the tower between 400 and 500 yards from the shoreline and lighted it on June 30, 1885. The third-order lens was eighty-five feet above sea level.

The choice of the site was not a good one, for within two years the sea had eaten away a third of the beach. Two years passed and the sea crept to within 200 feet of the tower. A year later only 144 feet of land separated the tower from the sea. Now fearful for the safety of the tower, the board requested and received money in 1890 to move it. Acquisition of another site at Cape San Blas dragged on, and in 1894 the board instituted condemnation proceedings. Meanwhile, the situation at the tower site was becoming more desperate, and in October of that year a storm extinguished the light, wrecked the two keepers' dwellings, and left the tower standing in water.

The Cape San Blas light was re-exhibited right away. Two years later, the board began moving the station to Black's Island in St. Joseph Bay; a temporary light served until the move could be completed. The work was about half done when the board changed its mind and in September, 1897, re-established the light in the old tower. The board wanted to erect a new tower at a different place and in 1903 received money for this purpose. But about this time the erosion pattern changed and the shore began to make out, so the board decided to leave the tower where it was. Everything was fine until 1916, when the sea once again threatened the site, and in 1919, the Cape San Blas light was moved a quarter mile north, where it has since remained.

### St. Joseph Point Light (1839)

Cape San Blas had a predecessor light. Established at the entrance to St. Joseph Bay in 1839, the St. Joseph Point light had served but a few years when the collector recommended it be discontinued in 1847, replaced by the Cape San Blas lighthouse. Subsequently the Lighthouse Board recommended from time to time that the light be reactivated to mark St. Joseph Bay as a harbor of refuge for the large fishing fleet that plied those waters. Finally, in 1898, Congress appropriated funds for a lighthouse. The board, however, determined that the tower would be more useful situated on the mainland and not on St. Joseph Spit as it had formerly been. The board obtained the land in 1901 and on

August 2, 1902, the keeper lighted the third-order lens in the new lighthouse. It served for 58 years until a steel skeleton tower replaced it.

### Egmont Key Light (1848)

To the southward the increasing activity of Tampa Bay resulted in a lighthouse being established there in 1848, the year the military turned over the 160 acres of the Fort Brooke reservation to the local government. It formed the basis of the city and is now downtown Tampa. Situated on the north end of Egmont Key, the lighthouse, built by Francis A. Gibbons of Baltimore, who was later to be one of the contractors to build the first lighthouses on the Pacific coast, had been in existence a half dozen years when shifting sand threatened to undermine the structure. Efforts to halt the undermining proved to be only temporary measures, and in 1858 a new tower, with a light eighty-five feet above sea level, replaced the old one. Damaged by the Confederates, the Egmont Key light was re-established in 1866. Today a light still beams from this more-than-a-century-old tower.

The Cedar Keys lighthouse (1854), the Gasparilla Island lighthouse (1890)—now called Port Boca Grande light—at the entrance to Charlotte Harbor, and the Sanibel Island light across the bay from Fort Myers Beach rounded out the principal lights erected on the west coast of Florida. This latter light was established when the board recognized that increasing coastwise trade required a light between Egmont Key and Key West. At the time of the beginning of construction the ship carrying the iron work for the tower was wrecked within two miles of the lighthouse site at the east end of Sanibel Island. Before the ship sank, the captain was able to off-load part of the cargo; the remainder went down. The district engineer exercised his imagination and initiative and utilized the crews of the two tenders, as well as the work crew, and a diver to salvage the materials. They retrieved all parts of the lantern except two small brackets, which the engineer was able to have duplicated in New Orleans. Work proceeded pretty much on schedule and the keeper displayed the Sanibel Island light on August 20, 1884. The light of this skeleton iron tower was ninety-eight feet above sea level. This light, as well as the one at Charlotte Harbor, continues in use. The Cedar Keys light was discontinued in 1916.

Mobile Point lighthouse. Established in 1822 near the subsequent location of Fort Morgan at the entrance to Mobile Bay, this tower underwent heavy shelling during the Union fleet's bombardment of the fort in 1864. *From* Frank Leslie's Illustrated Newspaper.

## Shot out by the federals

### LIGHTS IN ALABAMA

Of the states bordering the Gulf of Mexico, the one with the least amount of coast is Alabama. Indeed, its only major harbor is Mobile Bay, and since that state's shipping activity has been centered around that bay, the development of lighthouses in Alabama has been at Mobile Bay.

### Mobile Point Light (1822)

Mobile Bay is a roughly rectangular body of water that extends about thirty-five miles from its entrance to the city of Mobile at its head. An island on one side and a peninsula on the other narrow the entrance to less than five miles. Naturally enough the first lighthouse at the bay was placed at its entrance. Established in 1822 at Mobile Point on the east side of the entrance, where Fort Morgan is now located, the light has served from the beginning as a harbor light, not a coastal one. Indeed, the Lighthouse Board later fitted it with a fourth-order lens—a lens it used only for harbor lights—in 1858. Because it was located close to Fort Morgan, the masonry tower was riddled by shot and shell during the Civil War when the Federals bombarded the fort. The tower was beyond repair, and in 1864, the Lighthouse Board re-established the Mobile Point light on the southwest bastion of Fort Morgan. This temporary light remained there for nine years when, in 1873, the board constructed a thirty-foot iron tower on the same bastion and equipped it with a fourth-order lens. That light has continued to serve through the years except for a brief period in the latter part of May, 1898, when the light was extinguished because "military regulations forbade shipping from entering or leaving the harbor at night." Today the structure is known as the Mobile Point Range Rear Light.

### Choctaw Point Light (1831)

In 1831, a light was established at the head of the bay at Choctaw Point. It served to aid vessels across Dog River bar at the city of Mobile. Eliminated by the Confederates during the Civil War, the light was never reactivated because Confederate obstructions had so altered the channel that there was no longer a need for the light. Toward the end of the

nineteenth century the station was made a buoy depot, and the Mobile, Jackson, and Kansas Railroad installed wharves there.

### Battery Gladden Light (1872)

In 1872, the Lighthouse Board erected a screw-pile lighthouse on Battery Gladden—a Confederate-created island—about five-eighths of a mile east of Choctaw Point. Today, its fourth-order lens no longer shines, although the unused lighthouse still serves as a daymark.

### Sand Island Light (1838)

Alabama's first, and only, coastal light was on Sand Island. It was established in 1838 to mark the approach to the entrance to Mobile Bay. The Lighthouse Board felt Sand Island should also serve as a coast light, and accordingly had a new tower built and fitted with a first-order lens and lighted in January, 1859. In 1864 the board was dismayed to find the Confederates had blown up the "magnificent tower at Sand island." Establishing a temporary light, the board laid plans to erect a new tower that had a light with a focal plane 125 feet above sea level. Lighted September 1, 1873, the new conical brick tower contained a second-order lens.

Within a few years the beach began to erode on the east side of Sand Island and by 1882, the remains of the old tower stood in water. The board began building jetties and bulkheads, or walls, to halt erosion, but these things only slowed nature, and in the early 1890's the dwelling had to be moved. Riprap placed around the foundation of the tower proved of little permanent use. In 1898, erosion ceased and the eastern beach began to make out. But a year later the southeast and southwest sides of Sand Island began to erode, and Congress so feared for the safety of the tower that it appropriated $65,000 to be used when necessary to rebuild the station. The tower remained, however, but in 1906, a storm swept away the keepers' dwelling, drowning the assistant keeper and his wife. Meanwhile, erosion continued and in 1914, the tower stood wholly in water. But again nature changed her mind and altered the pattern of erosion. Today the tower still stands as Alabama's only coastal lighthouse.

Cat Island Light Station, Mississippi, around 1900. This screw-pile lighthouse was completed in 1871. Shortly after this picture was taken, the tower was further stabilized by rocks piled under and around it. *U. S. Coast Guard photo 26-LG-35-44 in the National Archives.*

## LIGHTS IN MISSISSIPPI

### Natchez Light (1827)

Mississippi's door on the Gulf of Mexico is not much larger than Alabama's. As far as can be determined at present, Mississippi's first lighthouse was not on its coast, but rather was located at Natchez on the Mississippi River. Established in 1827, the lighthouse remained in operation until about 1839, when a tornado decommissioned it. "It never was of much use," said the fifth auditor, "and it is not intended to put another in its place."

### Cat Island Light (1831)

In 1831, a lighthouse went into service on Cat Island, off the coast of Mississippi near Gulfport. Damaged severely on several occasions through the years by hurricanes, the tower received repairs and continued in use until the Civil War when the Confederates did so much damage that the Lighthouse Board after the war decided to build a screw-pile lighthouse. During construction, as at many other sites in the south, malarial fevers bothered the workmen. Nevertheless, they completed the structure, and the keepers exhibited the Cat Island light for the first time on December 15, 1871. Stabilized in

1900 by rocks piled under the dwelling and around the base, the lighthouse continued in use until 1938.

### Pass Christian Light (1831)

Also in 1831, the federal government erected a lighthouse at Pass Christian near Gulfport. It was a short brick tower, just twenty-eight feet high, and by 1860 an adjacent store had grown up and obscured much of the light from the tower's fourth-order lens; and the owner wanted to raise the building another story. The district engineer recommended selling the property since it had high commercial value; the lighthouse was situated on the main street of the village. The problem, however, was soon settled, because the Confederates moved in and dismantled the lens. Lighthouse officials found it at the end of the war in storage in Pass Christian. Local people quickly petitioned the Lighthouse Board to re-establish the Pass Christian light, which it did in August 1866. By 1882, trees had grown up on adjacent property and they were reducing the effectiveness of the light. The owner of the trees refused to cut them down or even trim them. This problem caused the Lighthouse Board to reassess the value of the Pass Christian lighthouse, and it concluded that the light should be discontinued since it was "of so little benefit to navi-

## Dismantled by the confederates

gation or commerce." The light was discontinued in September, 1882, and the property sold the next year to Lawrence G. Fallon for $1,225.

### Round Island (1833), East Pascagoula River (1854), and St. Joseph's Island (1865) Lights

In 1833, the government established a light at Round Island off Pascagoula Bay to guard shipping against the shoals of the island. In 1854, it placed a lighthouse not far away at East Pascagoula Bay.

The St. Joseph's Island lighthouse was built in 1859, but because of land ownership problems it was not exhibited until 1865. It remained in operation until 1889, replaced by the Lake Borgne light. During its last year, the Lighthouse Board condemned the structure because of erosion and placed an eight-day lantern on the lighthouse, which the keeper tended from his home in Bay St. Louis.

### Merrill's Shell Bank Light (1847)

Merrill's Shell Bank was guarded first in 1847 by a light vessel, but in 1860, a screw-pile lighthouse went into service there. Although taken out by the Confederates, it was not damaged and the board relighted the structure in 1863. In 1880, a fire on the wood shingle roof did a little damage, and three years later the structure burned to its pilings. Within three months the board built a new lighthouse—this time with a slate shingle roof—and lighted it November 20, 1883. The Merrill's Shell Bank station, however, is no longer in service.

### Ship Island Light (1853)

The Lighthouse Board established a light on the western end of Ship Island in 1853. During the Civil War, the Union forces erected Fort Massachusetts near the tower. The original light tower remained in service until 1886 when the board condemned it and built a new one—this time a square, pyramidal tower. The Ship Island tower is still active today, and its fourth-order lens guides shipping between it and Cat Island.

### Biloxi Light (1848)

Perhaps Mississippi's best known lighthouse is the one at Biloxi. Located in the median strip between the lanes of U. S. Highway 90, the tower is a prominent landmark to autoists as well as seamen. Built in 1848, the cast-iron conical tower has survived through the years. The keeper had a scare in 1867 when the erosion of the bank caused the tower to tip two feet out of plumb. But workmen righted the tower when they dug away the ground from the other side.

Tradition has the Biloxi tower painted black after the assassination of President Lincoln. It is a good example of how fiction can get mixed up with fact. It is true that the tower at one time was painted black, but that color did not last long because the tower tended to blend in with the dark trees in the background, and thus the tower's value as a daymark was considerably lessened. The tower was actually painted black in 1867, two years after Lincoln's death.

The Biloxi lighthouse through the years had several women keepers. Mrs. Maria Younghans succeeded her husband in the job in 1867, and she did not retire until 1920. She was replaced by her daughter Miranda who remained keeper until 1929.

The tower is still active today, although it is about to become part of a Biloxi city park and will be open to visitation.

## LIGHTS IN LOUISIANA

Louisiana exposes considerably more of her shore to the Gulf than do Mississippi and Alabama combined. Moreover, it is a different type of coast with a vast number of bays and little indentations on its coast. Throughout the history of the state the importance of these bays fluctuates as the thickness of traffic increases and decreases.

*Passes* and *bayous* are two terms common to this section of the coast. Although most commonly identified with Louisiana, the use of the terms spills over into Texas and Mississippi. Passes are access ways to rivers, bays, lakes, and other bodies of water. Bayous are usually natural channels that may or may not be of sufficient size and depth to accommodate water traffic.

Louisiana's first lighthouse apparently goes back to the earliest days of the French settlement of the Pelican state. Around 1699 or 1700 French pioneers established a settlement they named Balise, near the very end of the state's greatest protrusion into the Gulf, at one of the branches of Pass à L'outre, an access from the Gulf to the Mississippi River. The word *balise* in French means beacon or seamark, indicating that the settlers had an aid to navigation at this point. At any rate, the records indicate that a beacon was definitely at the place by 1721.

About this time, shortly after the founding of New Orleans, smaller ships seeking an access to the city other than by way of the long trip up the Mississippi River against the current began going through Lake Borgne (really a bay), past The Rigolets into Lake Pontchartrain, and then to the city by way of Bayou St. John. To help these mariners the government placed lights at The Rigolets and at the entrance to Bayou St. John.

In 1767, the Spanish governors had a pyramidal tower about 120 feet tall erected on Balise Island to guide shipping through a new pass that had opened on the northern side of the mouth of the Mississippi.

Just how long these aids to navigation remained active is not known, but probably by the time of American acquisition of the state most were no longer in use.

The light at Bayou St. John, it would seem, had disappeared, for in 1811, the United States government erected a light at the entrance to the bayou. It was a small light, in 1855 being only a sixth-order lens.

A light was established at East Rigolets on Pleasonton Island near the mouth of the Pearl River in 1833. It remained there until 1874, when it was determined to be of no more use to navigators. Meanwhile, at West Rigolets a light was established near Ft. Pick at the east end of Lake Pontchartrain.

### Franks Island Light (1818)

But long before these two were erected, the federal government had a lighthouse built on Franks Island near the Northeast Pass, apparently in the vicinity of Louisiana's first aid to navigation. Built in 1818 by Winslow Lewis, the light tower had a poor foundation, and soon the light was out of operation. Lewis offered, for a sum totalling nearly $10,000, to rebuild the tower and, this time, guarantee the foundation. The fifth auditor had Lewis rebuild the light tower in 1822. This tower remained in operation until August 18, 1856, when the Pass à L'outre lighthouse was established.

### Pass à L'outre Light (1856)

The Pass à L'outre tower had originally been at the Head of the Passes. After its lighting in the new location the tower began settling, despite the fact it had been built on a brick foundation on piles. By 1877 it had settled five feet and the floor of the tower had been raised twice to keep the floor above high tide. By 1880 it apparently had ceased settling. In time Pass à L'outre decreased in importance, and the tower is today but a daymark.

### South Pass and Southwest Pass Lights (1831)

The two most important passes through the Mississippi delta to the Mississippi River are South Pass and Southwest Pass. Lighthouses were established at both passes in 1831. The one at Southwest Pass lasted only until 1840 when it had to be rebuilt. The new tower had two lights—one on top of the other with twenty-five feet separating them. But this light was not satisfactory because it was too far from the entrance to the channel. Congress in 1854 appropriated money to build a screw-pile lighthouse "as near the entrance to the channel of the Mississippi river at the Southwest Pass as might be found practicable. . . ." But the Lighthouse Board delayed taking action and the Civil War finally put a halt to all plans for the new light. After the war the board found the light tower was sinking. Moreover, erosion was destroying the station. There was no doubt now, the tower had to be rebuilt and the station moved. In 1869, the board began building a new tower, concentrating on a secure foundation. One hundred eighty-five piles were driven into the ground and concrete was forced among and about them. Next the builders placed a layer of 12″ x 12″ beams and concrete. The workmen then set on top of the timbers three layers of three-inch planking encased in concrete. It was a formidable foundation and on it the board built a skeleton iron tower whose first-order lens was 128 feet above sea level; the dwelling was built into the tower. In 1894, a fire in the dwelling damaged the light, putting it out of commission and necessitating installation of a temporary light. Repaired finally in 1899, the tower remained in operation until 1953, when the Southwest Pass East Jetty light was enlarged to become the Southwest Pass Entrance light.

## Barely escaping with their lives

The South Pass light was established in 1831 at "South Point, (Gordon's Island), entrance of Mississippi River, South Pass," as an early *Light List* read. It was a wooden tower on a keeper's dwelling. In 1851, Lt. David D. Porter, U.S.N., reported that it and the Southwest Pass light "are very fair, and can be seen plainly twelve miles." Eliminated by the Confederates at the outbreak of the Civil War, the light was restored in 1862 with the placing of a third-order lens in the tower.

In 1868, the Lighthouse Board called attention to the fact that South Pass was the first light made by Mississippi River–bound ships from Europe and the West Indies. This fact, it felt, was sufficient to warrant rebuilding the rotting 1831 lighthouse and installing a first-order lens. The board kept asking for eleven years before Congress appropriated the necessary funds. Receiving the money in 1879, the board tested and located a site and put up the iron-skeleton light tower originally intended for Trinity Shoals. Situated 100 feet southeast of the old tower, the new South Pass tower held a first-order lens. The light, 105 feet above ground, was displayed August 25, 1881. The tower was painted white in 1900 so that navigators could better distinguish it from the Southwest Pass tower. Still active, the 1881 tower is today the rear range light for the entrance to South Pass.

### Point au Fer Light (1827)

The Point au Fer Light Station on Eugene Island at Atchafalaya Bay has a history going back to 1827. In that year the Point au Fer tower, some 65 feet tall, was lighted at the mouth of the River Teche in Atchafalaya Bay. It remained in operation until 1859, when the Southwest Reef Bay light tower exhibited its light at the entrance to the bay. The board had it built to replace not only the Point au Fer light, but also the Atchafalaya Bay lightship. In the next few years this screw-pile lighthouse apparently did not experience severe weather, but in 1867, two years after relighting as a result of Civil War damage, a hurricane swept the coast and severely shook the lighthouse, ripping the walkway from around the building, caving in the iron floor, and destroying nearly everything inside. In addition, the storm came close to pushing the lighthouse over. When the workmen arrived to repair the tower after the storm, they found the original build-

ers had failed to put the bracing on the tower, "a very serious omission in so exposed a structure." Repaired, the lighthouse continued to function until about World War I. Although no longer in use, the old lighthouse survives as a daymark.

The third lighthouse in that area was the current Point au Fer light on Eugene Island at Point au Fer Shell Reef. The white wooden dwelling built on piles and with a light on top went into service in 1916.

### Barataria Bay Light (1857)

At Barataria Bay, the hang-out of the controversial Louisiana pirate Jean Laffite, the federal government erected a lighthouse in 1857. It remained in operation but two years; traffic did not warrant a lighthouse there. Five years later the army occupied Fort Livingstone nearby and requested reactivation of the light. The Lighthouse Board complied and the lighthouse remained in operation at its old site for nearly thirty years. In 1893 a storm severely damaged the light, and because the station was difficult to reach for repairs and the site rapidly eroding, the Lighthouse Board at this time requested permission of the army to erect a new tower on the "cover face" of the fort. The army granted permission, and in 1897 a contractor erected "a square pyramidal frame tower, painted white" on the "cover face" of the fort. The light, a 200-mm lens seventy-seven feet above sea level, shines from this tower today.

### Timbalier Island Light (1857)

Southwest of Barataria Bay is Timbalier Bay, and like its neighbor it, too, received its first lighthouse in 1857. Built on a low sand spit at the east end of Timbalier Island, the lighthouse remained there for ten years before erosion threatened its existence. In danger of toppling, the tower had its lens removed in February, 1867, and stored in the keepers' dwelling. The following month a hurricane struck that section of the coast and leveled everything on the island, including the keepers' dwelling. The keepers kept the temporary light going to the very last, "barely escaping with their lives," before the tower went over. They took refuge in an iron can buoy where they lived for several days.

Some years passed before the Lighthouse Board

placed another lighthouse at Timbalier Bay, but in 1875, a new screw-pile structure with a second-order lens went into use. The board had justified the new light partially on the basis of its importance as a coastal aid. For nineteen years the light shone brightly from the skeleton-frame tower at the entrance to the bay. In 1894, scouring of the channel undermined the structure, and it canted over, damaging the lens apparatus. Unable to save the tower, the board erected a temporary light about a half mile from the wreck of the Timbalier light. Feeling the coastal light was no longer justified, the board put up a lens lantern[1] for harbor use. Although no longer active, the present structure, a square tower built in 1917 on wooden piles and located on the east end of Timbalier Island, serves today as a daymark.

### Trinity Shoals Light (1859)

The power and effect of storms in the Gulf of Mexico is well illustrated in the building of the Trinity Shoals lighthouse. There had been a lighthouse on Shell Keys just south of Marsh Island and east of Atchafalaya Bay. First lighted in 1859, the iron screw-pile structure was "discontinued" by the Confederates and re-exhibited by the Federals in 1865. Two years afterwards, a hurricane plowed through that area and destroyed the lighthouse, drowning the keeper on duty. About this time someone discovered the nearby Trinity Shoals and realized what a hazard to navigation it posed. The board recognized the fact that the buoy it had placed there was wholly inadequate and recommended that a lighthouse, the light of which would be 131 feet above sea level, be erected at the shoals. Congress accepted the board's recommendation and appropriated money so that work could begin in 1873.

Construction presented a unique problem. The site was twenty miles from the nearest land; consequently, some way had to be found to provide living quarters for the men at the site. The decision was reached to build a platform at the shoals and

---

[1] A lens lantern was a small one-unit light that did not require housing to protect it from the weather as did a regular Fresnel lens. The glass sides of the lantern served the same function as the lens, refracting and magnifying the light from the lamp.

house the workmen on it while the ship remained close with the materials for construction. Although weather hampered work, the men drove piles into the shoal and built their platform, completing it in October. About the time they finished it, two ships arrived with the ironwork for the lighthouse's foundation. The workmen began installing the foundation, but weather again soon interfered. On November 15, 1873, a storm hit the area, and winds drove one of the material-laden ships, the *Guthrie,* onto the shoal. The ship began to leak and the captain headed to sea, hoping to stay afloat by using the ship's pumps. But this scheme didn't work, and the captain turned his ship back to the shoal. The ship sank there in eleven feet of water. The other ship picked up the crew of the wrecked vessel, and the *Guthrie's* captain sought refuge on the construction platform. In time the winds eased, and everyone breathed easier. Several hours later, though, the winds increased and became so intense that they swept away the platform and dumped the sixteen-man work force into the churning Gulf. The workmen were picked up immediately, but the captain of the *Guthrie* and the superintendent of construction were dragged out to sea. The two men clung desperately to floating debris for three hours before rescuers arrived to pluck them from the sea.

The Lighthouse Board dispatched a vessel to the area to help salvage materials, but little could be saved. About this time the board decided that the site did not rate a lighthouse, and that they would be wiser placing a light vessel on the shoals. A lightship arrived there in 1881, and took up its duties at that time. The tower intended for Trinity Shoals was later used at South Pass.

### Chandeleur Island Light (1848)

Over on the eastern side of the state the fifth auditor had had a lighthouse erected on Chandeleur Island in 1848. Situated on south Chandeleur Island, the light remained but four years when it was destroyed. In 1856, a new brick tower was completed on the north end of Chandeleur Island. Abandoned in 1861, the light was back in operation by the autumn of that year, aiding the federal blockading squadron. The light continued to function, but in October, 1893, a storm nearly destroyed the station. Congress appropriated adequate funds for a new lighthouse, and the Lighthouse Board in 1896 built

Chandeleur Light Station, Louisiana, after the storm in 1893 that did so much damage to the second tower, built in 1856. A crew inspects the damage from a small boat to the right of the tower. In 1896, this brick tower was replaced by the present iron-skeleton structure. *U. S. Coast Guard photo 26-LG-35-1A, National Archives.*

nearby an iron-skeleton tower whose light was 102 feet above sea level. At the same time the light was increased to third-order because of its importance to those vessels seeking the Ship Island anchorage. The old brick tower was broken up and used to fill in around the foundation of the new Chandeleur Island lighthouse. The 1896 light tower survives to the present.

Louisiana has had many lighthouses that no longer exist. Generally, buoys have been adequate in recent years to fill the need the lighthouses supplied. Port Pontchartrain (1838), New Canal (1838), Pass Manchac (1839), Bon Fouca (1848), and Pointe Aux Herbes (1875) are but a few of these lighthouses that no longer exist.

### The Lights at the Sabine River (1856, 1906, 1908)

The border dividing Louisiana and Texas is the Sabine River, and the river has given its name to three important lighthouses: the red, conical, caisson-foundation Sabine Bank light built in 1906; the red, skeleton-tower Sabine Pass East Jetty light erected two years later and rebuilt in 1943; and the Sabine Pass light constructed in 1856. The latter light, located at the mouth of the Sabine River on the Louisiana side, was put out during the Civil War and relighted in 1865 after hostilities ended. A hurricane in 1886 swept away everything at the station except the tower, and this tower still stands. Disestablished in 1952, the light station is today a Louisiana state park.

## LIGHTS IN TEXAS

The Texas coast is reminiscent of North Carolina in that most of the state's mainland is protected by an outer rim of sand banks. Separating these elongated islands from the mainland are long, narrow bays. Texas has none of the huge sounds that make North Carolina distinctive. As in North Carolina, though, there are inlets every so often in these banks or long islands, and these inlets are the primary entrances to the ports and harbors of Texas.

Not long after Texas was annexed to the United States, Congress authorized several lighthouses, including one at the entrance to Matagorda Bay and one at the entrance to Galveston Bay. Although authorized in 1847, neither of these lights was established until 1852. Both were cast iron towers, and in 1858 both were equipped with third-order lenses. Thereafter their histories diverge.

### Galveston Bay Light (1852)

During the Civil War the tower at Bolivar Point on the north side of the entrance to Galveston Bay was

149

dismantled and removed. A temporary light was put in its place in 1865, and in 1872–73 the Lighthouse Board had a brick-lined, sheet-iron tower erected. Lighted on November 19, 1873, the tower served well, performing especially nobly in September, 1900, and August, 1915, when a number of local people sought refuge in the tower from the hurricanes and floods of those months. During the latter storm, some sixty people spent the night huddled on the tower's spiral stairway and watched while the water gradually rose in the tower to shoulder height. The assistant keeper maintained the light all night despite the fact he had to turn the lens by hand. The next two nights the light was out because the storm had destroyed the oil house, and the keepers had used all the other oil up the night of the storm. The Bureau of Lighthouses discontinued the light on May 29, 1933.

### Matagorda Light (1852)

At Matagorda, the Confederates attempted to destroy the light tower by dynamiting the foundation. They succeeded in throwing it partially over. This condition plus the threat of sea erosion persuaded the Lighthouse Board in 1867 to take down the tower and put its iron plates in storage. Later casting new plates to replace the blown-out ones, the board re-erected the ninety-foot tower two miles from its original site. The keeper exhibited the light at its new location on the west side of Pass Cavallo at the entrance to Matagorda Bay on September 1, 1873. In August, 1886, a storm swept the coast and destroyed all buildings at the station except the tower and keeper's dwelling. The tower was rocked so hard, however, that a piece of lens bounced out of the frame and smashed on the tower deck. The tower required considerable repair, and the dwelling had to be rebuilt. This tower, now painted red, is still active.

### Point Isabel Light (1853)

Point Isabel, near Brazos Santiago light east of Brownsville, in 1853 received a brick tower whose light was eighty-two feet above sea level. Taken out by the rebels, the tower was relighted in 1866 and remained in use until 1888 when the board had the light discontinued. About this time the board discovered that the federal government did not own the land on which the tower stood, a military reser-

vation known as Fort Polk. It seems that at the time of the Mexican War, General Zachary Taylor simply appropriated the land for a camp and depot. When it was discovered that the federal government had no title to the military reservation, the owners reclaimed the land and became the possessors of the tower and other buildings of the light station.

Once it had lost the property, the board began to reconsider and felt that the light was indeed needed at Point Isabel. The owners of the land offered to sell the station and land at what the board considered an eminently fair price, $8,000. Congress appropriated the money and the board obtained a deed. The Justice Department, however, was not happy with the deed and instituted condemnation proceedings. This action dragged the whole mess out for an additional four years, and the light was not re-established until July 15, 1895. It remained in operation ten years and then the Lighthouse Board again discontinued it. The station was sold to the highest bidder in 1927.

### Brazos Santiago Light (1854)

In the same year the Point Isabel tower was lighted, a square wooden tower painted black was placed on Padre Island on the north side of the entrance to Brazos Santiago near the United States–Mexico border. Nearby is the town of Brownsville. The following year, in 1854, the tower received a fifth-order lens, making its light thirty-five feet above sea level; in other words, it was simply an entrance light. The Confederates destroyed the tower during the Civil War. As replacement, the board installed a temporary light in 1864, and began pleading with Congress for a new iron tower. In 1874, a hurricane swept away the temporary light, and Congress finally appropriated $25,000 for a new tower. After considerable difficulty in obtaining the site from the state of Texas, the board began building a frame dwelling on screw piles in 1878 and placed the lantern on top of the dwelling. The keeper exhibited the light on March 1, 1879. Rebuilt in 1943, the light is still active and remains the last United States lighthouse before reaching the Mexican border.

### Three Lights in Galveston Bay (1854)

In 1854, Galveston Bay received three lighthouses.

Aransas Pass Light Station, Texas. Established in 1855, the tower was seriously damaged in a Confederate attack and its top twenty feet had to be rebuilt. Note the heavy screen around the lantern, probably to ward off birds attracted by the light. *U. S. Coast Guard official photo.*

All were small lights, having only sixth-order lenses. Red Fish Bar light was erected to guide vessels over the shoals at that point into Galveston Bay. Rebuilt in 1868 after having been burned by the Confederates, the light remained active until 1900 when a new cut was dredged through Red Fish Bar. The new passageway received a new tower that lasted until 1936, when a red skeleton tower was put into service. Inside the bay, a light went on Halfmoon Shoals to guide shipping past that hazard. Today a buoy serves the same purpose. Not far away, a screw-pile lighthouse served shipping passing through the channel at Clopper's Bar. It continued in use until 1880, when it was determined to be "of no further use to the navigation of the bay."

### Aransas Pass Light (1855)

In 1855, a fourth-order light went into service "on a low island, inside Aransas Pass." But the light had limited use, since the bar shifted so often that ships were advised not to cross it without a pilot. In December 1862 the Confederates attempted to blow up the brick tower and succeeded in damaging seriously the upper part of the tower so that the top twenty feet had to be reconstructed. While repairs were being made, a Texas phenomenon called a "blue norther" came blowing in. "The cold was so intense," the Lighthouse Board reported, "that fish, thrown ashore by the hundreds, were frozen, and birds of all sorts sought refuge in the tower and camp of the workmen, where they perished in large numbers." Repairs were finished in 1867, and the octagonal tower was relighted. The tower and its fourth-order lens went out of service in 1952.

The board placed a light near Fort Point off the northeast end of Galveston Island in 1881. An iron, screw-pile structure, the light remained in service until 1909. A fog-signal station continued there until December, 1950.

A light at the mouth of the Brazos River went into service May 30, 1896. An iron-skeleton tower 103 feet tall, it had a three-and-one-half-order lens that was still in use in 1952. The Brazos River light remains in service, but probably no longer equipped with its original lens.

### Swash Light (1858) and
### Decros Point Light (1872)

Texas has had many other lighthouses through the years, and some of them had a brief history. In Matagorda Bay, for example, the Swash Light Station built in 1858 and destroyed by the Confederates in 1861, and the Decros Point Light Station built in 1872 and destroyed by a hurricane in 1875 are two lighthouses that were never rebuilt after they met disaster. The Decros Point station consisted of two lighthouses, both of which disappeared, drowning four keepers.

The Decros Point disaster is little known. Since four men drowned, it was twice as great a tragedy as the far better known one at Minot's Ledge in Massachusetts where two keepers met their end. The point, of course, is that the keepers of the Gulf coast faced just as great dangers from storms as did those on the Atlantic coast, but the lighthouses of the Atlantic coast have had a better "press," and their histories are better known. Hopefully, historians of the Gulf States will turn their attention to aids to navigation in their areas; there is much that yet needs to be said.

# X

# Lighthouses of the West Coast:

## *San Diego to Cape Flattery*

THE WEST COAST of the United States proved unique. When this country acquired California at the end of the Mexican War, and secured sole possession of the Oregon Territory as a result of the treaty with England in 1846, it found there was not a single lighthouse nor other aid to navigation from the southern end of California to the northern tip of Washington, nor had there ever been one. This territory had no local tradition for the location of lighthouses or for the architectural design of towers, dwellings, and outbuildings. Presented with this clean slate, the lighthouse service reacted like the ordinary individual and drew upon its own knowledge and background, displaying, for various reasons, a typical lack of imagination. For the design of its lighthouses, the service turned to New England and chose a Cape Cod structure, a rather incongruous style amidst California's Spanish culture.

There are reports of past private efforts to provide signals to aid mariners. For example, some evidence exists that Spanish officials in San Diego hung a lantern on a stake at Ballast Point whenever a supply ship was expected from San Blas, and that a lady in Monterey placed a lamp in her window to assist vessels that arrived in the bay at night. But these were at best sporadic and temporary aids.

Neither the Spanish government, nor, later, the Mexican government made any effort to provide beacons of any sort to the seaman who sailed the Pacific coast. Consequently, the United States had a long coast—some 1,300 miles—that was a virgin territory to be developed as the government saw fit. But two things complicated the placing of aids to navigation: (1) the coast was unknown, and (2) the rule of the fifth auditor as general superintendent of lights was coming to an end. Both factors greatly influenced the course of the establishment of aids to navigation on the West Coast.

## THE FIRST SIXTEEN WEST COAST LIGHTS

Congress was quick to authorize lighthouses for the West Coast. In 1848, the act establishing the territory of Oregon provided for lighthouses at Cape Disappointment and New Dungeness, as well as for buoys in the Columbia River and in Astoria Harbor. At this point, however, Congress concluded that perhaps someone should look the sites over to determine if it were indeed feasible to put lighthouses at those two places, and logically selected the Coast Survey to perform the task. In addition, Congress also charged the survey with the duty of recommending sites for other lighthouses on the West Coast.

Arriving on this country's Pacific verge in the spring of 1849, the Coast Survey party had to remain in San Francisco through the summer for lack of transportation. But finally a vessel became available, and before too many months had passed, the

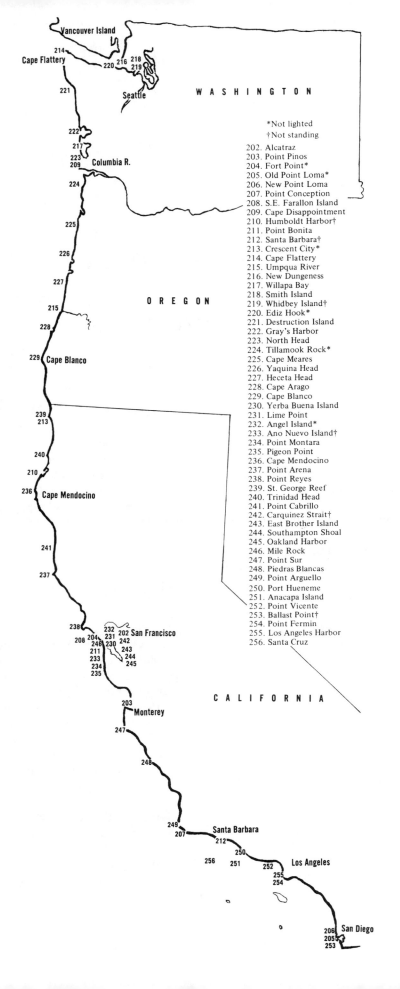

WASHINGTON

*Not lighted
†Not standing

202. Alcatraz
203. Point Pinos
204. Fort Point*
205. Old Point Loma*
206. New Point Loma
207. Point Conception
208. S.E. Farallon Island
209. Cape Disappointment
210. Humboldt Harbor†
211. Point Bonita
212. Santa Barbara†
213. Crescent City*
214. Cape Flattery
215. Umpqua River
216. New Dungeness
217. Willapa Bay
218. Smith Island
219. Whidbey Island†
220. Ediz Hook*
221. Destruction Island
222. Gray's Harbor
223. North Head
224. Tillamook Rock*
225. Cape Meares
226. Yaquina Head
227. Heceta Head
228. Cape Arago
229. Cape Blanco
230. Yerba Buena Island
231. Lime Point
232. Angel Island*
233. Ano Nuevo Island†
234. Point Montara
235. Pigeon Point
236. Cape Mendocino
237. Point Arena
238. Point Reyes
239. St. George Reef
240. Trinidad Head
241. Point Cabrillo
242. Carquinez Strait†
243. East Brother Island
244. Southampton Shoal
245. Oakland Harbor
246. Mile Rock
247. Point Sur
248. Piedras Blancas
249. Point Arguello
250. Port Hueneme
251. Anacapa Island
252. Point Vicente
253. Ballast Point†
254. Point Fermin
255. Los Angeles Harbor
256. Santa Cruz

## The first sixteen

members were sending back to Washington their recommendations for the location of lighthouses.

In time, as a result of these recommendations, as well as blandishments from its members from the Pacific coast, Congress authorized lighthouses for Fort Point, Fort Bonita, and Alcatraz Island in San Francisco Bay, Point Pinos at Monterey, Point Loma at San Diego, Santa Barbara, Point Conception, the Farallon Islands off San Francisco, Humboldt Harbor, and Crescent City, all in California; Smith Island, Cape Flattery, and Willapa Bay in the territory of Washington; and at the mouth of the Umpqua River in Oregon Territory. Between the years 1852 and 1858, the Lighthouse Board erected these sixteen lighthouses, the first ones on the West Coast.

All of these lighthouses had a basic design: a Cape Cod dwelling with a tower rising through the center. Some of the towers were taller than others, and in a few cases, an on-site decision at the time of construction caused a separation of the tower and the dwelling. Nevertheless, all lighthouses retained the basic design, which had been devised by Ammi B. Young, a prominent nineteenth-century architect who was employed at the time by the Treasury Department.

The Treasury Department decided to take the various monies appropriated up to that time and let a contract to erect eight lighthouses on the West Coast. In a case of questionable ethics, the contract was let to a Treasury Department official, with the apparent connivance of even higher officials, and then sold to experienced builders. In the end, a Baltimore partnership of Francis X. Kelly and Francis A. Gibbons wound up with the contract. Gibbons was an experienced builder of lighthouses, having erected a number, including the one at Bodie Island. Once their contract was legally established, Gibbons and Kelly in 1852 dispatched a ship, the *Oriole*, loaded with men and materials, to the West Coast to build lighthouses at San Diego, Point Conception, Point Pinos, the Farallon Islands, Fort Point, Alcatraz Island, Humboldt Bay, and Cape Disappointment.

Arriving in San Francisco in December, 1852, the workmen began laying the foundation for the Alcatraz lighthouse; meanwhile, back east, at about the same time, the secretary of the treasury, who had been handling directly affairs related to West-Coast lighthouses, turned responsibility for them over to the new Lighthouse Board.

While work was progressing on the Alcatraz lighthouse, part of the workmen shifted operations to the entrance to San Francisco Bay—the Golden Gate—and began erecting the Fort Point light. Although work on these two structures continued until the summer, in March part of the work crew headed south to Monterey and commenced the construction of the Point Pinos lighthouse.

A month later workmen converged on Southeast Farallon Island to put up the lighthouse there, but here they ran into unforeseen trouble. Egg-pickers, who were gathering the eggs of sea birds to sell on the San Francisco market, were fearful that a lighthouse would drive the birds away and refused to let the builders land. When the collector of customs in San Francisco (the local superintendent of lights) heard about the action of the egg-gatherers, he dispatched a Coast Survey steamer with an armed contingent to Southeast Farallon to reason with the egg-pickers, who, upon seeing the sailors fairly bristling with weapons, assumed a more amenable posture and welcomed the lighthouse builders.

Although delayed for two weeks, the workers went about construction with a will on this difficult site. The spot selected for the lighthouse was not only difficult of access because it was on a high point on this craggy island, but also it was large enough to provide space only for the tower. The dwelling had to be built separately, on a much lower and flatter area.

Finishing their work on Southeast Farallon in August, and pausing briefly at San Francisco, probably for a little recreation for the work force, the contractors pointed their ship north to the Columbia River and Cape Disappointment. As the vessel entered the mouth of the river, it struck nearby shoals and quickly sank. Everyone was rescued, but all the material to build the four remaining lighthouses went down with the vessel.

Despite this blow, Gibbons and Kelly went about gathering additional material and within a few months resumed construction of the remaining lighthouses on a stepped-up schedule, splitting their work force in an effort to meet the contract deadline. After the Cape Disappointment lighthouse was well underway, a portion of the work party began work on the light at Humboldt Bay and not much later another group dropped down to Point Conception and commenced building the structure there. As the Point Conception lighthouse neared completion, the contractors' principal foreman took

Alcatraz lighthouse in San Francisco Bay, California, around 1855. This was the first lighthouse on the West Coast. This watercolor was done by the district engineer after a sketch by Major Hartman Bache, early-day district lighthouse inspector on the Pacific Coast. *U. S. Coast Guard photo 26-LG-63-4, National Archives.*

a crew to San Diego to start the lighthouse at Point Loma. Work went surprisingly smoothly on all four lighthouses, and by the end of August, 1854, the last lighthouse had been completed and accepted by the government.

Thus were built the first eight lighthouses on the United States' Pacific coast. But these were just buildings, for on only two did a light shine.

### Alcatraz Island Light (1854)

The original contract to build these eight lighthouses called for lamps with parabolic reflectors to be placed in each lighthouse by the contractor. At this time, however, the country was shifting its thinking to Fresnel lenses for new lighthouses, and the secretary of the treasury had the contract changed to read that the United States would provide the illuminating apparatus for the eight lighthouses.

The secretary, in the meantime, had dispatched a naval officer to Paris to buy eight Fresnel lenses. The officer purchased the first two lenses, both of the third order, and had them shipped to San Fran-

cisco, where they arrived in the fall of 1853. Finally locating someone locally to install the lens on the Alcatraz tower, the keeper touched the lucerne to the wick on the evening of June 1, 1854, and the West Coast had its first light.

### Point Pinos Light (1855)

The other lens had been acquired for the Fort Point light, but that lighthouse, which stood where the army wanted to build a fort, had been torn down by the army just three months after the workmen completed it. With the lighthouse gone, the district inspector, Major Hartman Bache,[1] decided to alter the top of the Point Pinos tower and used the Fort Point lens on it, and on February 1, 1855, the West Coast had its second light.

---

[1] Major Bache, inspector of the Twelfth Lighthouse District, at heart a historian, believed that the lighthouse service archives should contain pictures and plans of all lighthouses. He made sketches, which were eventually rendered into watercolor, of a number of these structures, thus providing us with the best surviving contemporary views of these early West Coast lighthouses.

# The first sixteen

### Six Lights in Nine Months (1855)

The remaining six lenses arrived in San Francisco in later 1854 and early 1855. But for the lanterns and lenses to fit properly most of the other towers had to be altered, and two, Point Conception and Southeast Farallon, had to be torn down and completely rebuilt. Meanwhile, the district inspector had a new tower at Fort Point erected and lighted it on March 21, 1855. In San Diego, the Point Loma tower received alterations and a third-order lens, which the keeper lighted November 15, 1855. February 1, 1856, saw the reconstructed Point Conception tower lighted. In January, 1856, the Southeast Farallon light blinked on, and on October 15, 1856, the Cape Disappointment light, the first on the Oregon coast, came into being. Two months later, on December 20, 1856, the last of the eight lighthouses, Humboldt Harbor, displayed its light.

In the meanwhile, other lighthouses were being erected and lighted. These structures were built by local contractors at a cost considerably less than Gibbons and Kelly had been paid for the first eight.

### Point Bonita Light (1855)

A local contractor built the lighthouse at Point Bonita, which was on the opposite side of the Golden Gate from Fort Point. Lighted on April 30, 1855, this station had the first fog signal on the West Coast: a cannon obtained from Benicia Arsenal. The district inspector hired an ex-army sergeant to man the fog signal. It went into operation on August 9, 1855, and by the first part of October, the ser-

The present light tower atop fortifications at Fort Point, San Francisco, California, in 1969. Congress recently established Fort Point National Historic Site, and as part of the development of the site, the National Park Service plans to restore this lighthouse. *Photo by Joshua Freiwald for HABS.*

Point Bonita lighthouse at the entrance to San Francisco Bay, California, around 1856. This station was equipped with a fog cannon which, during a heavy fog in 1855, was fired almost ceaselessly for three days and three nights by one man. Watercolor after a sketch by Major Hartman Bache. *U. S. Coast Guard photo 26-LG-67-1 in the National Archives.*

geant was yelling for help. One of those San Francisco fogs rolled in, and for three days and three nights the sergeant had been able to get only two hour's rest. Nevertheless, the fog cannon continued in use until 1857.

### Santa Barbara and Crescent City Lights (1856)

A year after the lighting of the Point Bonita light the district inspector contracted to have a lighthouse constructed at Santa Barbara. Completed in the summer of 1856, the tower, rising through the center of the Cape Cod dwelling, did not exhibit its fourth-order light until December 1, 1856. Meanwhile, the inspector had a lighthouse erected at Crescent City; nine days after the displaying of the Santa Barbara light, the lighthouse at Crescent City on California's redwood coast went into service.

### Cape Flattery, Umpqua River, and New Dungeness Lights (1857)

In 1857, three lighthouses were built and lighted: at Cape Flattery, at Umpqua River, and at New Dungeness. At the two former sites, there was trouble with Indians, and it became so bad at Umpqua that a minor battle took place between the aborigines and the construction crew.

### Willapa Bay and Smith Island Lights (1858)

During 1858, two lighthouses were established. The Cape Shoalwater, or Willapa Bay, Light Station exhibited its light on October 1, and the light on Smith, or Blunt's, Island in the Straits of Juan de Fuca went into service on October 18.

Thus were built the first sixteen lighthouses on the West Coast.[2] What happened to them over the years?

---

[2] In addition to the sixteen lighthouses, the board placed a bell boat on the West Coast. It was stationed off the entrance to San Francisco Bay.

## An egg-pickers' war

### The Fate of the First Sixteen

The first lighthouse—Alcatraz—still survives as a light station, but without its original structure. Within a few years of its building, the army began constructing fortifications on the island, and in time the simple, peaceful, Cape Cod lighthouse took on a distinct military cast, with artillery installations nearby and stacks of cannon balls in its yard. In 1902, the original third-order lens was replaced by a fourth-order one. Displayed at the Panama-Pacific Exposition in San Francisco in 1915, the lens thereafter disappears.

Meanwhile, Alcatraz lighthouse was torn down in 1909 to provide room for the maximum-security prison built there. A new light tower—octagonal and much taller—went up at the same time just outside the prison walls. The light, visible twenty-one miles, is still in use, although it was shut down briefly when Indians occupied the island in 1970 to dramatize their efforts to reclaim the island for a park commemorating aboriginal culture. The Coast Guard relighted the tower in mid-1971 when United States marshals evicted the Indians from the island.

The Fort Point light, rebuilt in 1855, remained at its site just outside Fort Winfield Scott until 1864, when expansion of the fort necessitated moving the light to the northwest corner of the fort. Today, plans are underway to make a national monument of the fort, and the National Park Service plans to incorporate the now-discontinued light in the interpretive developments at the fort.

At the other side of the Golden Gate, the Point Bonita lighthouse had considerable difficulty keeping a supply of chimneys for the lens's lamp; the chimneys kept popping. After some anguish and threats to fire the keeper, the district inspector found that the lens had been installed off-center in the lantern. Quick adjustments resulted in reducing to normal the breakage of lamp chimneys. This tower remained in use until 1877, when the Lighthouse Board decided it was too high and had a new tower built at a lower point; the light in the new tower was 124 feet above sea level. This light is still in use and can be seen seventeen miles.

Off San Francisco, the Farallon light went into service after the tower had been rebuilt. This tower has witnessed a war between groups of egg-pickers, as well as several shipwrecks, and has had as its companion a unique fog signal powered by

waves. The light tower has never been rebuilt and continues in use, but with another lens. Its original lens is now in the possession of the San Francisco Maritime Museum.

The oldest active lighthouse on the West Coast today is the Point Pinos light at Monterey. Its first keeper was killed acting as a member of a posse pursuing a bandit, and his wife was appointed keeper in his stead. The earthquake of 1906 severely shook the lighthouse, and the structure received ex-

Farralon Island light tower about the time of the Civil War. The structure in the foreground is the sleeping shanty for the keepers. Major Hartman Bache's fog signal, a locomotive whistle mounted over a natural blowhole, was in use at this station from 1859 to 1871. *Photo courtesy of the Society of California Pioneers.*

Point Pinos lighthouse near Monterey, California, is today the oldest active lighthouse on the West Coast. It withstood the earthquake of 1906 that destroyed San Francisco; and its original third-order lens, now electri- fied, is still in use. This picture, after a sketch by Major Hartman Bache, though dated 1859, was made in 1855. *U. S. Coast Guard photo in the National Archives.*

tensive repairs and alterations in 1907. The original third-order lens, now electrified, still flashes its light to warn the mariner. The lighthouse, one of the features of Monterey's historical drive, is being opened to the public on a limited basis by the Pacific Grove Natural History Museum.

All the way to the northwest corner of the continental United States, the Cape Flattery, Washington, light, now with a fourth-order lens, continues to function as, among other things, a mark to the entrance to Juan de Fuca Straits.

In the straits, lights still beam from the stations on Smith Island and at New Dungeness. Both stations have received major overhauls: New Dungeness in 1927, and Smith Island in 1957 when the tower was rebuilt.

The Willapa Bay lighthouse continued in service until 1941 when erosion toppled it. Rebuilt several times since then—the last time in 1959—the Willapa Bay light, 113 feet above water, is an aid to coastal shipping as well as to those vessels entering the bay.

About six years after construction, erosion so threatened the Umpqua River lighthouse that the

board ordered the lens removed. Workmen had barely gotten the lens out when the tower began to shake, and, as the workmen stood watching, it toppled. It was replaced by a light at Cape Arago. In the 1890s, the Lighthouse Board determined that a light was needed at Umpqua River also, and in 1894, a light was exhibited from the new tower there. Over 160 feet above the sea, the light is visible nineteen miles and continues to aid shipping travelling along that coast.

For years the lighthouse at Humboldt Harbor fought a losing battle with the sea. The first damage occurred in 1865, when high tides swept across the low sand spit that bore the lighthouse and swirled sand away from the foundation of the structure. Filling back in and undertaking some preventive measures such as the burying of logs to prevent the washing of the sand, the Lighthouse Board fended off disaster for twenty years. A storm in November, 1885, pushed water once again across the sand spit, and when the water subsided, the district engineer found the building unsafe for occupancy. In 1892, the Lighthouse Board re-established the light on

Cape Flattery Light Station, Washington, in 1898. *Left:* the keepers and their families; *right:* the steam-powered fog signals. *U. S. Coast Guard photo 26-LG-61-4 in the National Archives.*

Table Bluff. Erosion continued to eat at the old abandoned lighthouse and, despite shoring, the walls of the dwelling in time crumbled, leaving only the tower standing awkwardly alone, showing scars where the dwelling once fitted around it. In time the sea took the tower, too.

Cape Disappointment's first-order lens remained in use until 1898, when the lens was moved to the newly created North Head station two miles away. Cape Disappointment received a new fourth-order lens that flashed red and white. Since then, the light has continued to aid vessels through that dangerous area into the Columbia River.

The Crescent City lighthouse remained in operation for many years, despite the fact that the Lighthouse Board felt it was inadequate as a coast light and of little use as a harbor light, since vessels could not enter Crescent City Harbor at night. Nevertheless, the light continued to function and was improved in 1907, when a lens of a newer design was installed. The light was made automatic in 1953, but a few months later the light was discontinued and the lighthouse was leased to the Del Norte Historical Society.

The light at Point Conception has remained, re-

built and relocated. By 1875, the dwelling had settled so much that a serious crack had appeared. Feeling the structure was beyond permanent repair, the Lighthouse Board erected a new tower at a lower point in 1882. That light, 133 feet above sea level and visible twenty-six miles, has remained in service to the present.

A little to the south is Santa Barbara, and the lighthouse there remained active until it was toppled by an earthquake in 1925. For forty years (1865–1905) a woman, Mrs. Julia F. Williams, tended the light, and she gave up at the age of eighty-one only because she broke her hip. From 1925 to 1935, the Bureau of Lighthouses maintained a temporary light at Santa Barbara. In 1935, it erected a white tower whose light today is visible twenty-five miles.

The West Coast's southern-most lighthouse has survived the years, but not on the same tower. For thirty-six years the Point Loma light served both as a coast light and as a harbor light for San Diego. It could function as both because its light was 462 feet above sea level—the highest light in the United States—and was visible both from the harbor and from the sea. But its height was its undoing. Often,

The New Dungeness Light Station in 1898. It was established in 1857 in the Straits of Juan de Fuca, Washington. *Photo in the National Archives.*

low clouds obscured the light, whereas a light nearer sea level could be seen by ships. So, reluctantly, the Lighthouse Board had to build another light tower situated at the lower elevation. The board selected a site at the tip of Point Loma just a few feet above sea level. Here the board erected a skeleton tower whose light has a focal plane eighty-eight feet above the water. Lighted in 1891, this tower remains in use.

After 1891, the old dwelling and tower on the summit of Point Loma fell on evil days. The lighthouse was neglected and gradually it deteriorated

through vandalism and the weather. Many tourists to San Diego visited the lighthouse because from its slowly disappearing tower one could obtain a magnificent panorama of ocean, islands, harbor, mountains, and undulating countryside. It was always a principal stop on a tour of San Diego. In time tourist guides began calling this old Cape Cod structure the "Old Spanish Lighthouse," and for decades it was listed in chamber of commerce literature by that name. These people had a sense of romance, but certainly not a sense of architecture or history.

The abandoned Humboldt Bay lighthouse, California, around 1910. Erosion slowly ate away at this structure, which had been built in 1856 on a low spit of land, and before too many more years passed, devoured first the dwelling, then the tower. *Photo from Carl Christensen collection.*

Cape Disappointment's first-order light tower, Washington, around 1855. For a short time, this point of land was known as Cape Hancock. Today, this tower displays a fourth-order light flashing red and white. After a sketch by Major Hartman Bache. *Photo 26-LG-61-2 in the National Archives.*

Point Conception lighthouse, California, about 1855. This structure was replaced by a new tower at a slightly lower location in 1882. This section of the California coast had a reputation as the "graveyard of the Pacific." After a sketch by Major Hartman Bache. *Photo 26-LG-65-9 in the National Archives.*

In 1913, Cabrillo National Monument, embracing one-half acre of ground surrounding the old lighthouse, came into being. Since the monument commemorated the 1542 voyage of Juan Rodriguez Cabrillo, who discovered and explored the west coast of the United States, the lighthouse was scheduled for demolition. The instigators of the monument wanted to erect a 150-foot statue of Cabrillo on the site. But not long afterwards, interest faded, and the lighthouse remained, continuing in its deteriorating state.

Cabrillo National Monument was turned over to the National Park Service in 1933, and that organization began laying plans to restore the old lighthouse. The work was completed in 1935, and from then until 1965 the lighthouse served as visitor center, tea shop (later bookstore), historic house, and monument offices. In 1965, the National Park Service completed a museum–visitor center at the monument and moved all operations out of the lighthouse. Since then park personnel have tastefully

refurnished the lighthouse with period pieces, and it is today on display as a historic house whose object is to give to the visitor an idea of the life and times of a nineteenth-century West Coast lighthouse keeper and his family.

## LIGHTS IN WASHINGTON

### Whidbey Island Light (1861) and Ediz Hook Light (1865)

With the completion of the sixteen lighthouses, the West Coast was basically lighted to meet the shipping needs of the times. Lighthouses built subsequently to these sixteen came into being as the need for them evolved with the growth of maritime activity and the opening of new ports. As traffic in Puget Sound increased, for example, the board contemplated a lighthouse there, and in 1861 built one on Whidbey Island to mark Admiralty Inlet at the entrance to Puget Sound. The light lasted until

The Santa Barbara lighthouse, California (lighted 1856), about 1900. The woman on the porch is Mrs. Julia Williams, keeper from 1865 to 1905. An earth-quake destroyed the lighthouse in 1925. The station now has a white tower whose light is visible twenty-five miles. *Photo in the author's collection.*

The old Point Loma lighthouse at San Diego, California, today. Lighted in 1855, at 462 feet above sea level, its light was for thirty-six years the highest in the United States—so high, in fact, that it was often obscured by low clouds. It was replaced in 1891 by a light near sea level that could be more easily seen by ships. This old structure, now included within Cabrillo National Monument, has been refurnished as of the late nineteenth century. *Photo courtesy of Cabrillo National Monument, National Park Service.*

1903, when the army displaced it with fortifications. Four years after the lighting of this lighthouse, in 1865, the Lighthouse Board established the Ediz Hook light near Port Angeles in the Straits of Juan de Fuca to replace a privately maintained one. Ediz Hook was in turn replaced by an aero beacon on the air control tower at Port Angeles Air Station in 1946.

### Destruction Island Light (1892)

Major lights subsequently built along the Washington coast include Destruction Island, Gray's Harbor, and North Head. They run geographically in that order from north to south. The third-order light at Destruction Island went into service on January 1, 1892. It is an iron tower lined with brick, and its light is visible twenty-four miles.

### Gray's Harbor Light (1898)

Overlapping the beam of this light is the one at Gray's Harbor. Lighted in 1898, this light would have been in service sooner but the Lighthouse Board realized, after it had already asked Congress for a harbor light, that actually a seacoast light was needed. Several years passed before Congress appropriated additional funds to build the more imposing structure. The octagonal brick tower at 107 feet turned out to be the tallest lighthouse on the Washington coast. It was equipped with a third-order lens, and today the light is visible, on a clear day, about twenty-two miles.

### North Head Light (1898)

Also in 1898, the Lighthouse Board, feeling the Cape Disappointment light was inadequate as a

Heceta Head Light Station, Oregon. This first-order light is 206 feet above the sea, and can be seen from twenty-one miles away. *U. S. Coast Guard official photo.*

coastal light, displayed a new one on the north side of the entrance to Columbia River, two miles north of the old Cape Disappointment tower. The board moved the Cape Disappointment first-order lens to the new lighthouse and installed a fourth-order lens at Cape Disappointment. With the lighting of this tower, called North Head, the board felt the coast was "well supplied with lights of the first order from Cape Flattery to Tillamook Rock."

## LIGHTS IN OREGON

### Tillamook Rock Light (1881)

Tillamook Rock light on the coast of Oregon went into service on February 1, 1881, and marked the southern approach to the Columbia River. Tillamook was a rough, crag-like rock surrounded by an insane sea. Only one side of the rock presented the possibility of securing a foot-hold to make a landing. After the board decided to place a lighthouse there, surveyors attempted for several weeks to effect a landing. Finally, one man with nothing but a pocket tape successfully reached the rock, and he made crude measurements from which plans were drawn. Further difficulty occurred in landing quarrymen to level the rock to receive the light station's buildings. Wind, salt spray, and the sea constantly hampered their efforts to carve a foundation out of the hard rock. From October, 1879, until January 21, 1881, workmen labored under the most horrendous circumstances, leveling the spot and building the lighthouse and the station's other buildings. They were constantly threatened or assaulted by the wind and the sea. To facilitate landing people and materials, the workmen installed a derrick with a long boom, and it remained after the builders left, so that everything landed at the station through the years was hoisted onto the rock, a method more frightening, but much safer, than the one the first arrivals at the rock had to use.

Duty at the station was both dangerous and arduous for light keepers over the years. Storms have sent seas taller than fifteen-story buildings over the station. And the sea has tossed rocks through the sides and roof of the tower's lantern, at times smashing the panels of the lens. In January, 1883, storm-tossed rocks broke through the iron roof in twenty places, and in 1912 green water broke over the station, caving in the roof of the fog signal station and the west side of the dwelling. A storm on December 9, 1894, threw stones, fish, and sea weed into the lantern and smashed thirteen panels of the lens. The station has witnessed other storms, some of which were more severe and smashed the panes of the lantern, putting out the lighthouse's illuminant. But the keepers have maintained the light, keeping it burning under the most nerve-shattering conditions. By the 1950's, the lighthouse was well out of shipping lanes, and in 1957 the Coast Guard discontinued the light.

### Cape Meares Light (1890)

Just south of Tillamook Rock is Cape Meares, where a squat iron tower was placed in 1890. Although the light from its first-order lens is but seventeen feet above the ground, the high promontory upon which the tower rests puts the focal plane of the Cape Meares light 232 feet above the sea, making it visible over twenty-two miles. Refitted in 1963, the iron tower still guides ships along the rugged Oregon coast.

### Yaquina Head Light (1873)

Yaquina Head, or Cape Foulweather, is the next coast light below Cape Meares. Lighted August 20, 1873, the station had been difficult to build, primarily because of the craggy shore below that inhibited landing with materials. The construction crew lost two loaded lighters, and at another time part of the lens. The brick tower was completed and today the light is 93 feet above ground and 162 feet above the sea. Still active, the station has the second oldest active light tower on the Oregon coast.

### Heceta Head Light (1894)

On March 30, 1894, the keeper displayed the Heceta Head light for the first time. It was a coast light with a first-order lens, and had been erected because there was no light between Cape Foulweather and Cape Arago, a distance of ninety miles. The white, conical masonry tower's light is 56 feet above the ground, but 206 feet above sea level; it is visible over twenty-one miles.

### Cape Arago Light (1866)

The second light on the Oregon coast was at Cape Arago, and it was established November 1, 1866.

Cape Arago Light Station, at the entrance to Coos Bay, Oregon. This tower replaced the original (1866) iron tower in 1934. Its light is 100 feet above the sea.  *U. S. Coast Guard official photo.*

Although primarily a coast light, Cape Arago also serves as an approach light to Coos Bay, a busy lumber port. The present masonry tower, on a rocky islet just north of Cape Arago, replaced the original iron tower in 1934, and its light is 100 feet above sea level.

## Cape Blanco Light (1870)

Eleven years previous to the erecting of the lighthouse on Tillamook Rock, the Lighthouse Board put one at Cape "Orford"; at that time someone was trying to eliminate the time-honored (since 1603) name of Cape Blanco and give the place a more Anglo-Saxon name. Fortunately, the new name didn't take, and by 1889 the Lighthouse Board was back to calling the white-faced cliff the more appropriate Cape Blanco.

At the time the lighthouse was built, the board desired to use local brick. The first batch of 80,000 arrived and the builders found them to be of only fair quality. The next delivery was even worse, and the construction superintendent rejected them outright. Finally, the workmen obtained enough brick to complete the tower, and in December, 1870, the keeper lighted the first-order lens, which was 59 feet above the ground and 245 feet above the sea.

From land the cliff is beautiful. Wildflowers grow in profusion and the view of sea, land, sky, and rugged shore is magnificent, but to the mariner the area abounds in treacherous waters, and it is a section of the coast to be avoided. Many ships have run afoul of its rocks and shoals and have been pounded to death by the surging sea. It is a distinctive landmark and was known to the seventeenth-century Spanish seamen whose galleons plied these waters. Indeed, the first vessel to learn the danger of the rocks of the area may well have been one of these early Spanish vessels.

With the coming of the lighthouse, shipwrecks here did not cease, and from time to time an unlucky vessel met her agonizing end on the rocks below Cape Blanco. But when one thinks of the number of wrecks that might have occurred had there been no aid at this point, one has a tendency to want to get on his knees and salaam to the tower which still sends its warning beam to the mariner.

## LATER CALIFORNIA LIGHTS

California has a long coast, and a busy one as far as shipping is concerned. From the time of the United States' first arrival on the West Coast as owner, California has had a heavy traffic, and as a result its coast received the bulk of the first lighthouses erected on this country's Pacific verge. As time moved on, particularly in the nineteenth century, this state continued to receive the greater number of the lighthouses built in the three states of the country's western shore.

### Fog Signals into Lighthouses

Fog was an especial problem on the California coast and a number of light stations were first fog signal stations. A fog bell was placed at Yerba Buena Island in San Francisco Bay in 1874, a year before a light went into service there. Lime Point, near the Golden Gate, received a fog signal in 1883 and a light eighteen years later. Similarly at Angel Island, a fog signal went into operation in 1886, but fourteen years passed before a light came into use there.

At Ano Nuevo Island, south of San Francisco, a fog signal came into service in 1872 and a light twenty-five years later. The Point Montara Light Station, on California State Highway 1 just south of Pacifica, did not receive a light until 1900; it had been a fog signal station for twenty-five years before that. One of the principal coastal lights, Pigeon Point, heard the raucous sound of the fog horn over a year before builders completed the light tower, over 100 feet tall, in 1872.

### Cape Mendocino Light (1868)

The majority of the lights, of course, were established to provide assistance to coasting vessels, and to a great extent the story of California lighthouses subsequent to the initial ones describes the lighting of darkened areas along the coast or at a prominent cape. One of the latter, where coasting vessels altered their course, was Cape Mendocino. According to the fourth edition of the *Coast Pilot,* "Cape Mendocino is the turning point for nearly all vessels bound north or south, and in view of the dangers in its vicinity, should be approached with considerable caution in thick weather. . . . The meteorological conditions northward of the cape are quite different from those southward. Fog is more prevalent southward and the rainfall heavier northward."

Mendocino had been a landmark for the Spanish Manila galleon when the English were just beginning to secure a toe-hold on the New World's Atlantic coast. Coming from the west, these galleons picked up the coast in the vicinity of Cape Mendocino and followed it south to their destination at Acapulco.

The building of the lighthouse at Cape Mendocino presented problems. The ground on which the tower was to rest was a chameleon. During the dry summer months, the ground was as hard as well-cured concrete, but in the rainy season the ground became soft and landslides were not unknown. To compensate for this latter factor, the builder excavated a hole two feet deeper and larger in circumference than originally planned and filled it with concrete. On this foundation the construction crew built a 16-sided iron pyramidal tower. Although the light was but forty-three feet above ground, the high promontory on which the tower stood made it 422 feet above sea level; after 1891, when the original Point Loma lighthouse was closed down, it became the highest light in the lighthouse service.

During the construction of this lighthouse, the lighthouse tender *Shubrick,* named for the first chairman of the Lighthouse Board, ran up on the rocks thirty miles south of Cape Mendocino. Aboard were materials for the then-building lighthouse. Although the *Shubrick* was later gotten off her perch, the building materials were lost.

Lighted on December 1, 1868, the Cape Mendocino tower survived the winter, but uneven settling occurred and a few small cracks appeared in the tower. Two years later, an earthquake so rattled the station's dwelling that it had to be torn down and rebuilt. The tower, however, was not damaged. Another earthquake in 1873 left a crack in the ground that ran within fifteen feet of the tower. The district engineer "bandaged" the rent by having concrete rammed into the hole.

Strong winds and storms, too, proved a problem at the light station. The dwelling became so loosened by the wind that it had to be braced with 12″ x 12″ timbers. In 1883, the lighthouse service built a sleeping shanty at the tower, because it was too dangerous on stormy nights for the keepers to travel between the dwelling and the tower.

Despite these vicissitudes and other earthquakes over the years, the light tower has survived and today sends out a light rated at 900,000 candlepower.

### Point Reyes and Point Arena Lights (1870)

Cape Mendocino is one of three prominent points on the California coast north of the entrance to San Francisco Bay. The other two are Point Arena and Point Reyes. These two latter points had lights installed on them in 1870. The Lighthouse Board had attempted to erect a lighthouse at Point Reyes as early as 1855. Indeed, the district inspector's negotiations for the site, which took an inordinate amount of time, had been one of the reasons for the slowness of getting lights on the West Coast's first eight lighthouses. At the time, however, there was a muddle over the ownership of the land, and the Lighthouse Board had to give up its efforts then for a lighthouse at Point Reyes. Later, after the Civil War, the Lighthouse Board began once again to obtain land for a lighthouse at Point Reyes, but this time the owners of the land wanted such an exorbitant price that the board had to resort to condemna-

tion proceedings. This action brought the land owners to a more amenable frame of mind, and they offered the land at a reasonable price. The board accepted their offer in 1869, and shortly thereafter began construction of a lighthouse at Point Reyes. The builders had to land the materials at Drakes Bay and haul it up to the top of the steep bluff and then lower it part of the way back down to the site of the light tower. Despite these vicissitudes the builders erected the squat iron tower, and the keeper lighted it December 1, 1870. The fog signal at the station later became famous during the days of radio when its two-tone bleat became the basis of a bath soap commercial. Still active, the station today is at Point Reyes National Seashore.

Point Arena lighthouse was built on a site just 50 feet above sea level, and had a light whose focal plane was 150 feet above the Pacific Ocean. In contrast, the Point Reyes beam is 294 feet above sea level. Lighted May 1, 1890, the Point Arena lighthouse served faithfully until April 18, 1906, when an earthquake—the same one that so devastated San Francisco—wrecked the tower and first-order lens, as well as the keepers' dwelling. Workmen salvaged the lantern from the wreckage, placed it on a temporary frame tower, and installed a second-order lens. The keeper lighted it January 5, 1907. Later, the Lighthouse Board had a reinforced concrete tower built at the station. The light from the new tower's first-order lens is about thirty-five feet lower than its predecessor.

### St. George Reef Light (1892)

Although not at a turning point in the coast, another important California lighthouse north of San Francisco is the one at St. George Reef just north of Crescent City. In addition to lighting a darkened area between Cape Blanco and Cape Mendocino, the purpose of the light was to warn coasting vessels of the dangerous reefs and rocks off Point St. George. The danger of the area had been sharply pointed up in 1865 when a side-wheeler, the *Brother Jonathan,* struck a sunken ledge off Point St. George and sank with a loss of 215 passengers and crew. At first the Lighthouse Board planned to place the light directly on Point St. George, but by 1875 it felt a light on the reef would be more effective. In 1881, the board selected Northwest Seal Rock off Point St. George as the site, and the

St. George Reef Light Station, California, at low tide *(above)*, and during a storm *(opposite)*. Because of its location—one of the most exposed on the Pacific coast—this lighthouse was ten years in the building and cost $704,-000. It sits on a rock only 300 feet in diameter, located six miles at sea. *U. S. Coast Guard official photos.*

following year engineers with considerable difficulty made a survey of the rock. In 1883, workmen began preparing the site, but work halted for the next three years because Congress failed to appropriate necessary funds. Work resumed in 1887 with the hauling of cut stones to the site. By the end of the year the builders had laid eight courses of stone. Construction continued for the next four years, and on October 20, 1892, the keeper lighted the first-order lens. The lighthouse was a square pyramidal tower built on a pier. The light was 144 feet above sea level.

Despite the stormy seas that swept over the rock, slowing construction—in one instance the workmen's quarters were smashed in a gale—work went surprisingly smoothly. Only one workman lost his life, and that occurred when a wave swept the poor fellow off the rock. The lighthouse cost $704,633.78, and was the most expensive one built in the United States up to that time.

Through the years it has been a dangerous place to work. At least one keeper perished at the rock when the station boat overturned in a rough sea. But the granite lighthouse has survived the turmoil of the sea and is still active.

### Trinidad Head Light (1871)

Two smaller lighthouses built to illuminate unlighted areas of the northern California coast between large first-order lighthouses were Trinidad
Head and Point Cabrillo. Both had less powerful
lenses and each was intended primarily as an aid
to those vessels that tended to hug the shore.
Perched on the slope of Trinidad Head like a nesting sea gull, the squat white tower is eighteen feet
tall, but the height of the site puts the focal plane
of the light from the fourth-order lens 196 feet
above sea level. It was lighted December 1, 1871,
and continues to serve its intended purpose.

### Point Cabrillo Light (1909)

The lighthouse at Point Cabrillo in design looks

like the first lighthouse erected on the West Coast.
The lantern of the lighthouse sits atop the Cape
Cod dwelling and was lighted in 1909. Today the
light of this lighthouse is measured at 700,000 candlepower, and, because its focal plane is but eighty-
four feet above the sea, it can be seen only fifteen
miles. That distance, however, is adequate to reach
out to the main coastal shipping lanes, so that after
a vessel has altered course at Point Arena, she
may shortly take bearings on the Point Arena and
Point Cabrillo lighthouse to determine if she is on
the proper course.

### Lights in San Francisco Bay (1874–1910)

San Francisco Bay is well endowed with lighthouses. In addition to the West Coast's first light-

house, Alcatraz, there are ones at Carquinez Strait (1910) on the route to Suisun Bay, East Brother Island (1874) marking the entrance to San Pablo Bay, Southampton Shoal (1905) off Angel Island, Yerba Buena Island (1875) south of Treasure Island, and Oakland Harbor (1890).

One of the more interesting lights associated with San Francisco Bay, both from construction and purpose points of view, is the Mile Rock light, located just outside the Golden Gate on the south side of the channel. Erected to warn ships of the rocks and shoals in that area, the lighthouse was built on a rock just thirty feet by forty feet in size. During construction, because the rock faced the sea, water often swept over it, hampering the efforts of the workmen. Because of the configuration of the rock, the base of the lighthouse is elliptical in shape. Rising from this base are concrete walls four feet thick and thirty-five feet tall, all encased in steel plates. The metal tower, containing living quarters and a watchroom, rests on this foundation. The third-order lens was lighted in 1906 and today its light, forty-nine feet above the sea, is visible twelve miles.

### Pigeon Point Light (1872)

Several important lighthouses were erected between San Francisco and Point Conception. Pigeon Point light near Pescadero marks a break in the coast where coasting vessels make a small course change. This point, named for the ship *Carrier Pigeon* which wrecked here in the early 1850's, received its light in 1872. The light rose 148 feet above the sea on a tall, white, brick tower. Still in service, the aero beacon now on its tower, looking like a wart on an upright finger, can be seen eighteen miles.

### Point Sur Light (1889)

South of Monterey is Point Sur. Here coasting traffic alters course, so the point was significant to north- and south-bound shipping. The Lighthouse Board erected a fifty-foot stone tower on a high bluff. Lighted August 1, 1889, the lens is 270 feet above sea level. A number of ships have gone down here, including the *Los Angeles* in 1873 and the *Ventura* in 1879. In 1935, the navy dirigible *Macon* crashed off the point, and this disaster figured decisively in the curtailment of the navy's dirigible program. Point Sur's light is still active with one of

those new wart-like aero beacons surmounting its tower.

### Piedras Blancas Light (1875)

South of Point Sur, about halfway between Point Conception and Monterey is Piedras Blancas lighthouse. It serves to mark a darkened area along that coast and was, and is, valuable to coasting vessels. The white conical tower, lighted in 1875, is still in use; its light is visible eighteen miles.

### Point Arguello Light (1901)

Twelve miles north of Point Conception is Point Arguello, the scene of one of the greatest peacetime disasters in the history of the United States Navy. The light at Arguello was important to coast traffic rounding the dangerous Point Conception. The Lighthouse Board began asking for a lighthouse there in 1888. But eleven years passed before Congress appropriated the necessary money. Lighted on George Washington's Birthday in 1901, the illuminant, 148 feet above the sea, was a fourth-order lens. The light today is more powerful, having a rating of 1,300,000 candlepower.

In 1923, seven destroyers, unknowingly off course, piled up on the rocks just north of Point Arguello. Not only were the four-stackers lost, but twenty-two sailors died in the disaster, and several very promising naval careers, including the squadron commander's, perished in the calamity.

### Channel Lights at Santa Barbara

Point Conception marks the north end of the Santa Barbara channel, and two lights aid vessels entering the channel here: the lighthouse on the mainland and an untended beacon on Richardson Rock off San Miguel Island. At the south end of the channel, the Lighthouse Board erected a light at Port Hueneme on the mainland and later the Bureau of Lighthouses built a light station on the other side of the channel at Anacapa Island. Port Hueneme's fourth-order lens was first exhibited on December 15, 1874, and today its 200,000 candlepower beam is visible thirteen miles.

Anacapa Island, one of three islands now composing Channel Islands National Monument, is actually three high, precipitous islets that are the tops of a mountain chain that long ago sank beneath the sea. The lighthouse service built the light tower on the southernmost islet in 1912. The Lighthouse Board had asked Congress for a light there in 1868, and eventually had to settle for the light at Port Hueneme. The 1912 tower was a square, pyramidal, skeleton tower, but twenty years later the Bureau of Lighthouses built a short cylindrical tower there; its light was 277 feet above sea level. Although homes were built on this isolated island for the keepers and their families, no one lives in them today, since the light is tended from the Port Hueneme station and the Coast Guardsmen and their families live on the mainland. Today, sickly white rabbits hop about over the islet, feeding on the unique native vegetation. Apparently placed there by the navy in World War II to provide sport for the wartime inhabitants, as well as meat should Anacapa be cut off from the mainland by enemy action, these rabbits have multiplied and their descendants are much in evidence.

### Point Vicente Light (1926)

Between Port Hueneme and the Point Loma light in San Diego, the principal light is the 600,000-candlepower Point Vicente light. Situated on a cliff, the white cylindrical tower with its light 185 feet above the sea went into service in 1926 and serves as a coastal light and a guide to Los Angeles Harbor.

### Harbor Lights (1869–1913)

A number of harbor lighthouses have been erected on the coast south of San Francisco through the years. Most of them are small lights and have no other purpose than to guide seagoing traffic into and about a harbor. The Ballast Point lighthouse (1890) marks the entrance to San Diego Harbor. Point Fermin (1874) and Los Angeles Harbor (1913) lighthouses guide vessels into Los Angeles Harbor, and the Santa Cruz light (1869) denotes the entrance to that harbor, which is located at the north end of Monterey Bay.

The chief significance of the lighting of the West Coast is that the establishment of the first lighthouses virtually coincided with the beginning of the Lighthouse Board as this country's manager of aids to navigation. Consequently, one can say that the West Coast was the Lighthouse Board's show, and on the whole the board did a remarkably fine job. The board cannot be faulted for the fact that many of the early lighthouses had to be relocated; their original sites were selected before the Lighthouse Board gained responsibility for the West Coast. After the building of these first lights, the board kept up with the needs of shipping traffic, and it achieved some remarkable engineering feats with the building of such lighthouses as the ones at Tillamook Rock and St. George Reef.

# XI

# Lighthouses of the Great Lakes and Lake Champlain

THEY ARE called lakes, but from the lighthouse point of view they have virtually all the characteristics of the ocean. The Great Lakes presented all the difficulties and problems of lighting that the nation's ocean coasts presented. Coastal lights, harbor lights, lightships, and channel lights were all needed, and lighthouses and beacons had to be built on precipitous bluffs, low sandy coasts, at the end of piers, and on shoals in a storm-angered sea.

## LIGHTS ON LAKE ERIE

### Presque Isle Light (1819)

As in the remainder of the country, aids to navigation on the Great Lakes followed commerce and population. One of the two first lighthouses on the Great Lakes was the one built at Presque Isle, as Erie, Pennsylvania, was then called. The place had been of military importance for many years. The French, during their occupancy of the place, erected Fort Presque Isle. Abandoned for some years after the Americans came on the scene, the fort was reactivated in 1795. During the War of 1812, Oliver Hazard Perry built here the ships that defeated the British squadron at Put-in-Bay; it was after this fight that Perry sent his famous message, "We have met the enemy and they are ours."

The government placed the lighthouse on Presque Isle at the entrance to the bay in 1819, and in 1837 the light consisted of ten lamps. In that year the inspector marvelled at the good shape the station was in, and considered it one of the most useful on the south shore of the lake. The light, however, had the same fault that most lights of the period possessed: the lamp chimneys were too short and did not extend above the reflectors, thus blackening them quickly and unnecessarily.

About this same time, but before the inspector arrived, a beacon possessing four lamps was erected on the pier in Erie Harbor. Later, in 1858, it was rebuilt.

The Presque Isle light tower was rebuilt in 1867, and in 1870 the Lighthouse Board changed the name of the station to Erie Light Station. The reason for the change, apparently, was the desire to build a lighthouse on the north shore of the peninsula forming Erie Harbor—the peninsula now comprising Presque Isle State Park. This new lighthouse, with its fourth-order lens fifty-seven feet above the lake, went into service on July 12, 1873, and became the Presque Isle Light Station.

The Erie Light Station, meanwhile, continued in use until 1881, when the board discontinued it and sold the property. Realizing it had made a mistake, the board repurchased the land three years later, and in 1885 relighted the tower. Twelve years later the tower had to be raised seventeen feet so that its light would beam above the trees that had grown up near it.

Today the Erie Pierhead light is carried in the Coast Guard's *Light List* as the direct descendant of the United States' first lighthouse on the Great Lakes.

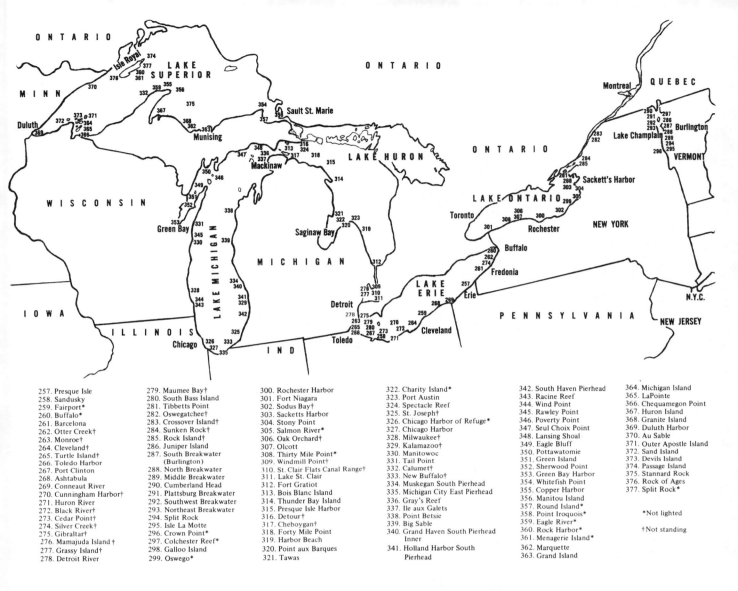

## Sandusky Light (1821)

The oldest light tower still standing is the one erected near Sandusky, Ohio, in 1821. Known as the Sandusky Light Station until 1870, when the Lighthouse Board changed it to Marblehead, the tower served both as a coastal light and as a mark of the entrance to Sandusky Bay. Although the keeper's dwelling was rebuilt in 1881, the old, conical, white tower has remained in its original state except for the replacement of the upper eight feet of the stone tower with a vertical brick wall to enclose a watch room. Through the years its light has consisted of thirteen lamps and reflectors, a fourth-order lens, and, in 1903, a third-order lens.

## Fairport Light (1825)

At Fairport, Ohio, at the mouth of the Grand River, the fifth auditor had a light established on the West

Pier in 1825 and ten years later a beacon placed on the East Pier. This latter light was discontinued in 1860. The 1825 tower was falling apart by 1868, and the Lighthouse Board had iron bands placed around the tower to hold it together. But the tower was too far gone, and before long, one of the bands, unable to stand the strain, snapped, so the board had no choice but to erect a new tower. This time it had one built with a pile and grillage foundation on which the workmen laid a limestone base. On this base masons built a tower of Berea sandstone. Lighted on August 11, 1871, the light station continued in service until 1925.

## Buffalo Light (1819)

At the same time the contractor built the Presque Isle Light he also erected the Buffalo Light. Some controversy surrounds the date of this lighthouse.

## The Great Lakes and Lake Champlain

George R. Putnam, the former Commissioner of Lighthouses, states that the lighthouse was built in 1818 and rebuilt in 1833. One cannot ignore any statement about lighthouses that Putnam makes, but the records of the old lighthouse service now reposing in the National Archives are not in agreement with Putnam, for they state that the lighthouse was erected ten years later, in 1828, and rebuilt in 1838, not 1833. The 1836 date seems more likely since an inspector in 1838 reported, "I found the (Buffalo) lighthouse was situated on the extreme outer end of the mole, and that it was a new building in perfect order."

As for the date of the initial lighthouse and whether it was indeed the first one on the Great Lakes, the controversy is settled by *The American State Papers*, v. II, pp. 459–60 it states the Presque Isle and the Buffalo lights were erected by the same contractor in 1818 and each cost $7,750. Apparently both were lighted in 1819.

The 1836 lighthouse was a stone, octagonal tower, according to a picture of the period. It was raised three feet in 1857–58 and received a third-order lens. The tower went out of service in 1914, and at least as late as 1937 it was still standing.

### Barcelona and Otter Creek Lights (1829)

The year 1829 saw the advent of two lights that did not long survive: the Barcelona and Otter Creek lighthouses. The Barcelona, or Portland, light near Fredonia, New York, used gas and was tended by "a deaf, superannuated clergyman having numerous female dependents." The use of gas caused problems, since water collected in the two miles of pipe leading out to the light, and someone had to take them up every so often and drain them. The board discontinued this harbor light in 1859 because it learned there was no harbor at Barcelona. Otter Creek light was discontinued ten years earlier upon exhibiting of the Monroe, Michigan, light.

### Cleveland Light (1829)

Cleveland, Ohio, received its lighthouse in 1829. Located at the corner of Main and Water Streets, the light was considered unnecessary by two separate inspectors in 1837 and 1838. Both felt that the beacon that had been established on the end of the pier in 1831 would be quite adequate, if it were

Presque Isle lighthouse at Erie, Pennsylvania, in 1870. This was one of the first two United States light stations on the Great Lakes. *U. S. Coast Guard photo 26-LG-46-79 in the National Archives.*

## Smacked by ships and tows

beefed up with a few more lamps. Finally, in 1854, the beacon was fitted with a fourth-order lens and the main light was discontinued. The light was out but five years when an act of Congress ordered its re-establishment. By 1867, the structure was in danger of toppling, since the city had been removing dirt from around its foundations to grade Cleveland's streets. The board in 1873 rebuilt the lighthouse on the old site, although it tried to convince Congress that it would be better to build on the end of East Pier so that one light could serve the same purpose as two. The new lighthouse continued in use for nineteen years when the board announced it was no longer needed as a coast light and that the three beacon lights on the pier were quite adequate to navigate the harbor. The old dwelling, which was attached to the discontinued tower, remained in use for some years while the tower was cannibalized for metal items to be used in the Braddock Point Light Station.

### Turtle Island Light (1832)

In 1832, the Turtle Island light in Maumee Bay went into service and thirty-five years passed before it had to be rebuilt. The island in that time eroded from eight acres to one and a half acres. The light was replaced in 1904 by the Toledo Harbor light.

### Pierhead Lights of the 1830's

In the 1830's, a number of beacon or pierhead lights were erected to guide ships into harbors. Port Clinton (1833), Ashtabula (1834), Conneaut River (1835), Cunningham Harbor (1835), Huron River (1835), Black River (1836), and Cedar Point at Sandusky Bay (1839), all in Ohio, and Silver Creek, New York (1838), are places, mostly small harbors, that received beacon lights.

### Lights on the Detroit River (1838–1885)

The last important navigation way on Lake Erie not already mentioned is the Detroit River. The first lighthouse to aid vessels through that waterway was built in 1838 at Gibraltar on the western channel of the river eighteen miles from Detroit. In 1838, it was regarded as the last lighthouse in a line that began at Buffalo, New York. Rebuilt in 1873, the light was discontinued six years later. In

1895, the property, including buildings, was sold.

In 1849, the Mamajuda Island light in Fighting Island Channel of the Detroit River went into service, as did one on Grassy Island. The Detroit River light at the entrance to the river was activated in 1885. Its main purpose was to prevent vessels from grounding on Bar Point, "a dangerous shoal jutting out from the Canada shore." The structure was a cast-iron, conical tower built on a wooden crib filled with concrete. As a result of its exposed position, the lighthouse has been smacked several times over the years by ships and tows.

### Maumee Bay Light (1855) and South Bass Island Light (1897)

Lake Erie has seen many other light stations established over the years, such as the Maumee Bay screw-pile lighthouse (1855) and the South Bass Island light (1897). Time has seen the importance of the lake's harbors wax and wane, and it has seen lighthouses come and go. Although many of these aids to navigation are still in use on Lake Erie, today aids of lesser magnitude, such as buoys, daymarks, range marks, and small beacons are in greater abundance.

## LIGHTS ON THE ST. LAWRENCE RIVER (1827–1848)

The passage to the sea from the Great Lakes is the St. Lawrence River. Early in the navigational development of the lakes, the government began erecting lighthouses to guide vessels into and around the natural hazards of the St. Lawrence River. Tibbetts Point at the Lake Ontario entrance to the river received a lighthouse in 1827. It was rebuilt in 1854 and received major repairs to its parapet walls twenty-nine years after that. Lighted with a fourth-order lens, the lighthouse survives to the present. Another one was built at the confluence of Oswegatchee River with the St. Lawrence near Ogdensburg, New York, in 1834. Four years later the government placed a lighthouse at tiny Crossover Island about mid-point of the Thousand Islands. This small sixth-order light continued in use until 1941. Also in the Thousand Islands, a light went on Sunken Rock about a half mile below Alexander Bay in 1848. The rock was only large enough to hold first a brick tower, later (1884) an iron one;

Cleveland Light Station, Ohio, about 1890. The tower was originally lighted in 1829 and rebuilt in 1873. Superseded by the beacon on Cleveland's East Pier in 1892, it no longer stands. *U. S. Coast Guard photo 26-LG-44-63 in the National Archives.*

so the keeper's dwelling was ashore. In 1848, a light went on Rock Island below Alexandria near Thousand Island Park. Originally a lantern on the keeper's dwelling, in 1882 the Lighthouse Board had an iron tower built to hold the light.

Through the years other aids have been added, including buoys, daymarks, range lights, and small light towers or beacons. Powerful lights are not needed on the twisting St. Lawrence River.

## LIGHTS ON LAKE CHAMPLAIN

Long and skinny, Lake Champlain is connected to the St. Lawrence River by the Richelieu River and to the harbor of New York by the Champlain Canal and the Hudson River. By no means as large nor as active in shipping as the Great Lakes, Lake Cham-

plain nevertheless has had sufficient shipping to warrant the building of aids to navigation.

### Juniper Island Light (1826)

The Juniper Island lighthouse, east of Burlington Bay, was built only seven years after the completion of the Presque Isle lighthouse on Lake Erie, the first light on the Great Lakes. Lighted with ten lamps and reflectors, the tower was much out of repair by 1838. An iron tower replaced the original tower in 1846, and this structure, with its light 100 feet above the lake, survives to the present.

### Burlington Lights (1857)

Ships were guided into Burlington Harbor by lights

180

on the South Breakwater and the North Breakwater. Both lights went into service in 1857, and in 1890 a Middle Breakwater light was added. The towers were rebuilt on the Middle and North breakwaters in 1925 and on the South Breakwater twenty-five years later. All three today are black skeleton towers on square concrete bases.

## Cumberland Head Light (1838) and Plattsburg Breakwater Lights (1867)

In 1838, the Cumberland Head lighthouse at the east entrance to Cumberland Bay went into service as a guide into Plattsburg Harbor. Rebuilt in 1868 and again in 1934, the light is still active, but is aided in its duties by the Plattsburg Breakwater Southwest and Breakwater Northeast lights, both of which the Lighthouse Board had installed in 1867. The Bureau of Lighthouses rebuilt the towers in the 1920's, and they, like the ones at Burlington, are skelton towers on concrete bases.

## Split Rock Light (1838)

Another light was erected in 1838 near the lower end of the lake. Located at Whallon Bay, the Split Rock lighthouse guides vessels through a section where the lake narrows considerably. Rebuilt in 1867 and again in 1934, the tower today is a red skeleton tower similar to breakwater lights of this lake.

## Isle la Motte Light (1857)

In 1857, the Lighthouse Board, at the instigation of local pilots and seamen, placed a small light on the north end of Isle la Motte, a few miles south of where Richelieu River enters Lake Champlain. A steamboat company had maintained a light there up to that time. The board erected a stone pyramid and placed an "ordinary lantern" on it. A local farmer tended the light, but the lantern was unreliable on stormy nights, and in 1868, the board recommended a small lighthouse in its stead. Congress, however, failed to act, and the Lighthouse Board continued to recommend the lighthouse. By 1877, increased traffic, according to the board, made Isle la Motte "one of the most important lights on Lake Champlain." At last Congress responded, and in 1880–81 the board built an iron skeleton tower and

frame dwelling on the island. The light was exhibited in 1881. It was rebuilt in 1933, still an iron skeleton tower.

In 1858, the board erected a stone tower just south of Isle la Motte where vessels coming around the island have to alter course to avoid the shore. The original tower is still active.

## Crown Point Light (1859)

As early as 1838, a naval officer recommended erecting a lighthouse at Crown Point near the southern end of Lake Champlain. In 1853 others noted the need of a lighthouse "to enable vessels to pass with safety through the dark narrow channel at Chimney Point." Upon the Lighthouse Board's recommendation Congress authorized a lighthouse here, and construction of a short tower began in 1858 near the site of historic French and English fortifications. The following year the keeper displayed the light; its focal plane was eighty-seven feet above the water, but less than thirty feet above the ground.

The Champlain Memorial Commission began to look about for a way to commemorate the memory of the great French explorer Samuel de Champlain and struck upon the idea of a memorial lighthouse at Crown Point. In 1912, the Bureau of Lighthouses gave the commission permission to erect the memorial lighthouse on the site of the Crown Point light tower. Using a part of the base of the old tower and the brick stair cylinder, the workmen erected an ornamental granite cylindrical tower surrounded by eight Doric columns. Above this tower was an equally elaborate, granite cornice, as well as a watchroom and lantern parapet. Topping it all was a lantern containing a fifth-order lens. Statues of Champlain and others were placed about the lower part of the tower. Carl Heber, and not Auguste Rodin as has been claimed by some, did the statuary. Rodin did a medallion that the French delegation presented at the ceremonies for later placing on the memorial. Completed in August, 1912, the tower exhibited a fixed white light. The light was discontinued in 1926, and the Bureau of Lighthouses transferred the site to the state of New York.

## Colchester Reef Light (1871)

One of Lake Champlain's best known lighthouses went into service in 1871. Located in the lake a mile from Colchester Point, Vermont, the Colchester Reef lighthouse warned shipping bound to Burlington from the north of three dangerous shoals that lay in the way. The lighthouse continued in use until 1933 when it was closed. It lay deteriorating for nearly twenty years when the Shelburne Museum obtained it. In 1952, the museum moved the lighthouse, piece by piece, from its foundation in the lake and transported the pieces to the mainland where workmen reassembled it near the museum. Today it is a historic lighthouse–maritime museum.

## LIGHTS ON LAKE ONTARIO

### Galloo Island Light (1820)

To assist ships from Lake Ontario to the St. Lawrence River entrance in 1820 the government established a lighthouse on the west side of Galloo Island. Rebuilt in 1867, and still in use today, the light, fifty-five feet above the ground, has been important not only because of its relationship to the river, but because it also serves to guide ships past the islands and shoals in the vicinity and into Sacketts Harbor.

### Oswego and Rochester Harbor Lights (1822)

Two years later a lighthouse went into service at Oswego, New York. Situated at the mouth of Oswego River, the light served as a guide into the harbor. It was moved in 1837 to the end of west pier where it would be more effective to ships entering the harbor. In 1869, the board increased its role to that of a coastal light by raising the tower fourteen feet and installing a third-order lens.

Also in 1822, Rochester Harbor received a lighthouse. It was replaced by a new structure in 1931. The Oswego light has been replaced by other aids.

### Fort Niagara Light (1823) and
### Sodus Bay Light (1825)

The following year, in 1823, a light was placed on the mess house of Fort Niagara. A low wooden tower supported the lantern, whose light served as a guide to the entrance to the Niagara River. By 1868 the old mess house had been made into officers quarters, and the wooden tower was in a dilapi-

dated condition. The Lighthouse Board erected a stone tower outside the fort's walls in 1872, and in 1900 the board raised the tower a little over eleven feet to provide a watchroom. The gray octagonal tower is still in service.

At Sodus Bay a light went into use in 1825. Rebuilt several times, the last in 1870, on a bluff three-fifths of a mile west of the bay entrance, the light was discontinued in June, 1901.

### Lights of the 1830's

A lighthouse went into service at Sacketts Harbor in 1831. The fifth-order lens, installed in 1855, guided ships into the harbor. Rebuilt in 1870 and in 1957, the light is still active.

In 1838, two lighthouses exhibited their lights on Lake Ontario. Stony Point light at Henderson, New York, at the end of the lake is still active, but the Salmon River light near Port Ontario was discontinued in 1859.

### Lights of the 1870's

In the 1870's, several lighthouses went into use. Oak Orchard light (1871), at the harbor by that name, was also a coastal light until 1905 when the board reduced it to a five-day lens lantern. Olcott light (1873) on the end of the west pier is still active, but the present structure dates from 1931. The Thirty Mile Point light (1876) was also a coast light and was equipped with a third-order lens. It is now inactive and the station forms part of Golden Hill State Park.

Lake Erie and Lake Huron are connected by the Detroit and St. Clair rivers. Between these two rivers is Lake St. Clair, a formidable body of water. It has seen several lighthouses, including Windmill Point (1838), St. Clair Flats Canal Range (1935), and the Lake St. Clair light (1941) near the middle of the lake.

## LIGHTS ON LAKE HURON
### Fort Gratiot Light (1825)

In Lake Huron one of the first lights was at the lake's entrance and it served primarily to guide shipping into the St. Clair River. Erected and illuminated in 1825 near Fort Gratiot, the station took its name from that installation. By 1875 it was

Thirty Mile Point Light Station, New York, on Lake Ontario in 1970. Lighted in 1876, but replaced by another structure in 1959, this old lighthouse is now in Golden Hill State Park. *Photo by J. Carl Burke, Jr., for HABS.*

not only the oldest light station in the Eleventh Lighthouse District, but it was also one of the most important, since 33,000 vessels passed it annually. Rebuilt in 1861, the tower still is in service, its light, eighty-two feet above the sea, sending out a beam rated at 25,000 candlepower.

### Bois Blanc Island Light (1829)

Four years after the exhibiting of the Fort Gratiot light, a lighthouse went into service at the other end of Lake Huron. Situated on Bois Blanc Island, the light assisted ships entering the Straits of Mackinac which leads into Lake Michigan. Rebuilt in 1839 because the original station had been eroded away, and again in 1941, the light tower still serves its original purpose.

### Thunder Bay Island Light (1832) and Presque Isle Harbor Light (1840)

The entrance to Thunder Bay received a light in 1832, and eight years later Presque Isle Harbor,

Michigan, received a small light. In 1868, the board realized that a coast light was needed at Presque Isle and that it should be built a mile to the north at the turning point for north- and south-bound vessels. Three years afterwards, a third-order lens, 100 feet above the ground, went into use. The old brick tower is still in use and supports a light measured at 40,000 candlepower.

### Detour Light (1848) and Cheboygan Light (1852)

The Detour lighthouse at the mouth of the St. Mary's River exhibited its light in 1847. This light station was replaced by the Detour Reef light in 1931. On the other side of the lake nearly opposite Detour a fifth-order light went into service in 1852. Three miles east of the Cheboygan River, the Cheboygan light guided ships through the Straits of Mackinac on the south side of Bois Blanc Island. The Cheboygan light grew in importance, and by 1870 is was, as the Lighthouse Board said, "the turning point between Lake Huron and the south channel of the straits [of Mackinac], the one almost exclusively used by sailing vessels and steamers plying between Lake Michigan and the lower lakes." After thirteen years of pleading to Congress, the board received a third-order lens for this tower in 1883. The Cheboygan Light went out of service in the early 1940s.

### Forty Mile Point Light (1897) and Harbor Beach Light (1858)

In subsequent years the board requested a coastal light to light the darkened middle portion of the fifty-mile-long coast between Presque Isle and Cheboygan. In time Congress appropriated the money and on May 1, 1897, the Forty Mile Point lighthouse went into service. Rebuilt in 1935, the lighthouse today is a square brick tower attached to a dwelling. It is at P. H. Hoeft State Park.

In 1858, the Harbor Beach lighthouse displayed its light. Located at the first turning point for north-bound vessels, particularly those going to Saginaw Bay, the original structure is still in use.

### Lights in Saginaw Bay (1848–1878)

Through the years the large Saginaw Bay received several lighthouses to aid the navigator in safely reaching the head of the bay. The first light was installed at the entrance to the bay at Point Aux Barques in 1848, and a half-dozen years later the Tawas light at that point went into service. It was on the opposite side of the bay's entrance from Point Aux Barques. The point at Tawas made out steadily and in less than twenty years the light was over a mile from the point. The Lighthouse Board built a new tower at the end of the point and lighted it in the spring of 1877. Seventy feet above the water, the light today delivers a maximum intensity of 20,000 candlepower.

Charity Island, near the center of the bay, received a light in 1857, and Port Austin, near Point Aux Barques at the entrance to the bay, was lighted in 1878 to warn vessels of the reef there. Port Austin and Point Aux Barques lights are still in use, but Charity Island today has lighted buoys to warn the navigator.

### Spectacle Reef Light (1874)

The greatest engineering achievement in lighthouse construction on Lake Huron, and one of the outstanding feats in the lighthouse service as a whole, was the erection of the Spectacle Reef lighthouse at the eastern end of the Straits of Mackinac. Located a little over ten miles east of Bois Blanc Island, the reef was, according to the Lighthouse Board, "probably more dreaded by navigators than any other danger now unmarked throughout the entire chain of lakes." It estimated a light would cost $300,000, a hefty sum in those days, but, the board pointed out, the value of the two ships that were wrecked there in the autumn of 1867 was far greater than that amount.

Congress in 1869 authorized the lighthouse and work began on the structure the following year. Major O. M. Poe, the engineer supervising the project, selected a point on the reef that had but eleven feet of water over it. The work crew had to clear away the wreckage of the *Nightingale,* an iron-ore-laden schooner, before they could start work on the foundation.

Construction proceeded much as it had at Minots Ledge in Massachusetts. A crib dam, pre-constructed ashore, was placed around the site so that the water could be removed, thus permitting the crew a dry site on which to work. After the crib dam had been placed and the water pumped out, the men levelled the foundation and bolted pre-shaped stones to the rock. The bolts were three feet long, and twenty-one inches of that length was sunk into the base rock. Subsequent courses of stone were bolted to each other and to the stones of the course below. Each bolt was set in pure portland cement which today is as hard as the stone itself.

The circular tower is a solid mass of stone for the first thirty-four feet and thereafter it rises five stories to the lantern. Although four years passed between the beginning of construction and the displaying of the light, only twenty work months were invested in the construction of the tower.

Ice is the biggest winter-time problem in the Great Lakes, and Spectacle Reef was baptized early. When the keepers came to the light in May after the winter of 1873–74 they found ice piled all around the lighthouse to a height of thirty feet. In order to get into the tower they had to hack their way through the ice.

Lighted in June, 1874, the light tower has served well through the years, and today the light exhibits a maximum candlepower of 400,000. For nearly 100 years this light has guided lake vessels past the dangerous reef and toward the Straits of Mackinac which lead into Lake Michigan.

## LIGHTS ON LAKE MICHIGAN

### St. Joseph and Chicago Harbor of Refuge Lights (1832)

One of the earliest lights established on Lake Michigan was the St. Joseph lighthouse at the entrance of the St. Joseph River. Exhibited in 1832, it lasted until 1886 when the pierhead light was enlarged and made more powerful.

Also in 1832 a light went into service at the mouth of the Chicago River on the south side. The light was not powerful, even by the standards of those days, but its primary purpose was to guide vessels into the harbor of refuge there. This light continued in use until 1893 when the Chicago Harbor light was displayed.

### Chicago Harbor Light (1893)

The lens installed in the Chicago Harbor lighthouse was a prize-winning one. Originally ordered for the new Point Loma, California, lighthouse, the red and white panelled third-order lens was so highly regarded by the Lighthouse Board that that body ordered it exhibited at the Paris Exhibition and later at the Columbia Exposition in Chicago in 1891. The lens won prizes at both places, and it remained on display until the Columbia Exposition closed. In the meantime, the Lighthouse Board found another lens for Point Loma, and at the end of the Exposition had the award-winning lens moved over to the then-completed Chicago Harbor lighthouse.

*River Entrance Lights (1838–1849)*
*and Pierhead Lights (1838–1851)*

Many of the early lights on Lake Michigan, and on much of the Great Lakes for that matter, were erected at the mouths of rivers, mainly because the settlements were near there. Some of these lights and/or settlements are little more than a memory today. For the most part these lights were simply harbor lights and had little function in the scheme of coastal navigation. Milwaukee (1838), Kalamazoo (1839), Manitowoc (1840) in Wisconsin, Tail Point (1848) near Green Bay, and Calumet (1851) are but a few lighthouses on Lake Michigan that were at the entrances to rivers. New Buffalo (1840) was another light erected at the entrance to a river, but erosion threatened the site, and in 1859 it was discontinued. All movable property was hauled away and the buildings were sold at public auction in 1861–62. The land itself was sold to F. R. Perkins in 1902 for $75; the site had originally cost the fifth auditor $200.

The Muskegon South Pierhead light, built in 1903, traces its lineage to the Muskegon light erected at the harbor entrance in 1851. Michigan City's East Pierhead light has a similar history, except that its original light goes back to 1838.

*Coastal and Pierhead Lights on*
*the Eastern Shore (1839–1936)*

Prominent coastal lights along the east coast of Lake Michigan include Gray's Reef light (1936), which replaced a lightship that had been there since 1891; Ile aux Galets (1850), which was rebuilt in 1886; Point Betsie (1858) near Crystal Lake, one of the most important lights on that coast because it was a turning point for several routes up and down Lake Michigan; and Big Sable light-

house (1867) at the present Ludington State Park, a conical tower whose light is 106 feet above the water. Southward of Big Sable, there are only pierhead lights, and these lights are adequate for vessels staying close to shore. Ships bound southward for the principal ports of Chicago and Gary follow shipping lanes farther out in the lake after passing Big Sable. Northbound vessels from these two ports pick up the coast again about Big Sable. Some of the pierhead lights south of Big Sable are: Grand Haven South Pierhead Inner light (1839), which was rebuilt in 1905 as a red conical tower fifty-one feet tall; Holland Harbor South Pierhead light (1907), now a red square tower erected in 1936, whose light is visible fourteen miles; and the South Haven Pierhead light (1872), whose rebuilding in 1913 made the light high enough to be seen thirteen miles.

*Coastal Lights on the Western*
*Shore (1854–1928)*

Prominent coast lights on the west side of Lake Michigan are Racine Reef light (1906) rebuilt in 1961; the white, conical tower of Wind Point lighthouse (1880) just to the north of Racine; the Rawley Point light (1854), whose present skeleton tower went up in 1894, marks an important position point for north- and southbound vessels; the Poverty Point lighthouse, which had a temporary light installed in July, 1874, when construction funds ran out, but whose white conical tower was completed and lighted a year later; the Seul Choix Point light (1892), whose 450,000 candlepower light can be seen seventeen or more miles; and the Lansing Shoal lighthouse (1928) forty miles west of the Straits of Mackinac.

*Lights on Green Bay (1837–1935)*

The largest bay in Lake Michigan is Green Bay and through the years a number of lighthouses have been placed along its shores to aid traffic bound for the city of Green Bay. In addition to the Tail Point and the Eagle Bluff lights, there are Pottawatomie light (1837) at the entrance to the bay, Green Island light (1864) off Menominee River, Sherwood Point light (1883) at the entrance to Sturgeon Bay, and the Green Bay Harbor entrance light (1935) on the west side of the channel.

## LIGHTS ON LAKE SUPERIOR

North of Lakes Michigan and Huron is Lake Superior, sitting like a crown above the other lakes. It has led an active shipping life, though this activity began later than on the other lakes.

### Whitefish Point and
### Copper Harbor Lights (1849)

The two oldest, active lights on Lake Superior are at Whitefish Point and at Copper Harbor. Both were erected in 1849. Whitefish Point was rebuilt in 1861, an iron skeleton tower eighty feet tall. Its 1,000,000 candlepower beam guides ships into Whitefish Bay and to the passage that leads to Lake Huron.

Copper Harbor light, located on the north side near the end of the Keweenaw Peninsula, went into service just five years after the discovery of a rich copper vein near there. Situated near Fort Wilkins, the light's keeper occupied one of the quarters at that installation. Rebuilt in 1866, the light remained active until 1884, when the board discontinued it. Called back into service four years later, the Copper Harbor light is still active, beaming out its 90,000 candlepower light to mark the entrance to the harbor. Though still standing, the old tower went out of service in 1933. Today the light is atop a steel skeleton tower located on the light station grounds.

### Manitou Island Light (1850)

Off the tip of Keweenaw Peninsula and east of Copper Harbor is Manitou Island. The light there was exhibited in 1850 and its purpose has been to guide ships to and around the peninsula, particularly those vessels entering Lake Superior through Whitefish Bay. Rebuilt in 1861, its iron skeleton tower has a flashing white light rated at 250,000 candlepower.

### Lights of the 1850's

The Lighthouse Board established a number of lighthouses on Lake Superior in the 1850's; many in time became no longer useful and were discontinued. Those that fall into that category include Round Island and Point Iroquois, both erected in 1855 at the entrance to St. Mary's River; Eagle River (1857) west of Copper Harbor on Keweenaw Peninsula; and the Rock Harbor light (1855) on

Isle Royale. This latter lighthouse is included within Isle Royale National Park and has been out of service since 1879, when the board decided that the Menagerie Island light (1875), just off shore, was quite adequate for vessels to navigate the harbor safely. Somehow the structure survived and in recent years the National Park Service has made efforts from time to time to stabilize the structure and keep it from sliding off its rock base into the water. Unfortunately, endeavors to save the lighthouse from the weather have generally been inadequate.

Lighthouses put up during this decade that are still active include Marquette light (1853), which was last rebuilt in 1867; Grand Island light (1855) near Munising, though now atop a white column; Michigan Island light (1857) in the Apostle group, which was last rebuilt in 1930; and La Pointe and Chequamegon Point, both established in 1858 at Chequamegon Bay and both rebuilt in 1897.

### Huron Island Light (1868) and
### Granite Island Light (1869)

In the 1860's increasing traffic between Marquette and Portage on the Keweenaw Peninsula called attention to two islands on the route. The Huron Islands, the board reported, "are a constant source of anxiety to the navigators, wrecks having frequently occurred at this point." Selecting a site on the highest point of West Huron Island, the board built a tower and lighted it October 20, 1868.

The following year the board built a gray, square, granite tower on the appropriately named Granite Island which lay across the route of several shipping lanes. The keepers lighted the lens lamp in the spring of 1869. Both Granite and Huron Islands have active lights today.

### Duluth Harbor and Au Sable Lights (1874);
### Lights of the Apostle Islands

The Duluth Harbor light (1874) came into use because that port's activity had grown with the extension of the railroad to that city, which resulted in a need for ships to get into the harbor on foggy days and at night. The Au Sable light, a few miles west of Grand Marais, went into service August 19, 1874, to light the darkened coast between Whitefish Point and Grand Island Harbor. The Apostle group received a light on Outer Island in 1874 and on Sand Island in 1881. Both lights were in response

Big Sable Light Station, Michigan, in 1914. This light is still active as one of the most prominent coastal lights on the eastern shore of Lake Michigan. *U. S. Coast Guard photo 26-LG-69-1 in the National Archives.*

to the growing traffic at the west end of Lake Superior, an increase of activity centering around the bustling Duluth. Devils Island, also in the Apostle group, received a temporary light in 1891 and a permanent one ten years later.

## Passage Island Light (1882)

Passage Island light was illuminated on July 1, 1882. An increase in traffic had occurred because of the discovery of silver on the lake. The light was installed to mark the passage between the island and the much larger Isle Royale, now a national park.

## Stannard Rock Light (1882)

Lake Superior's three most spectacular lighthouses are Stannard Rock, Rock of Ages, and Split Rock. Stannard Rock is a shoal, about forty miles north-northeast of Marquette, Michigan, and about twenty-five miles southeast of Manitou Island, that rises a few feet above the water, and the board in 1866 considered it "the most serious danger to navigation in Lake Superior." But Congress did not respond, and the board in 1867 placed a daymark on the rock. Over the next five years, traffic increased considerably and the board urged that a lighthouse be placed "on this danger, so much dreaded by vessels. . . ." Finally, in 1877, Congress appropriated the money to build a lighthouse similar to the one that had been built at Spectacle Reef in 1874. The tower went up and exhibited its light on Independence Day of 1882. The Stannard Rock lighthouse remained active, but in 1962 an electrical short caused the diesel fuel tank to explode, destroying much of the interior of the tower and killing one of the three men aboard at the time. It remained in service until the following year when the 1,400,000 candlepower light was replaced by a minor light of but 3,000 candlepower.

## Rock of Ages Light (1908)

The Rock of Ages light, on a brick tower with a concrete foundation located on a long, narrow, rock ridge off the western end of Isle Royale, went into service on October 22, 1908. For two years a temporary lens beamed from this light, but finally a permanent second-order lens, 117 feet above lake level, began guiding vessels past Isle Royale. It has been especially useful to ships bound to and from Duluth along the north coast of Lake Superior, particularly

Rock of Ages lighthouse in Lake Superior guards the western tip of Isle Royale. Its light, 117 feet above the lake, guides Duluth-bound shipping along Superior's north coast. *U. S. Coast Guard official photo*.

The Stannard Rock lighthouse, erected in 1882. This tower is located in Lake Superior some twenty-three miles from the nearest land. In this 1954 picture, a small boat from a Coast Guard cutter is approaching the tower to remove the keepers at the close of navigation on the lake for the winter. The light has been automated since 1961 and is now untended. *U. S. Coast Guard official photo.*

during storms, when vessels travel in the lee of Isle Royale rather than the southerly, and rougher, course. Still active, the lighthouse is viewed today by many visitors to Isle Royale National Park.

### Split Rock Light (1910)

The light station at Split Rock, Minnesota, on Lake Superior was established in 1910 on 7.63 acres of land that cost the government $200. That particular site was selected because, as the Lighthouse Board reported, "The unusual local magnetic attractions and the impossibility of getting reliable soundings in the neighborhood make navigation difficult in thick weather." The thirty-eight-foot, octagonal, brick light tower rests on a rock that juts out into the lake. This tower, along with the oil house, fog signal house, boathouse, three 3-bedroom, 2-story dwellings with basement cisterns, and three barns cost the government $72,541. The tower's second-order lens, with incandescent oil vapor lamp, gave out a light rated at 1,200,000 candlepower. In later years a third-order lens was substituted and the candlepower of the light was reduced to 450,000. The Split Rock lighthouse is no longer in operation.

# XII

# Lighthouses of Alaska, Hawaii, Puerto Rico, and the Virgin Islands

THROUGH the years, the United States government has maintained lighthouses at its various possessions and territories, including the Philippine Islands, the Panama Canal, Guam, Midway, and Samoa, as well as at the better-known Virgin Islands, Puerto Rico, Hawaii, and Alaska. At several of these territories, particularly Puerto Rico, the Virgin Islands, and the Philippines, the government inherited a going lighthouse system, with the result that all that was necessary was to adapt the system to the United States' way of doing things and to expand and improve on the lighthouse service already in existence.

Generally, the Lighthouse Board, and later the Bureau of Lighthouses, ran directly the lighthouse systems in the possessions. In a few cases, such as Guantanamo in Cuba, Samoa, and Guam, however, it was more efficient and economical, at least in the early years, to let the U. S. Navy administer aids to navigation. At these places the aids to navigation were few, the distance to these possessions was great, and the work there was not sufficient to warrant stationing administrative personnel. The lighthouse service, nevertheless, retained nominal control over these aids, since money to operate and maintain them came from appropriations made to the lighthouse establishment.

Alaska, Hawaii, Puerto Rico, and the Virgin Islands had or required complex systems of aids to navigation, and consequently their operation be-came integrated into this country's lighthouse establishment, and the administration of their aids to navigation followed the general methods and procedures in the older, functioning districts on the mainland.

## LIGHTS OF ALASKA

The first possession whose aids to navigation the Lighthouse Board became responsible for was Alaska. When the United States acquired the territory in 1867, it found that the Russians had maintained a light at Sitka, and it apparently was turned over to the Lighthouse Board. This light, located in the cupola of the Baranof Castle, consisted, so several historians of the Russian period in Alaska reported, of seal oil lamps and a huge reflector. For some reason the board did not continue this aid, probably because of Congress's failure to provide adequate funding. Congress was by no means convinced of the wisdom of the purchase of Alaska—even at two cents an acre—and subsequently made little provision for governmental activity in that territory. The Lighthouse Board apparently relied upon the army to keep up the light, and when the army departed in 1877, so did acting ordnance sergeant George Golkell, who had been appointed keeper in 1867.

For many years the board made no effort to introduce other aids in Alaskan waters. Its first action in

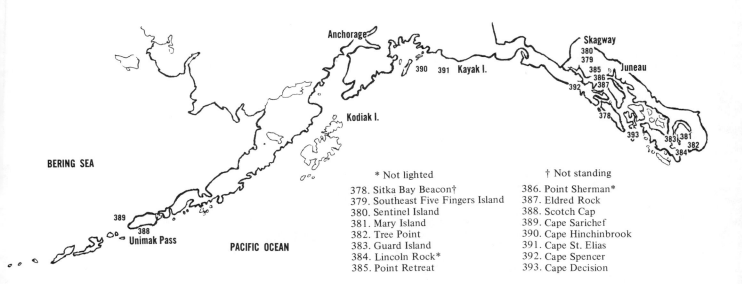

BERING SEA

Anchorage

390 391 Kayak I.

Skagway
380
379
385
386
387
392
378
393 383 381
382
384

Juneau

Kodiak I.

389
388
Unimak Pass

PACIFIC OCEAN

| * Not lighted | † Not standing |
|---|---|
| 378. Sitka Bay Beacon† | 386. Point Sherman* |
| 379. Southeast Five Fingers Island | 387. Eldred Rock |
| 380. Sentinel Island | 388. Scotch Cap |
| 381. Mary Island | 389. Cape Sarichef |
| 382. Tree Point | 390. Cape Hinchinbrook |
| 383. Guard Island | 391. Cape St. Elias |
| 384. Lincoln Rock* | 392. Cape Spencer |
| 385. Point Retreat | 393. Cape Decision |

that territory came in the spring of 1884 with the placing of fourteen iron buoys. And these fourteen buoys, plus a beacon light established in Sitka Harbor in 1895, were all the aids to navigation available to the ship masters who brought supplies, materials, and people to Alaska in the busy and frantic gold rush years of 1897–98. The navigator had to guide his ship through tortuous channels and along precipitously rocky and often fog-enshrouded coasts, with little but instinct fortified with experience and luck to aid him. On too many occasions, one or more of these ingredients was not present and a ship found its destiny as it broke apart on a rock-bound coast or was pulled beneath the surface by a sea surging through a gaping hole gouged into the ship's bottom by an unmarked rock.

Perhaps it was the frightful loss of lives and vessels that prodded Congress in 1900 to appropriate $100,000 to establish lighthouses in Alaskan waters. The Lighthouse Board apparently had been lax in its leadership, since it was unprepared for this windfall and had to dispatch the district inspector and the district engineer northward to examine proposed sites. Hardening of the arteries had set in in this once vigorous and aggressive organization, and within ten years the board was to be supplanted as the manager of the country's aids to navigation. On their return, the two lighthouse officials recommended eleven lights for the southeast coast of Alaska and four for the western coast. They gave priority to lighthouses at Southeast Five Fingers Island on the route to Juneau and Skagway, Point Retreat and Sentinel Island not far from Skagway, and Fairway Island in Peril Strait.

*Lights on the Inside Passage (1902–1905)*

In June, 1901, a year after the appropriation, the Lighthouse Board let contracts to build lighthouses at Southeast Five Fingers Island and at Sentinel Island. Work on them was completed the following year, and on March 1, 1902, these two lighthouses went into service. In the next three years, seven other lighthouses were established on this inside passage to Skagway: at Mary Island (July, 1903) and Tree Point (April, 1904) in Revillogigedo Channel; at Guard Island (September, 1904) at the entrance to Tongass Narrows in Clarence Strait; on Lincoln Rock (December, 1903) also in Clarence Strait; and at Point Retreat (September, 1904) and Point Sherman (October, 1904) in the Lynn Canal to Skagway. The following year, in 1905, the Eldred Rock light went into use; today it is the only one of these early lighthouses of the inside passage that has not been rebuilt, mainly because it was constructed of concrete while most of the others had been of frame construction. Lincoln Rock's frame tower, for example, was so badly damaged by the storms of 1909 and 1910 that a new iron tower was placed in its stead in 1912.

*Scotch Cap Light (1903)*

For those vessels that travel the outside passage, several coastal lights have been established to guide them. Two of the first to go into service were but seventeen miles apart and were two of the most isolated lighthouses in the United States' lighthouse service. Families were not permitted at these sta-

191

Sentinel Island Light Station, Alaska, in 1915. Lighted in 1902, this station exhibited one of the first U. S.– constructed lights in Alaska. *U. S. Coast Guard photo 26-LG-60-92 in the National Archives.*

tions, and, consequently, the civilian keepers were given one year's leave in every four years. Located near the west end of Unimak Island, these lights mark Unimak Pass, the main passage through the Aleutian Islands into the Bering Sea. Scotch Cap light on the Pacific side of the pass, went into use on June 18, 1903, and was Alaska's first coastal lighthouse. An octagonal wooden tower supported the light, which was ninety feet above the sea, until April 1, 1946, when an earthquake and tidal wave swept the station, with its five keepers, into the sea. A temporary light marked the site until 1950, when the Coast Guard completed construction of a new rectangular, flat-roofed, white building on top of which is a tower whose light is 116 feet above the sea.

### Cape Sarichef Light (1904)

On the Bering Sea side of the island, the Cape Sarichef tower was lighted July 1, 1904, and has been the only manned lighthouse on the shores of the Bering Sea. Like its sister lighthouse at Scotch Cap, the Cape Sarichef tower was rebuilt and relighted in 1950. Today its light is 177 feet above the sea.

### Cape Hinchinbrook Light (1910)

In 1908, the Lighthouse Board let a contract to build a lighthouse at Cape Hinchinbrook at the entrance to Prince William Sound. Since exhibiting its third-order lens on November 15, 1910, the station

Cape Hinchinbrook lighthouse, Alaska, in 1912. This station was lighted in 1910 and rebuilt in 1934; today, it is one of Alaska's most important coast lights. It dis- plays a third-order light. *U. S. Coast Guard photo 26-LG-60-10 in the National Archives.*

has served not only as a mark to the entrance of the sound, but also as a coast light and a warning to navigators of the dangerous Seal Rocks nearby. Rebuilt in 1934, the light station continues as one of Alaska's principal coast lights.

### Cape St. Elias Light (1916)

About 150 miles to the southeast, the Bureau of Lighthouses established a lighthouse on the south- ern end of Kayak Island. Lighted on September 6, 1916, the light station became known by the name Cape St. Elias because its purpose was to identify this important landfall to navigators. Never rebuilt, this light station is still manned and active.

### Cape Spencer Light (1925)

For those vessels that wished to avoid the storms of the open sea, the Bureau of Lighthouses built a lighthouse at Cape Spencer marking the northern entrance to the inside passage. The light station, its buildings of reinforced concrete, went into service in 1925 and is still active today, with its original structures.

### Cape Decision Light (1932)

The last of Alaska's coastal lights went into service in 1932. The Cape Decision Light Station, its rein- forced concrete buildings situated on the coast at one of the middle entrances to the inside passage, today exhibits a light measured at 350,000 candlepower.

Almost as important as the light, the fog signal is a necessity in Alaska. All of the principal stations have one.

Servicing lighthouses in Alaska, because of the cold, the fog, and stormy weather, as well as the rocky, treacherous shores, was not a task performed with ease. Early in this century, Dr. Henry S. Pritchett, a member of the Lighthouse Board, recognized this difficulty and urged that no more major lighthouses be built and that the hazards of the Alaska coast be marked with acetylene buoys and beacons. These lights required servicing only about every six months. Although in subsequent years major lighthouses came into existence, the bulk of lights on the Alaska coast have been of a type requiring infrequent servicing.

## LIGHTS OF HAWAII

In 1898, the United States acquired two major possessions on opposite sides of the world: Puerto Rico and Hawaii. Puerto Rico, which came to this country by way of the Spanish-American War, had a more sophisticated lighthouse system than did Hawaii. In Puerto Rico the Spanish had erected modern lighthouses with up-to-date illuminating apparatuses. Hawaii, on the other hand, had primitive structures on which it rested its equally primitive lights, which often consisted of little more than household lamps.

Although the Lighthouse Board received responsibility for Puerto Rico's aids to navigation in 1900, it wasn't until January 1, 1904, that President Theodore Roosevelt transferred Hawaii's aids to navigation from the territorial government to the Board. To administer these aids more effectively, the Lighthouse Board made Hawaii a subdistrict of the

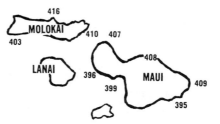

| * Not lighted | † Not standing |
| --- | --- |
| 394. Diamond Head | 406. Kawaihae |
| 395. Kanahene Point† | 407. Nakalele Point |
| 396. Lahaina | 408. Pauwela Point |
| 397. Laupahoehoe | 409. Hanamanioa |
| 398. **Mahu Kona** | 410. Hawea Point |
| 399. Maalaea* | 411. Kaena Point |
| 400. Waiakea | 412. Kahala Point |
| 401. Paukaa Point | 413. Makahuena Point |
| 402. Barbers Point | 414. Hanapepe |
| 403. Kalaeokalauu* | 415. Kakole |
| 404. Pepeekeo | 416. Molokai |
| 405. Napoopoo | 417. Makapuu Point |
| | 418. Kilauea |

## A red cloth around a lantern

Diamond Head light tower, Oahu, Hawaii, in 1915. When the Lighthouse Board assumed control, Diamond Head was the only tower in Hawaii mounting a Fresnel lens. *U. S. Coast Guard photo 26-LG-68-1B in the National Archives.*

Twelfth Lighthouse District and appointed an inspector and an engineer to be directly responsible for aids to navigation in the islands.

When the Lighthouse Board took charge in the Hawaiian Islands there were nineteen lighthouses, twenty daymarks, and twenty buoys, as well as some sixteen private aids maintained by the Inter-

Island Steamship Company and others. Only one of the lighthouses—the one at Diamond Head—had a Fresnel lens. The condition of the others had been pretty well summed up in a previous report by a civilian investigator:

> The lighthouses are generally of a very crude character, the one on the top of the custom house in Honolulu being a lantern with a red cloth tied around it. . . . On the island of Hawaii there are but six lights, and they are all "fixed," so called, two small colored and four white ones, all very cheap and of short range.
>
> The lights used in the light-houses throughout the islands, except Diamond Head light, are ordinary oil lights, either double wicks or circular burners.

On inspecting the various established lights in the islands, the subdistrict inspector found that generally the light towers were wooden trestles with little rooms at the top where the lamps were placed. At Kanahene Point on the south coast of the island of Maui, "two ordinary kitchen lamps" marked the low lava spit that ran into the ocean and caused many ships to founder. Similar illuminating apparatuses were found at Lahaina, also on Maui, and at Laupahoehoe and Mahu Kona on the island of Hawaii. The light at Maalaea Bay on Maui consisted of an "ordinary red lantern hung from a post," while the Waiakea light, located on the "southeast side of Hilo Bay, in rear of wharf near entrance to Waiakea Creek," consisted of a city arc light with a red screen in front of it. The entrance to Hilo Bay was equipped with a little better light which was composed of three small reflector lights situated on Paukaa Point. There is some evidence to indicate that the Barbers Point light and the Kalaeokalauu light on Molokai Island may have been truer lighthouses, with more substantial towers and small Fresnel lenses.

When it moved into Hawaii the Lighthouse Board took three courses of action. It immediately went about installing Fresnel lenses of the lower orders at many of the established stations, and at others it placed lens lanterns, at the same time rebuilding some of the towers and improving living conditions at others. The board instituted a policy of taking over private aids to navigation as money became available. And lastly, the board conducted an evaluation to determine where additional lights were

Landing supplies for the Paukaa Light Station at the entrance to Hilo Bay, island of Hawaii, in 1904. This station was displaying three small reflector lights when the Lighthouse Board took it over that year. Consider-ing the forbidding rocks in the vicinity, contemporary mariners must have wished for a better light at this location. *U. S. Coast Guard photo 26-LG-64-4 in the National Archives.*

needed for the convenience and safety of naviga-tion.

In subsequent years the Lighthouse Board, and later the Bureau of Lighthouses, placed lighthouses and beacons to mark harbor entrances and to warn navigators of nearby rocks and shoals. Pepeekeo light (1907) north of Hilo Bay, Napoopoo light (1908) on Cook Point, Kawaihae light (1906) at the bay of that name, all on Big (Hawaii) Island; Nakalele Point light (1908), Pauwela Point light (1910) at Kahului Bay, Hanamanioa light (1918) on the cape by that name, and Hawea Point light (1911), all on Maui; Kaena Point light (1920), on Oahu; and Kahala Point light (1908) at the en-trance to Anahola Bay, Makahuena Point light (1908), Hanapepe light (1912) at the entrance to the bay, and Kakole light (1908) on the point, all on Kauai Island, are some of the lights that were placed in the islands to make the navigator's job easier and the seaman's life safer.

### Molokai Light (1909)

The board also placed several large coastal lights in the islands in these early days. In 1909, the board erected an octagonal concrete tower 138 feet tall at a cost of $60,000 on the north shore of Molokai Island. Known simply as Molokai light, the tower survives to the present, supporting an illuminant whose light measures 2,000,000 candlepower.

### Makapuu Point Light (1909)

In the same year, a light went into service on Maka-puu Point at the eastern extremity of Oahu Island. The need for a light here early struck the Light-

## A million-candle landfall

house Board, and in 1905 it said, "All deep-sea commerce between Honolulu and Puget Sound, the Pacific coast of the United States, Mexico and Central America, including Panama, passes Makapuu Head, and . . . there is not a single light on the whole northern coast of the Hawaiian Islands to guide ships or warn them of their approach to land, after a voyage of several thousand miles." Congress responded in 1906 with an appropriation of $60,000.

The site the board selected was nearly 400 feet above the sea; consequently, there was no need for a tall tower. The towers erected placed the focal plane of the light 420 feet above sea level. Lighted October 1, 1909, the tower supports one of the new hyper-radiant lenses, the largest lens still in use in a United States lighthouse. It measures eight and one-half feet in diameter.

### Kilauea Point Light (1913)

In 1913, the Kilauea Point Light Station on the island of Kauai went into service. Its prime purpose was to provide an aid for traffic from the west as Makapuu Point light served shipping from the east. In other words, it was a landfall light for ships coming from the Orient.

The site of the tower was 180 feet above the sea and, consequently, the tower, "slightly conical in shape," was short, just tall enough to put the focal plane of the second-order lens thirty-seven feet above the ground. Today this tower, which has never been rebuilt, emits a light equivalent to 1,000,000 candles.

Today the Hawaiian Islands are well lighted, and many stations trace their ancestry back to the pre-Lighthouse Board days. Barbers Point, first lighted in 1888, now possesses a tower that exhibits a 700,-000 candlepower light; Laupahoehoe (1890) light today has a skeleton tower built in 1947 and displays a 5,000 candlepower light, which, though small by today's standards, is quite an improvement over the power of the "ordinary house lamp" the station first had; and Diamond Head light (1899) whose present occulting (disappearing and reappearing) white and red light on its 1917 tower is more distinctive than its original fixed, white light. These are a few of the surviving early light stations of Hawaii; there are a number of others.

### LIGHTS OF PUERTO RICO

Meanwhile, in the Caribbean, as mentioned earlier, the United States had acquired Puerto Rico, and in time it was to obtain the Virgin Islands. Both territories already had lighthouses, but additional ones were sorely needed.

On May 1, 1900, a presidential order turned over Puerto Rico's lighthouses to the administration of the Lighthouse Board. Thus the board inherited thirteen lighthouses and a badly-out-of-condition buoy system.

The first step the board took was to bring administration to the area's lighthouses. It put the island under the Third Lighthouse District and appointed a navy lieutenant as sub-district inspector with headquarters in San Juan. The board next began to bring Puerto Rico's aids to navigation up to full standing. It sent buoys, paints, and lighthouse supplies to San Juan, and the sub-district inspector saw to the repair of the war-damaged lighthouse on El Morro, the old Spanish fortification at the entrance to San Juan Harbor which had undergone bombardment in 1898 from the ships of the United States Navy. In addition, the inspector saw to the finishing of the lighthouse on Mona Island.

### Mona Island Light (1900)

Mona Island was located in the passage between Puerto Rico and Santo Domingo. It was uninhabited and had no harbor, but for years vessels had been coming to obtain the guano and phosphate which were in plentiful deposits there. Ships had to anchor off the island, and, as the Lighthouse Board dryly noted, the winds and currents were such that when the crews went ashore, their vessels sometimes followed them. Eleven ships had wrecked on the island in the two years prior to the completion of the light station.

But the main purpose of the lighthouse was to guide ships through the Mona Passage. To this end the Spanish had deposited materials on the island to build a light tower, but the Spanish-American War halted their activity. The materials lay there, some of them rusting and some of them being stolen, so that when the Board of Public Works, which administered Puerto Rico's lighthouses before the Lighthouse Board arrived on the scene, decided to take up where the Spanish left off, it had to transport additional material to the island. All

Lighthouse on El Morro, the old Spanish fortification that is part of San Juan National Historic Site, Puerto Rico. This tower, completed in 1908, replaced the one built by Spain that had been rendered useless by bombardment during the Spanish-American War. *Photo by Jack Boucher for HABS, 1960.*

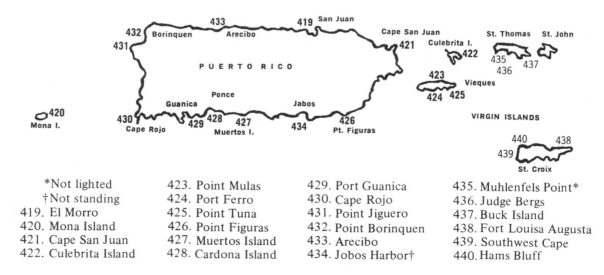

|  |  |  |  |
|---|---|---|---|
| *Not lighted | 423. Point Mulas | 429. Port Guanica | 435. Muhlenfels Point* |
| †Not standing | 424. Port Ferro | 430. Cape Rojo | 436. Judge Bergs |
| 419. El Morro | 425. Point Tuna | 431. Point Jiguero | 437. Buck Island |
| 420. Mona Island | 426. Point Figuras | 432. Point Borinquen | 438. Fort Louisa Augusta |
| 421. Cape San Juan | 427. Muertos Island | 433. Arecibo | 439. Southwest Cape |
| 422. Culebrita Island | 428. Cardona Island | 434. Jobos Harbor† | 440. Hams Bluff |

## A spoiled symmetry

the material to build the lighthouse had to be carried from the beach over a mile to a site nearly 200 feet above the sea. The surface up the side of the island was so rough that the workmen had to blast a trail to the top. Through persistence and hard work the workmen transported the parts to the top, and soon began erecting a skeleton tower whose second-order lens was to be fifty-two feet above the ground. The keeper exhibited the light April 30, 1900. The following year the Lighthouse Board completed the other buildings of the station and laid a track to facilitate movement of lighthouse supplies from the boat landing to a cave where supplies were stored. The work crew put in a track from the cave to the tower.

### Lights Taken Over from Spain

The thirteen active lights comprising the Spanish lighthouse system in Puerto Rico consisted of the beforementioned one at El Morro Castle, as well as lighthouses at Cape San Juan, Culebrita Island,

Point Mulas, Port Ferro, Point Tuna, Point Figuras, Muertos Island, Cardona Island, Port Guanica, Cape Rojo, Point Jiguero, and Point Borinquen.

The light at El Morro had been damaged severely during Admiral Sampson's bombardment, and could no longer be used. The tower, which the Spanish had erected in 1853 on the centuries-old fort, had to be rebuilt in 1899 by the military government. The gray, octagonal, iron tower did not hold up, and in 1907–08 the Lighthouse Board had a new tower constructed. The designers of the new tower, which is still active, tried to blend it in architecturally with the old fort, and they botched the job. The tower is like a dissonant chord in a grand symphony. When one visits El Morro, which today is part of San Juan National Historic Site, and his eye sweeps over the massive and magnificent fortifications that took centuries to evolve, one is pleased by the balance, continuity, and symmetry—until his gaze brings the lighthouse into view; then the senses are jarred, as if one had been travelling over a smooth road and all of a sudden hit a washboard

Culebrita Light Station, Puerto Rico, about 1910. Built by Spain in 1885, the light is 305 feet above the sea, and is today rated at 20,000 CP.  *U. S. Coast Guard photo 26-LG-40-28 in the National Archives.*

section. The castellated walls of the tower are miniaturized and look exactly what they are: phony. The Spanish had not tried to hide the fact that their structure was a lighthouse, and achieved a pleasing effect with their tower of traditional and simple lighthouse lines. On the other hand, the Lighthouse Board tried to hide the fact that their structure was a lighthouse, and placed a lump on the fort.

The Spanish placed a cylindrical tower rising from a rectangular building at Cape San Juan on the north coast of Puerto Rico. Established in 1880 to guide vessels along the north and east coasts of the island, the lighthouse still stands, having never been rebuilt. Originally equipped with a third-order lens, the tower later received one of the first order.

In 1885, the Spanish placed a similar lighthouse on Culebrita Island, on the west side of the Virgin Passage. The light from the fourth-order lens was 305 feet above the sea. Still active, the tower's light is now measured at 20,000 candlepower.

At Point Mulas in 1896 there was a sixth-order light to guide ships along the north shore of Vieques Island. The tower still has this small lens.

Also on Vieques Island, on the south side, the Spanish began a third-order light in 1896 to mark the entrance to Port Ferro. The United States completed it in 1899. It has never been rebuilt.

The Spanish also erected a light tower in 1893 at Point Tuna. This third-order light served to aid vessels navigating along the southeast coast of the island. Its original tower in 1951 still had a third-order lens.

On Point Figuras, at the entrance to Port Arroyo on the south coast of Puerto Rico, the Spanish built a small harbor light in 1893. The tower survived until 1938 when it was rebuilt.

In 1885, the Spanish placed a third-order light on Muertos Island. The light still serves as a guide to vessels travelling along the south coast of the island.

Not far away, at the entrance to Ponce Harbor, a light went into service in 1889. Built on Cardona Island, the short tower with its sixth-order lens was still active in 1951.

The Guanica light on Point Meseta at the entrance to Port Guanica was completed in 1893. Its sixth-order light, 117 feet above the water, beamed from the thirty-two-foot tower until 1950 when the Coast Guard had the lighthouse rebuilt.

Cape Rojo on the southwest point of Puerto Rico received a third-order light in 1882. The forty-foot hexagonal tower continues to aid vessels travelling the south coast of the island as well as those ships heading for the Mona Passage.

At Point Jiguero on the south side of Aquadilla Bay—where many contend Columbus first landed on Puerto Rican soil—the Spanish in 1892 placed a sixth-order light. The octagonal tower, thirty-two feet high, served as a guide through Mona Passage and in approaching Mayaguez Bay. Destroyed by an earthquake, the station was rebuilt and relighted in January, 1922.

The Spanish erected a forty-foot tower with a fourth-order lens on the north coast at Point Borinquen in 1889. Rebuilt in 1920 and again in 1947 at a higher elevation and equipped with a first-order lens because of the site's increasing importance as a landfall, the light, 292 feet above the water, serves also as a guide along that coast.

### Arecibo Light (1898)

These lighthouses served as the basis for the system of aids to navigation in Puerto Rico, and the bulk have never been rebuilt or relocated, which is a tribute to the skill of the Spanish. As the years went on, the United States added to the number. In 1898, the military government placed a third-order light at Arecibo on the north coast of Puerto Rico as a guide to the Arecibo Roads, and this was about the last of the major lights placed in Puerto Rico. Other lights subsequently established, such as the lens lantern at Jobos Harbor in 1902, have been small lights, more of either the beacon or range-light variety.

## LIGHTS OF THE VIRGIN ISLANDS

In 1916, the United States purchased the islands of St. John, St. Thomas, and St. Croix in the Virgin group from Denmark. The transfer of property was slow, and the government did not receive the island's lighthouse sites—some five in number—until 1919. It is not known when the Danes constructed these lights, but apparently they were established sometime just prior to 1919. These lights formed the basis for the lighthouse service in the Virgin Islands.

One of these was the Muhlenfels Point Light Station, located at the entrance to St. Thomas Harbor.

It was a steel skeleton tower, but was later rebuilt by the United States as a white cylindrical tower. Also in St. Thomas harbor are the Judge Bergs range lights, placed there some time between 1911 and 1919.

Just off the island of St. Thomas is the small Buck Island, which has a steel skeleton tower that the Danes placed there at least by 1913.

On St. Croix Island a lighthouse existed in 1919 on Fort Louisa Augusta, an old artillery installation situated on a promontory on the east side of the entrance to Christiansted Harbor. The lighthouse was a brick dwelling with a tower on top, and the Bureau of Lighthouses rebuilt it as a skeleton tower in 1931.

Lighthouses also existed on Southwest Cape at Fredericksted and at Hams Bluff some five miles away. This latter station had a cylindrical steel tower reportedly built in 1915.

As the years went by, a few other lights were added in the Virgin Islands, but they were small lights, usually of the range, harbor, and buoy type.

Through the years the United States has maintained lights at other places in the Caribbean, such as at Quita Sueno Bank (1919) and Little Corn Island (1924) off the coast of Nicaragua. The largest and most important of these lights was the one on Navassa Island about forty miles west of Haiti. An American company once mined phosphate on this two-mile long island which has steep bluffs and deep water close to it. With the opening of the Panama Canal this island increased in importance as a lighthouse site since it lay across the path of vessels bound through the Windward Passage and was the first landfall for vessels bound north from Panama. Strong and irregular currents in the vicinity sometimes forced ships to lay to at night until it was light enough to pick up the coast of Haiti.

In January, 1916, a contractor began building on the island at a site about 250 feet above the sea. The tower was of reinforced concrete and was 147 feet high. Its second-order lens, 395 feet above the sea, went into service the following year. It remained a manned station until 1930 when the Bureau of Lighthouses made the light automatic.

At one time the Lighthouse Board entered into an agreement with several other countries to maintain a lighthouse a considerable distance from United States soil. The United States and several European powers, including England, France, and Spain, entered into a joint agreement with the Sultan of Morocco to erect a light on Cape Spartel near Tangiers that would benefit coastal traffic. The agreement called for the Sultan to build the lighthouse and the other countries to maintain it. Situated opposite Cape Trafalgar on Spain's coast, the Cape Spartel lighthouse displayed its first-order, fixed, white light on October 15, 1864.

# XIII

# Fog Signals, Buoys, and River Lights

*Fog Signals*

Although the popular mind quickly associates fog signals with lighthouses, it may come as a surprise to many to learn that a vast number of light stations do not have fog signals. On the Atlantic coast south of Chesapeake Bay, a fog horn or siren is a rarity. Puerto Rico and Hawaii have no fog problem and, consequently, no warning devices. The principal lighthouses of the Gulf coast do not have fog signals, but there are separate fog warning stations at several harbors along that coast.

On the other hand, most of the lighthouses on the coast north of Chesapeake Bay have fog signals, as do the lighthouses of the Pacific coast and Alaska. Lightships also possess fog warning devices, as do the new Texas-type towers replacing lightships, no matter where their location.

The reason for the presence or absence of fog signals is simply that these warning devices are placed where they are needed, and on those coasts where fog is no problem, there are no fog signals. On the New England, Pacific, and Alaskan coasts, fog is a problem, and as much as 25 percent of the working time at some stations may be devoted to warning vessels traveling in fog. In 1918, for example, Libby Island light on the coast of Maine held the east-coast record for the greatest number of hours its fog horn was in operation: 1,906 hours. On the west coast, Point Reyes at San Francisco reported that their fog signal was active for 2,139

hours. The following year Moose Creek light, Maine, with 1,832 hours, was the record holder, while on the West Coast Alaska's Scotch Cap light was the most active with 1,346 hours.

In any discussion about fog warning devices, one factor should be kept in mind: it is one thing to have a fog signal, and another thing to get the sound to the vessel in the water. When it administered this country's aids to navigation, the Lighthouse Board made a number of studies on how sound travels. These tests were exhaustive and thorough, and certain principles were established. But experimenters learned that many variables, or combinations of variables, inhibit and/or distort the passage of sound and thus reduce the effectiveness of the fog signal. Temperature on the shore, temperature at sea, humidity, direction of wind, speed of wind, and tone of the fog signal are some of these variables. The Lighthouse Board did not find all the answers, nor have those who have subsequently experimented with sound and tried to unravel the mystery of how it travels. Even in this advanced scientific age, the problem has not been solved, and the latest issue of the Coast Guard's *Light List* carries the warning:

Fog signals depend upon the transmission of sound through air. As aids to navigation, they have certain inherent defects that should be considered. Sound travels through air in a variable and frequently unpredictable manner.

The fog cannon at Boston Light Station. The year "1700" is cut into the breech of the gun, indicating that this was probably the actual gun that was the first United States fog signal. This photograph was made in 1914. *U. S. Coast Guard photo 26-LG-5-48B in the National Archives.*

Mariners are . . . warned that fog signals can never be implicitly relied upon, and that the practice of taking soundings of the depth of water should never be neglected.

The nation's first fog signal was at the nation's first lighthouse: Boston light. It was a cannon and first went into service in 1719.

The use of a cannon as a fog signal is not unusual in the history of aids to navigation. The Trinity House in England as late as the 1860's was experimenting with cannon as a fog signal. In the United States, fog guns have been used at such places as West Quoddy Head light in Maine and at Point Bonita in California. The gun at Point Bonita, a twenty-four-pounder cannon obtained from the army, was the first fog signal on the west coast of the United States. During one fog (see pp. 157–158), the lighthouse service employee there was required to fire the cannon at regular intervals for three days and three nights straight, without relief.

Generally, though, for many years the mariner had to take his chances with fog and had to rely upon his own instinct and ability without assistance from a signal. In the 1820's, the situation improved when fog bells were introduced at several New England lighthouses. Over the next several decades other New England lighthouses, but by no means all, received bells.

At first these bells were rung by hand, but around 1860, the Lighthouse Board installed mechanisms to ring them mechanically. Engines were used at first, but the Lighthouse Board found it more practicable and reliable to adapt the clockwork system (i.e., a falling weight was the source of power) to ring the fog bells.

The Lighthouse Service continued to improve the machinery to ring the fog bell, and by the 1920's it had not only an electrically operated bell, but also a device that automatically turned on the sounding equipment when the weather became dangerously thick. The device was a hydroscope, and it was actuated by moisture in the atmosphere. When the humidity approached 100 percent, such as during periods of fog, rain, or snow, the hydroscope became saturated enough to trip the electric switch that turned on the power to the striking device. One of these automatic fog bells was in service at Lazaretto Depot in Baltimore Harbor in the early 1920's when the Francis Scott Key Memorial at nearby Fort McHenry was being dedicated by President Warren G. Harding and other dignitaries. Adding to the color of the occasion were the city of Baltimore's fire boats shooting streams of water into the air. A westerly breeze carried the moisture-laden air to the island on which the lighthouse depot resided. It was sufficient moisture to saturate the hydroscope and turn on the striking apparatus of the 2,000 pound bell. The sonorous notes of the fog signal drifted across the water to punctuate the remarks of the speakers.

Although simple and primitive-looking, fog bells have continued in use through the years. They can be found aboard today's lightships for utilization when the regular fog-signalling machinery breaks down.

In the 1850's, the Lighthouse Board undertook tests and experiments with whistles and trumpets operated by compressed air. One of these was a trumpet invented by C. L. Daboll. The largest model of Daboll's signal was huge. The trumpet was seventeen feet long, ending in a flared mouth thirty-eight inches across. The sound came from compressed air vibrating a reed ten inches long and over two-and-a-half inches wide. The trumpet was a megaphone to magnify the sound. Although used at some light stations, the Daboll trumpet was apparently not adopted for general use by the lighthouse service.

Experiments were also conducted with natural orifices as a source of power for fog signals. The most successful of these tests, all conducted in the nineteenth century, was the one undertaken by the West Coast district inspector, Major Hartman Bache, at the Farallon Island light in 1859. Over a blowhole that had a passage extending to the water's edge, he erected a brick structure that acted as a support and an air conductor. Bache then fitted a locomotive steam whistle to the support's opening. The surge of the sea sent water rushing into the passageway; the water raced forward, forcing air before it, and the air burst through the blowhole and into the whistle, which promptly gave off the sharp toot of the locomotive. Unfortunately, this fog signal did not last long, for a particularly vicious blast of air through the passageway was more than the whistle could handle, and the air, compressed tightly, blew apart the support structure. Undaunted, Major Bache put up another support, and this time he installed a safety valve to relieve the pressure of the more powerful surges. A visitor to the island in the early 1870's described this second fog signal:

The mouth-piece of the trumpet or fog-whistle is fixed against the aperture in the rock, and the breakers, dashing in with a venomous spite, or the huge bulging wave which would dash a ship to pieces and drown her crew in a single effort, now blow the fog-whistle and warns the mariner off. The sound thus produced has been heard at a distance of seven or eight miles. It has a peculiar effect, because it has no regular period; depending upon the irregular coming in of the waves, and upon their similarly irregular force, it is blown somewhat as an idle boy would blow his penny trumpet. It ceases entirely for an hour and a half at low water, when the mouth of the cave or passage is exposed.

Bache's fog signal remained in service for a dozen or more years, being destroyed, reportedly, in 1871. This time, it was not replaced, and in 1880 the Lighthouse Board installed a regular fog siren on the Farallones.

Through the years, the lighthouse service experimented with a variety of devices to warn the sailor during times of reduced visibility. In the mid-1850's,

Fog horn with trumpet extension at Boston Light Station about 1890. This trumpet is even larger than Daboll's largest. Note the man standing in the bell. *U. S. Coast Guard photo 26-LG-5-29, National Archives.*

the board ran tests on the steam whistle, but the experiments proved unsuccessful. Apparently, the unsatisfactory results were due to the small size of the steam whistle used, for a decade or so later the Lighthouse Board, perhaps shown the way by Bache's West Coast experiment, installed the large locomotive-type steam whistle at a number of lighthouses, and these whistles proved so successful that they continued in service well into the twentieth century.

The siren as a fog signal was developed by the United States, and this type of signal first went into service in 1868 at the East Beacon at Sandy Hook, New Jersey. Today, sirens along with diaphones, the latter an invention of the Canadian Lighthouse Service, and diaphragm horns, are the principal sound-type fog signals used by the United States

It might be remarked that these fog signals have not always been received happily by neighbors of lighthouses. On more than one occasion through the years, the administrators of lighthouses have received blistering letters from irate neighbors when a new fog horn or siren went into service. In 1905, for example, when the Lighthouse Board installed a siren to replace the fog horn on Captains Island,

the people of the shore towns around Greenwich, Connecticut, complained vehemently of the new instrument, whose sound one newspaper reporter described as a "screech like an army of panthers, weird and prolonged, gradually lowering in note until after a half minute it becomes the roars of a thousand mad bulls, with intermediate voices suggestive of the wail of a lost soul, the moan of the bottomless pit and the groan of a disabled elevator." It had hardly sounded the first wail on its first night when lights popped on in houses along the shore and people tumbled out of bed to investigate whether there had been a great natural disaster or an invasion by a foreign power—at least, so said the reporter, who had his tongue placed in the vicinity of his cheek.

On occasions such as this, the Lighthouse Board and its successor, the Bureau of Lighthouses, were sympathetic to those who lived near lighthouses. When they received complaints they did what was feasible to pacify neighbors, but at the same time keeping in mind the safety of seagoing traffic, the paramount consideration. Sometimes the problem could be resolved by putting deflectors on the shore side of fog signals. Often nothing could be done,

Making a spar buoy at Portsmouth Buoy Depot, New Hampshire, about 1885. Note, *background,* the side-wheeler tender with walking beam engine. *U. S. Coast Guard photo 26-LG-24-31 in the National Archives.*

and at such times Commissioner George R. Putnam of the Bureau of Lighthouses could only reflect on the words of a reporter who wrote after one of those complaints:

> Russian Hill should put to sea of a foggy night in a fisherman's boat or a three-master. It should see the skipper at the helm, holding his boat to an uncertain course through the blackness of space, while the wet sails drip in endless patter on the deck. There would be minutes of suspense and apprehension; then out of the night would come the siren, so friendly and intimate and re-assuring—almost beautiful. Then Russian Hill could go back and sleep in peace; the siren would have a sweeter tone ever after.

The last thirty or forty years has seen the development of the soundless fog signal: the radiobeacon. Not only is the radiobeacon useful during periods of reduced visibility, but it is also helpful to ships at sea out of sight of land in aiding them to determine their positions, no matter the weather.

George R. Putnam, first and long-time commissioner of lighthouses, considered the adaption and introduction of radio as an aid to navigation as one of the most significant and proudest achievements of his administration.

### Buoys

"Red right returning" is perhaps the first ditty the navigator learns, and it means simply that when returning to port keep the red buoy on your starboard side. In the United States, black and red buoys mark channels into harbors—black buoys designate the left hand side, inbound, and red buoys the right. In addition, white buoys mark anchorages, yellow buoys designate quarantine anchorages, and green buoys usually mark dredging or surveying operations. Such standard coloration has not always been used. Although buoys as aids to navigation have been used since colonial days, it wasn't until 1850 that Congress systematized their coloring.

The country's early buoys were made of wood;

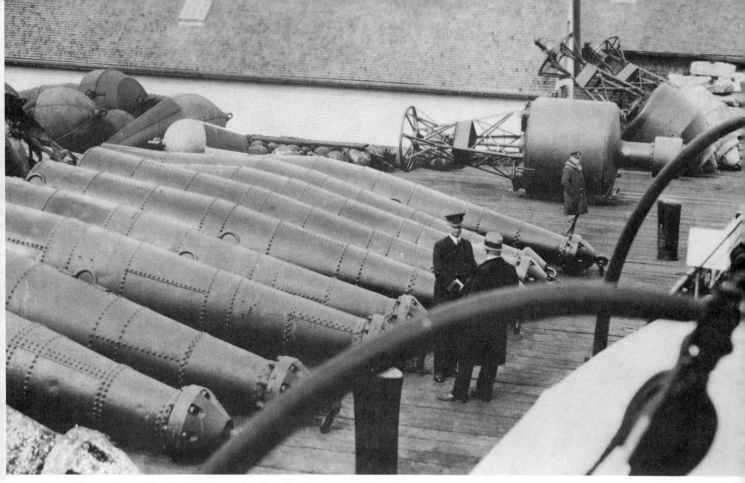

Can and nun buoys *(foreground)*, a whistling buoy, and lighted buoys *(right rear)* at Little Diamond Island De- pot (First District), Maine, in 1930. *U. S. Coast Guard photo 26-LG-3-7A in the National Archives.*

some were fashioned of wooden staves, while oth-ers were simply solid wooden spars. Held in place by heavy sinkers, several marked hazards in Dela-ware Bay at least as early as 1767. As the years wore on, more buoys were placed in navigable waters throughout the country, and by 1842, around 1,000 of them were in service. Twenty-five years later the number had doubled, and in another twenty-two years it had doubled again. By the mid-1930's, over 14,000 buoys of all types were in service.

For many years, wood was the only material used for buoys. And not only were these buoys placed in the calmer waters of harbors and bays, but also in more tempestuous places such as Diamond Shoals and Cape Lookout Shoals. Apparently around the middle of the nineteenth century, iron buoys were introduced, and they began to supplant the ones of wood. The wooden spar buoys held on for many years, though. Nothing more than shafts of wood varying in length from twelve to sixty feet, these buoys were fitted with iron sheaths so they could be moored to a desired location. Although pine and

spruce were used, cedar was the preferred wood for a spar buoy. Being wood, these buoys had to be re-placed regularly and taken ashore, where they could dry out and regain their buoyancy. Also, since they were of wood, they could be damaged easily by vessels, especially by a ship's propellers, which could slice them in two.

Iron buoys were a different story. Made of boiler iron and compartmented so they would not easily sink, an iron buoy could often give as good as it got. The commissioner of lighthouses reported that, once, a crew of a buoy tender raised a missing buoy and found a huge gash in it, and inside were pieces of a ship's propeller blade. The buoy had been sunk, but the vessel suspected of being the culprit had been seen limping away under tow.

At one time buoys were especially susceptible to injury from tugs towing barges. The tugs would cut too short and the buoy would foul the towline, with the result that the buoy would be either damaged, pulled out of position, or run over. Buoys were ex-pensive and the Bureau of Lighthouses grew rather

207

Whistling buoys *(center foreground)* and can buoys *(left and right rear)* beside the carpenter shop at the Staten Island Depot in 1890.  *U. S. Coast Guard photo 26-LG-16-13 in the National Archives.*

tired of replacing them because of the carelessness of tug operators. The bureau had saw-teeth placed on the buoys subjected most often to this abuse, and these teeth were capable of cutting a towline. Those heavy manila towlines were expensive and tugboat skippers were upset over the installation of these cutting devices, but they began passing the buoys with room to spare.

Sometimes buoys shift or break loose, and on these occasions they are not only a hazard to shipping but also misleading to the navigator. Despite the best efforts and the most advanced mooring techniques, buoys even today break loose or are pushed out of position by storms. The Coast Guard in its *Light List* warns the navigator against relying upon a floating aid to maintain its position.

Many buoys that have disappeared from their stations have never been found, but some have had remarkable journeys. One of the buoys at Frying Pan Shoals off the coast of North Carolina broke loose and drifted out into the Gulf Stream. Over a

year and 4,000 miles later, the twelve-ton buoy washed up on the shore of Ireland. The lighthouse service suitably rewarded the Irishmen who retrieved the buoy, and then brought the buoy back to its station at Frying Pan Shoals. In another, and even more remarkable instance, a buoy at Matanilla Shoal in the Florida Straits drifted off its station in a hurricane in 1926 and dragged its mooring chain and sinker into deep water. The buoy, its mooring keeping it half submerged, wandered about for several months before a buoy tender recovered and restored the aid to its station. At another time, a San Francisco buoy drifted for seventeen months before it was retrieved off the coast of Maui in the Hawaiian Islands.

To make buoys more effective, technology has developed various lights and signals for them. Acetylene gas came into use around the turn of the present century to light buoys. A charge of the gas would last quite a long time—in some cases over a year. Sun valves—sensitive to light—turned the flame

One of the large navigational buoys now replacing lightships. This particular buoy, equipped with a 7,500-candlepower light, fog signal, radiobeacon, and radar reflectors, is located where the old Scotland lightship was stationed, just off Sandy Hook, New Jersey. In addition to its navigational equipment, the 104-ton buoy also has instruments to gather meteorological and oceanographic information. *U. S. Coast Guard official photo.*

Eight-day post light, at Sand Shoal Inlet, Virginia, in 1928. The four crosspieces distinguish this light from otherwise similar ones in the vicinity. *U. S. Coast Guard photo 26-LG-24-39 in the National Archives.*

off during the day and back on at night. Incidentally, the development of the acetylene light for buoys led to the decision to adopt this form of automatic light for the Alaskan lighthouses, which thus eliminated the necessity of building expensive structures that had to be manned, since it meant that a light needing service only semi-annually could be placed along that rugged and forbidding coast.

Audible signals on buoys consist of either bells or whistles, both of which are actuated by the motion of the sea. J. M. Courtney is generally given credit for the invention of the whistling buoy, first used in the United States in 1876. His whistle was ingenious, designed to be blown by the air compressed by the up-and-down motion of the sea. Be-

fore development of the whistle buoy, the Lighthouse Board had used a bell boat, which apparently was introduced in 1852. It did not prove satisfactory, but the bell from it was adapted to buoys, and the bell even today clangs out its warning notes with the roll of the sea.

One of the remotest buoys in service is off the coast of Southern California at the Cortez Banks. This whistling buoy marks Bishop Rock nearly ninety miles off the mainland.

*River Lights*

Prior to 1874, traffic on the Mississippi, Missouri, and Ohio rivers was restricted to daylight hours.

## Beating off the rattlesnakes

Twists in the channels and obstacles in the rivers made navigation at night a gamble against highly unfavorable odds. These waterways were the principal transportation arteries into the interior of the United States, and each year $400 million in cargo passed through them. Consequently, when prodded by river transportation interests, Congress hesitated little in authorizing a study of these rivers to determine what aids should be placed on them to make navigation safer, particularly at night.

This survey resulted in the establishment of two lighthouse districts embracing these rivers. On creation of the districts, an inspector and an engineer appointed in each went about locating sites and establishing markers and lights. Each year, more aids were added on these three rivers, as well as on rivers in other lighthouse districts, so that by 1890, over 1,500 post lights illumined nearly 4,500 miles of eighteen rivers and the Puget Sound.

Known as post lights because they were lens lanterns hung from posts, these aids to navigation were relatively easy to maintain. Later, ease of maintenance was further enhanced when a light was developed that held an eight-day supply of oil. These eight-day lights were usually for more remote sites. One keeper, usually a farmer in the neighborhood, maintained several lights, and the devotion of these keepers matched that of keepers who maintained the big coastal lights. In 1912, the keeper of the post lights on the St. Johns River, near Jacksonville, Florida, suffered serious injury when a light's lamp exploded and threw him twenty-two feet to the ground, where he lay unconscious for two and a half hours. Coming to, he could find the lamp nowhere. Despite the agony of his injuries, he crawled nearly 100 yards to his boat, obtained another lamp, crawled back and ascended the twenty-two feet to the top of the post where he put the lamp into position and lighted it. He then worked his pain-racked body back down the post and across the ground to his boat, which he proceeded to row eight miles back to his home, where he received medical treatment and learned that he had, among other things, a contusion of the head and a broken leg.

On southern waters it was not uncommon for post light keepers to encounter rattlesnakes and water moccasins resting on these lights. One keeper tending a South Carolina river light discovered a rattlesnake on the platform supporting the lens. The keeper knocked the snake into the water with an oar. Angered, the rattler swam back to the post and began climbing it toward the keeper. This time, the keeper applied the oar more vigorously to the snake, and the reptile fell back into the water and floated off, apparently mortally wounded.

In the severe floods of 1927, keepers on the Mississippi kept their lights burning even though they had to move some of the lights, and their oil supplies, to a higher location when water rose above the posts. Many of the keepers' own homes were flooded to the roofs at this time.

# XIV

# Epilogue

THE FEEBLE FLAME of the 1716 Boston lighthouse gradually grew brighter, and in time illumined all the shores of the United States. But lighthouses and other aids to navigation have fought heavy seas in getting where they are today.

Now lighthouses are far more efficient, reliable, and effective than they have ever been in their long history. Technological advances have made them so. Powerful lights glow brightly on their towers so that the mariner does not have to peer into the dark seeking a dim beacon from a weak flame. Nor is the mariner nagged by doubts of whether he holds in view the right light, since adequate coastal charts and a *Light List* constantly kept current tell him where specific aids to navigation are, and a system of light characteristics eliminates all possibility of his mistaking one light for another. The mariner also can be reasonably assured that any navigational danger will be marked by some sort of aid, whether by a buoy or a full-fledged lighthouse. Moreover, the mariner has more effective fog signals to rely upon, and, if his vessel is so equipped, radio signals from many light stations can tell him his position no matter how thick the weather. Lighted and colored buoys mark channels guaranteed to be of a certain depth.

Indeed, the mariner has a veritable cornucopia of aids to help him safely navigate the shores, bays, harbors, and rivers of the United States. This condition stands as a monument to the Lighthouse Board, which first set this country on the path to systematically providing adequate and technologically advanced aids to bring a measure of safety to those who earn their livelihood on the sea.

The board's successors—the Bureau of Lighthouses and the U. S. Coast Guard—have carried on the tradition established, and over the years have worked constantly to take advantage of new developments and to adapt them to the needs of navigation. The introduction of radio signals and the more recent construction of Texas-tower lighthouses on former lightship stations are but two of many examples of how these organizations have adapted advancing technology to the needs of the navigator.

Perhaps the key word in the history of these improvements is "technology." Technology has provided the means whereby the navigator goes about his business with a considerable degree of safety. But at the same time, technology has depersonalized aids to navigation and has taken away virtually all of whatever humanness the aids once possessed. Buoys now mark many dangers where once lightships, manned with dedicated but bored men, strained at mooring chains. Grand masonry towers are rarely built now; a steel-skeleton tower is adequate to get a navigational light to the proper height. Auxiliary fog signals swing into action when the main signal fails; consequently, a keeper need no longer express his concern for his brothers by standing all night banging a fog bell with a hammer.

There is no question that today's modern lights are far superior to those of the past and that it is much less expensive to use the latest device to switch lights on automatically than to have a keeper

## A depersonalized service

present to do it manually. In view of this development, and the fact that there is no longer the routine cleaning and maintenance to be performed, there is little justification for lighthouse keepers; indeed, light keeping, at least in the old sense, is rapidly going the way of the dodo bird. It is with sadness that we note this depersonalization of aids to navigation. Our minds can easily conjure up the vision of the neat lighthouse and the faithful keeper, dutifully going about his lonely work, who, when the occasion demands, summons that extra courage to rescue the victims of a storm-aroused sea, despite the rigorousness of the effort or the danger to his own life. It is impossible to summon up any sentiment for an automaton.

Technology, therefore, has shown the way to build and maintain more effective aids to navigation, and in most cases at far less cost. The price that has been paid is depersonalization, which on the surface appears to be a melancholy and dreadful development. But one has to keep in mind that lighthouses, lightships, and other aids have but one purpose and that is to provide for the safety of the seaman and his vessel. Depersonalization of aids to navigation is a cheap price to pay for the measure of safety the technologically advanced lights provide.

The old masonry towers are not disappearing; they are still being utilized by the Coast Guard and will continue to be for as long as they are safe from the sea, easy to maintain, and at the proper place to warn the mariner most effectively.

As these towers become surplus to the needs of the Coast Guard, they are offered to federal, state, and local historical agencies for preservation. As a result, many of these old towers survive today in national, state, county, and city parks to be viewed, visited, and admired by millions of people. Some of these old structures have been restored and refurnished and re-equipped as of the period when they were active aids to navigation. A few lightships, too, are being preserved, so that many generations to come will be able to walk the metal decks of this dying breed of navigational aid.

Lighthouse lenses, tools, and other equipment are being preserved in maritime museums along our seaboards. Unfortunately, there is no full-scale aids-to-navigation museum in the country, and to see the various examples of this type of equipment, one has to travel pretty widely. No one park or museum, for example, has a complete set of the various sizes of Fresnel lenses. Nor is there one place possessing the various types of lamps used in these lenses. This writer knows of no place that preserves one of Winslow Lewis's old lamp-and-reflector lights. Moreover, small tools used to maintain and repair lenses and lamps are rarely seen.

It is unfortunate that more energy and thought are not going into the systematic collecting and preserving of specimens and examples of aids to navigation and related equipment, for, unquestionably, the evolution and technological development of lighthouses and lightships played a significant role in the nation's maritime history.

# The Light List

The *Light List* for the United States' coasts is generally regarded as having been introduced by the Lighthouse Board, and it usually comes as a surprise to learn that the fifth auditor, Stephen Pleasonton, issued a *List of Lighthouses, Beacons, and Floating Lights of the United States*[1] beginning, apparently, in 1838. There are some indications he produced a new list annually, but I have seen only a half dozen or so years represented between 1838 and 1849. We know Pleasonton issued one for 1851, for the 1852 *Light List*, the first one produced by the Lighthouse Board, refers to it.

As aids or guides to mariners, Pleasonton's *Lists of Lighthouses* were not very useful tools. One today can easily imagine the ship captain thumbing through one of these lists and then tossing it aside for the latest edition of the *American Coast Pilot,* which contained more useful information about lighthouses than did the government's own official list. Pleasonton's *List of Lighthouses* was simply not oriented to the requirements of the navigators; consequently, it stands today as further illustration of the abysmal lack of knowledge Pleasonton and his cohorts displayed when it came to the needs of the mariner. In the list, the organization of the lights was by states, which in most cases was all right, but within the states the arrangement was usually chronological.[2] In Maine, for example, the first lighthouse listed

was Portland Head light, which is located considerably down the coast; the West Quoddy Head light, the most northerly of the Maine lighthouses, was in the No. 6 position. The reason for this arrangement was that the first lighthouse erected in Maine was the Portland Head light and the sixth was West Quoddy Head.

Moreover, the geographical listing by states had many inconsistencies. Vermont's Juniper Island light on Lake Champlain, the state's only lighthouse, was included between the listings of coastal lights for Rhode Island and Connecticut. Pennsylvania's Presque Isle lighthouse on Lake Erie was inserted between the coast lights of New Jersey and Delaware, and New York's lights on the Great Lakes and the St. Lawrence River were listed along with that state's coastal lights. Furthermore, New York's listing did not follow the chronological arrangement of the previous states. New York's oldest lighthouse, Montauk Point, occupied, for example, the No. 13 position. Other states, too, showed inconsistencies. New Jersey reflected a geographical listing. North Carolina, South Carolina, and Georgia had neither geographical nor chronological order to their listings. Then to add further confusion, following Georgia came the listings for Ohio, Louisiana, Florida, Michigan, Alabama, and Mississippi, in that order.

Another defect of Pleasonton's *List of Lighthouses* was its failure to recognize the lighthouse as a useful daymark to navigators. The list gave no description, such as color or shape, of the light towers that would have assisted a navigator as he plotted his course along a coast.

---

[1] For 1838 and a few subsequent years this publication had a slightly different title: *The Lighthouses, Beacons, and Floating Lights of the United States.*

[2] Light numbers on the maps in this book correspond to the order in which lights are mentioned in the text.

## Bureaucracy vs. the navigator

As new lighthouses were built on the coasts, each was added on to the end of its state's listing. When aids were first built in previously unlisted states of the Great Lakes, those states, with their lights, were added at the end of the previous year's listing.

In trying to surmise what must have been the rationale behind the organization of this first light list, one has but two alternatives to consider: (1) the people who compiled the list did not know what they were doing, or (2) they were deliberately attempting to get out a light list that would be of little use to the mariner.

Over the years, as can be seen by the 1848 *List of Lighthouses* printed herein, few changes occurred to make the list more useful to the seaman. This list, by its own statement, had been "Carefully Revised and Corrected," and there was some improvement. It had the states running geographically down the coast to Louisiana, following which were the Great Lakes states. Occasionally, information was given on the type of construction material used in light towers, although little effort still was made to describe these structures so that they would be more easily recognized as daymarks. More information was given about the thirty-two "light-boats" listed, including tonnage, type of lights and their elevation above the sea, and special remarks, such as noting the two iron-hulled light vessels then in service.[3] Except for these few improvements, the *List of Lighthouses* had changed little in ten years of "experience."

The Lighthouse Board took over aids to navigation in 1852 and almost immediately went about revising the *List of Lighthouses, Lighted Beacons, and Floating Lights of the United States.* The board issued its first list as of July 1, 1852, and it embraced forty-seven pages and carried 357 lighthouses, beacons, and light vessels. So quickly had the board turned to the problem of the *Light List* that it had to rely on the fifth auditor's compilation of the preceding year. The board did, however, substitute the latitude and longitude of lighthouses when they had been determined by the Coast Survey and the Topographical Engineers.

Most important, the board in its first issue listed the lighthouses and lightships geographically, beginning with the light at West Quoddy Head, Maine. Primary seacoast lights were shown in bold letters, and lightships were indicated in italics. The lights of the Great Lakes were listed by lake.

Just as important, the board gave information on the light tower, such as color, and on unusual features of the light station and its surrounding land, so that navigators could more readily use the lighthouses as daymarks. The board also included a notation on the existence of a fog signal, if any, and remarks on peculiar hazards in the waters near a light station.

Over the next four years, the Lighthouse Board, to render the *List* even more useful to the mariner, continued to revise it, making changes in the format and correcting errors of past editions. In 1854, the publication showed Pacific Coast lighthouses for the first time, and new columns appeared for fog signals and order of lenses.

One of the important additions in the 1854 *Light List* reflected the earnest desire of the board to improve the nation's lighthouses. On the last page of the booklet was a statement by Commodore Shubrick, chairman of the Lighthouse Board, soliciting seamen to report "cases in which lights are not lighted punctually at sunset and extinguished at sunrise, or in which they are not properly attended to during the night, or in which light-vessels and buoys are out of position. . . ."[4]

By 1856, more information on the description of lighthouses and lightships was being included, and a year or two later a column showing the height of the focal plane of the light above sea level was included. By 1860, the list had grown so large that the board felt it better to carry the lights of the Great Lakes in a separate publication. Around 1870, each lighthouse district began issuing its own buoy list. And through the years to the present the *Light List* continued to be revised as information changed and as the needs of the navigator altered with changing technology.

The *Light List* today consists of five volumes (one for the Mississippi and Ohio Rivers), and each volume runs between 200 and 300 pages. In size it is certainly a far cry from the fourteen-page *List of Lighthouses* Pleasonton issued in 1838. Although the present list is a direct descendant of the 1838 one, it would, if it were possible, blush with embarrassment at its ancestor.

The 1848 list was somewhat of an improvement over the 1838 one, and it reflects the best effort of Pleasonton. At the time, though, it must have been virtually a useless publication, and today it is a historical curiosity. It does, however, give a good picture of the lighthouses in service in the middle of the nineteenth century just prior to the revolution that attended the coming of the Lighthouse Board. Incidentally, many of the light stations listed here are still in existence.

*Overleaf,* for comparison, appear pages from the early Light List and the present-day version.

---

[3] Also, in 1848 Pleasonton issued three maps of the United States coasts showing the location of the various lighthouses and light vessels. One map embraced the coast from Maine through Virginia, a second included the southern states and the Gulf Coast, and the third map depicted the light stations on the Great Lakes.

[4] This statement, dated October 14, 1852, may have been included in the 1853 *Light List.*

| No. | State, and name of light. | Place on which the light is situated. | Latitude. Deg. min. sec. | Longitude. Deg. min. sec. | Number of lamps. | Size of reflectors. Inch. | Fixed or revolving. | Time of revolution. Min. sec. | Distance at which they are visible in clear weather. Miles. | Height of lantern above the sea or highwater mark. Feet in. | Height of towers, from base to lantern. Feet in. | Year in which built. | Remarks. |
|---|---|---|---|---|---|---|---|---|---|---|---|---|---|
| | FLORIDA. | | | | | | | | | | | | |
| 194 | St. Augustine | On N. end of Anastasia Island, and S. side of entrance to St. Augustine. | 29 52 18 | 81 25 00 | 10 | 14 | Fixed | - | 16 | 70 00 | 40 00 | 1823 | |
| 195 | Musquito Inlet | Entrance of said Inlet, S. E. St. Augustine. | - | - | - | - | - | - | - | - | - | 1834 | Undermined by the sea, and destroyed. |
| 196 | St. John's River | Near mouth St. John's River, S. side of entrance. | 30 20 30 | 81 33 00 | 14 | 15 | Fixed | - | 16 | 65 00 | 65 00 | 1829 | Rebuilt in 1834. |
| 197 | Cape Carnaveral | On said Cape, S. S. E. of St. Augustine. | - | - | 15 | 21 | Revolving | - | 16 | 55 00 | 55 00 | 1847 | |
| 198 | Cape Florida | Off S. E. point of Florida, or on Key Biscayne. | 25 41 00 | 80 05 00 | 17 | 21 | - | - | 16 | 65 00 | 65 00 | 1825 | Burnt by hostile Indians in 1836; rebuilt in 1846. |
| 199 | Dry Tortugas | On Bush Island, one of the westernmost of the Florida Reef. | 24 37 20 | 82 52 22 | 17 | 21 | Fixed | - | 16 | 70 00 | 65 00 | 1825 | Refitted with new lantern and large plate glass, &c., in 1846. |
| 200 | Sand Key, | About 8½ miles S. W. by S. of Key West. | 24 28 30 | 81 49 30 | 14 | 21 | Revolving | 54 | 20 | 70 00 | 65 00 | 1826 | Refitted anew in 1843; destroyed by tornado in 1846. |
| 201 | Key West, | Key West Island, Florida Reef, S. Westerly of Cape Sable. | 24 32 32 | 81 48 30 | 13 | 21 | Fixed | - | 17 | 67 00 | 49 00 | 1825 | Destroyed by tornado in 1846, and rebuilt on new site in 1847. |
| 202 | Cape St. George | On said Cape, and about 2½ miles East of West pass to St. George's Sound. | - | - | 15 | 16 | Fixed | - | 15 | - | 65 00 | 1847 | In place of one on St. George's Island. |
| 203 | St. Mark's | East side of entrance to St. Mark's Harbor. | 30 04 00 | 84 11 00 | 15 | 15 | Fixed | - | 16 | 73 00 | - | 1829 | Refitted in 1844. |
| 204 | Pensacola | South side of entrance to Pensacola Bay, and N. W. of Fort on St. Rosa Island. | 30 20 48 | 87 17 00 | 10 | 16 | Revolving | 1 10 | 17 | 80 00 | 40 00 | 1824 | Refitted with new lantern, plate glass, &c., in 1847. |
| 205 | Amelia Island | South side of entrance to St. Mary's River, and on N. end of said Island. | 30 42 00 | 81 36 30 | 14 | 15 | Revolving | - | 15 | - | 50 00 | 1838 | |
| 206 | Cape St. Blas | On Cape St. Blas, about 2 miles from its south point. | - | - | 10 | 15 | Revolving | - | 15 | 65 00 | 65 00 | 1847 | In place of the former one at St. Joseph's Bay. |
| 207 | Dog Island | On said Island, E. side of middle entrance to St. George's Sound. | 29 46 20 | 84 38 09 | 14 | 16 | Revolving | 3 00 | 15 | - | 40 00 | 1838 | New frame tower in 1843, the old one having been injured in the gale of 1842 |
| 208 | Egmont Key | On said Key or Island, entrance of Tampa Bay. | - | - | 13 | 21 | Fixed | - | - | - | 40 00 | 1847–8 | |
| | ALABAMA. | | | | | | | | | | | | |
| 209 | Mobile Point | On Mobile Point, East side of entrance to Mobile Bay. | 30 13 42 | 87 58 00 | 21 | 16 | Revolving | 1 00 | 15 to 18 | 55 00 | 40 00 | 1821 | Refitted in 1835. |
| 210 | Choctaw Point | On Choctaw Point, a little S. of Mobile. | 30 44 00 | 88 12 00 | 11 | 14 | Fixed | - | 14 | - | 40 00 | 1831 | |
| 211 | Sand Island | About 3 miles S. S. Westerly from Mobile Point. | 30 13 00 | 88 10 58 | 14 | 16 | Fixed | - | 15 | - | 50 00 | 1838 | |

The 1848 list–two pages of which are here faced by a corresponding page from the current *Light List*–originally consisted of thirty-nine pages, and was preceded by a five-page, alphabetical index. As will be obvious from a comparison of the lists, the 1848 version lacked system: it was arranged neither geographically (the most logical approach from the mariner's viewpoint), nor chronologically (an approach that might conceivably make sense to an administrator who had not analyzed the purpose of what he was administrating). Note also that Pleasonton tended to exaggerate the distance his lights could be seen, apparently because he did not allow for the curvature of the earth. Compare his range of visibility for the Sand Key light (*above*) with the "Geographical Range" for the light given by the Coast Guard (*left*); the present light is even higher above the sea than the one displayed in Pleasonton's day.

*Above*, two pages from the fifth auditor's *List of Light-Houses, Beacons and Floating Lights of the United States in Operation on the 1st of July, 1848, with a Statement of Their Location, Heights, Distance at which They are Visible in Clear Weather, &c, &c.* From Record Group 26, National Archives.

*Left*, a page from U. S. Coast Guard, *Light List*, 1970.

| (1) No. | (2) Name / Characteristic | (3) Location Lat. N., Long. W. | (4) Nominal Range / Intensity | (5) Geographic Range | (6) Structure Ht. above ground / Ht. above water | (7) Remarks / Year |
|---|---|---|---|---|---|---|
| | | | | | | **SEVENTH DISTRICT** |
| | | **FLORIDA** | | | | |
| | **SEACOAST** | | | | | |
| 91 *J3006* | **SAND KEY LIGHT**...... Gp. Fl. W., 4 R. sectors, 10ˢ. 0.5ˢfl., 1.5ˢec. 0.5ˢfl., 7.5ˢec. 2 flashes | In center on low white sandy key, on seaward side of reefs. 24 27.2   81 52.7 | 9W 900 / 6R 200 | 16 | Brown, square, pyramidal skeleton tower inclosing stair cylinder and square dwelling; pile foundation. 120 / 109 | White from 199° to 231°, 270° to 072, 085° to 118° and 129° to 189°, red in intervening sectors. 1826–1853 |
| | (Chart 1252) | | | | | |
| | Western Dry Rocks Daybeacon K... | In 1 foot. 24 26.8   81 55.6 | | | Brown square daymark on pile. | |
| | Coalbin Rock Buoy CB............ | In 16 feet, on south side of shoal. | | | Red and black horizontal bands; nun. | White reflector. |
| 92 *J3052* | Cosgrove Shoal Light............ Fl. W., 6ˢ(1ˢfl) | In 14 feet. 24 27.5   82 11.2 | 10 1,300 | 12 | Small black house on red hexagonal skeleton tower on piles. 49 | 1935 White reflector. |
| | Marquesas Rock Buoy MR ...... | In 12 feet, on south side of reef. | | | Red and black horizontal bands; nun. | White reflector. |
| 93 | Twenty-Eight Foot Shoal Lighted Bell Buoy. I. Qk. Fl. W. | On southwest side of shoal. 24 25.7   82 25.4 | 150 | | Red and black horizontal bands. | Nun station buoy with white reflector. |
| | Halfmoon Shoal Wreck Buoy WR4A... | In 24 feet, 135 yards 239° from last reported position of wreck. 24 33.5   82 28.5 | | | Red nun. | Marks wreck of S. S. VALBANERA. Red reflector. |
| | (Charts 585, 1351) | | | | | |
| 94 *J3056* | Rebecca Shoal Light............ Gp. Fl. W., R. sectors, 15ˢ. 1ˢfl., 2ˢec. 1ˢfl., 2ˢec. 1ˢfl., 8ˢec. 3 flashes | In 12 feet, on south west edge of shoal. 24 34.7   82 35.2 | 9W 1,000 / 6R 200 | 13 | Small white house and square skeleton tower on brown pile foundation. 66 | Red from 254° to 302°. 1886–1953 |
| 95 *J3060* | **DRY TORTUGAS LIGHT** ........ Fl. W., 20ˢ. Resident Personnel. | On Loggerhead Key. 24 38.0   82 55.2 | 28 2,000,000 | 19 | Conical tower, lower half white, upper half black. 157 / 151 | RADIOBEACON: Antenna 365 feet 233° from light tower. See p. XVII for method of operation. 1826–1858 |
| | Tortugas Sea Buoy 8 ......... | In 21 feet, at southwest end of shoal off Garden Key. | | | Red nun | Red reflector. |
| 96 | Tortugas Outside Lighted Whistle Buoy 8A. Fl. W., 2.5ˢ | In 66 feet. 24 34.3   82 57.2 | 300 | | Red | |
| | Loggerhead Reef Buoy 10 ......... | In 48 feet, at southwest end of reef. | | | Red nun | Red reflector. |
| | (For Garden Key, see No. 945) | | | | | |
| | **GULF COAST** | | | | | |
| 97 *J3068* | Pulaski Shoal Light............ Fl. W., 6ˢ(1ˢfl) | In 15 feet, on east side of shoal. 24 41.6   82 46.4 | 10 1,400 | 12 | Small black house on hexagonal pyramidal skeleton tower on piles. 49 | 1935 |
| 98 | New Ground Rocks Lighted Whistle Buoy. 12. Fl. W., 4ˢ | In 36 feet, west end of shoal. | 200 | | Red | Nun station buoy with red reflector. |
| | Ellis Rock Buoy 1A ......... | In 7 feet, on rock. 24 39.0   82 11.0 | | | Black can | Green reflector. |
| 98.55 | Tortugas Shrimp Bed Lighted Buoy B. Fl. W., 4ˢ | In 84 feet. 24 46.3   82 23.1 | | | Orange and white vertical stripes. | Ra ref. Private aid. |

# References

## CHAPTER 1

Brown, Lloyd A., *The Story of Maps* (New York: c. 1964).

Heap, D. P., *Ancient and Modern Lighthouses* (Boston: 1889).

Majdalany, Fred, *The Eddystone Light* (Boston: Houghton Mifflin Co., 1960).

Morison, Samuel Eliot, *John Paul Jones: A Sailor's Biography* (Boston: 1964).

Putnam, George R., *Lighthouses and Lightships of the United States* (Boston: 1917).

Reynaud, Leonce, *Memoir Upon the Illumination and Beaconage of the Coasts of France*, translated by Peter C. Hains (Washington: G.P.O., 1876).

Scott, Kenneth, "The Sandy Hook Lighthouse," *The American Neptune* 25, no. 2 (April, 1965).

Smith, Fitz-Henry, Jr., *The Story of the Boston Light* (Boston: Privately Printed, 1911).

Smith, Milton B., "The Lighthouse on Tybee Island," *The Georgia Historical Quarterly* 49, no. 3 (Sept., 1965).

Stevenson, D. Alan, *The World's Lighthouses Before 1820* (London: 1959).

U. S. Coast Guard, *Historically Famous Lighthouses* (Washington: 1957).

## CHAPTER 2

Anonymous, *Lighthouse Construction and Illumination*, bound in *General Technology*, vol. 4, Library of Congress.

Clipping File, Oil, R. G. 26, National Archives.

*12th Cong., 1st Sess., Doc. No. 168, American State Papers, Commerce and Navigation, Class IV,* vol. 7 (Washington: Gales and Seaton, 1832).

*25th Congress, 2nd Session, Sen. Doc. No. 14* (Serial #314).

*25th Congress, 2nd Session, Sen. Doc. No. 138* (Serial #315).

*25th Congress, 2nd Session, Sen. Doc. No. 506* (Serial #319).

*25th Congress, 3rd Session, House Doc. No. 24* (Serial #345).

*25th Congress, 3rd Session, House Doc. No. 183* (Serial #422).

Conklin, Irving, *Guideposts of the Sea* (New York: Macmillan Co., 1939).

Fifth Auditor, "Lighthouse Letters," March 2, 1847, to July 24, 1847; January 1, 1838, to October 17, 1838; June 10, 1835, to February 15, 1837, all in Record Group 26, National Archives.

Holland, F. Ross, Jr., "A History of the Bodie Island Light Station," Division of History, National Park Service, February 1, 1967.

————, "A History of the Cape Hatteras Light Station," Division of History, National Park Service, September 30, 1968.

Johnson, Arnold B., *The Modern Lighthouse Service* (Washington: G.P.O., 1890). (Johnson was the long-time chief clerk of the Lighthouse Board, a position he took in 1869 after some years of service in other agencies of the Treasury Department. In 1908, at the age of seventy-three, the Lighthouse Board assigned him as superintendent of the Fifth Lighthouse District under the district inspector. With the reorganization of the lighthouse service in 1910 he became superintendent of the Seventh District. Nine months later he relinquished these duties to take over as assistant superintendent of the Second District. He died in 1915, aged eighty. See *Lighthouse Service Bulletin* 1, no. 38, February, 1915.)

Lewis, Steven H., "Historic Structures Report: Jones Point Lighthouse," Division of History Studies, National Park Service.

Morison, Samuel Eliot, *Old Bruin: Commodore Matthew C. Perry* (Boston: Little Brown & Co., c. 1967).

Putnam, George R., *Lighthouses and Lightships of the United States* (Boston: Houghton Mifflin Co., 1917).

*Report of the Officers Constituting the Lighthouse Board . . . 1851*, 32nd Congress, 1st Session, House Ex. Doc. No. 55.

Stevenson, Alan, *The World's Lighthouses Before 1820* (London: Oxford University Press, 1959).

Updike, Richard W., "Winslow Lewis and the Lighthouses," *The American Neptune* 28, no. 1 (January, 1968).

## References

### CHAPTER 3

Anonymous, *Our Lighthouse Establishment* (c. 1856), bound in *General Technology,* vol. 4, Library of Congress.

Burstyn, Harold L., *At the Sign of the Quadrant: An Account of the Contributions to American Hydrography Made by Edmund March Blunt and His Sons* (Mystic, Conn.: The Marine Historical Association, 1957).

Campbell, John F., *History and Bibliography of The New American Practical Navigator and the American Coast Pilot* (Salem: Peabody Museum, 1964).

Capron, Walter C., *The U. S. Coast Guard* (New York: Franklin Watts, Inc., c. 1965).

*25th Congress, 2nd Session, House Doc. No. 19* (Serial #322).

*25th Congress, 2nd Session, House Doc. No. 27* (Serial #322).

*25th Congress, 2nd Session, House Doc. No. 41* (Serial #322).

*25th Congress, 2nd Session, House Rept. No. 741* (Serial #410).

*25th Congress, 2nd Session, Sen. Doc. No. 138* (Serial #315).

*25th Congress, 3rd Session, House Doc. No. 24* (Serial #345).

*25th Congress, 3rd Session, House Doc. No. 158* (Serial #158).

*25th Congress, 3rd Session, House Doc. No. 160* (Serial #347).

*27th Congress, 2nd Session, House Rept. No. 811* (Serial #410).

*28th Congress, 1st Session, House Doc. No. 38* (Serial #441).

*32nd Congress, 1st Session, Sen. Ex. Doc. No. 28* (Serial #617).

*62nd Congress, 2nd Session, House Doc. No. 670* (Serial #6298).

Heap, D. P., *Ancient and Modern Lighthouses* (Boston: Ticknor and Co., 1889).

Holland, F. Ross, Jr., "A History of the Bodie Island Light Station," Division of History, National Park Service, February 1, 1967.

———, "A History of the Cape Hatteras Light Station," Division of History, National Park Service, September 30, 1968.

Lewis, Winslow, *Review of the Report of I. W. P. Lewis on the State of Lighthouses on the Coast of Maine and Massachusetts* (Boston: Tuttle and Dennett, 1843).

Macy, Robert H., "Consolidation of the Lighthouse Service with the Coast Guard," *United States Naval Institute Proceedings* 66, no. 1 (January, 1940).

Putnam, George R., "Beacons of the Sea," *National Geographic Magazine,* vol. 24 (January, 1913).

———, *Sentinel of the Coasts: The Log of a Lighthouse Engineer* (New York: W. W. Norton & Co., c. 1937).

Updike, Richard W., "Winslow Lewis and the Lighthouses," *The American Neptune* 28, no. 1 (January, 1968).

U. S. Bureau of Lighthouses, *Lighthouse Service Bulletin,* vol. 1, nos. 1, 8, 38; vol. 2, no. 15; vol. 3, no. 1.

U. S. Lighthouse Board, *Annual Report, 1903; 1910* (Washington: G.P.O., 1903, 1910).

*Washington* (D. C.) *Federal Times,* July 23, 1969.

Willoughby, Malcolm F., *Lighthouses of New England* (Boston: T. O. Metcalf & Co., 1929).

### CHAPTER 4

*25th Congress, 3rd Session, House Doc. No. 24* (Serial #345).

*32nd Congress, 1st Session, Sen. Exec. Doc. No. 28* (Serial #617).

Heap, D. P., *Ancient and Modern Lighthouses* (Boston: Ticknor & Co., 1889).

Holland, F. Ross, Jr., "A History of the Cape Hatteras Light Station," Division of History, National Park Service, September 30, 1968.

———, "Lighting the West Coast: The Story of the Building of the Pacific Coast's First Sixteen Lighthouses," Ms in possession of the author.

———, *The Old Point Loma Lighthouse* ([San Diego]: Cabrillo Historical Assn., 1968).

Hussey, John A., "Point Pinos Lighthouse," *Early West Coast Lighthouses* (San Francisco: Book Club of California, 1964).

Johnson, Arnold B., *The Modern Lighthouse Service* (Washington: G.P.O., 1890).

Maxwell, True H., "Santa Barbara Lighthouse," *Early West Coast Lighthouses* (San Francisco: Book Club of California, 1964).

Nordoff, Charles, "The Lighthouses of the United States," *Harpers Magazine,* vol. 38 (March, 1874).

Putnam, George R., *Lighthouses and Lightships of the United States* (Boston: Houghton Mifflin Co., 1917).

———, *Sentinels of the Coasts* (New York: W. W. Norton, c. 1937).

Ragusin, Anthony V., "Lighthouse Tended by Woman," *The Mentor*, vol. 13 (July, 1925).

U. S. Bureau of Lighthouses, *Lighthouse Service Bulletin*, vols. 1 & 2.

U. S. Coast Guard, *Historically Famous Lighthouses* ([Washington]: G.P.O., 1957).

U. S. Lighthouse Board, *Instructions and Directions to Guide Light-House Keepers and Others Belonging to the Light-House Establishment* (Washington: 1870).

U. S. Lighthouse Board, Letters to 5th Dist. Inspector, 1860-1871; Lighthouse Board, Letters to 5th Dist. Engineer, 1868-1873; Lighthouse Board, Letters to Inspectors, 12th L.H. Dist., July 1, 1889-Dec. 31, 1891; Clipping Files, Civil Service, Nantucket (Great Point) Light Station, and Uniforms and Civil Service; and Ledgers entitled "Lighthouse Keepers and Assistant Keepers," and "Records of Lightkeepers," for the various lighthouse districts, all of the above in Record Group 26, National Archives.

U. S. Lighthouse Board, *Management of Lens Apparatus and Lamps* (n.d.).

U. S. Lighthouse Board, *Rules, Regulations, and General Instructions, 1857* (Washington: 1857).

U. S. Lighthouse Board, *Notes on Inspecting Lights, Lampists' Duties, Masters of Tenders, Masters of Supply Vessels, Provisions for Crews* (Washington: 1871).

U. S. Lighthouse Board, *Instructions to Light-Keepers, July, 1881* (Washington: G.P.O., 1881).

U. S. Lighthouse Board, *Instructions* (1853).

[U. S. Lighthouse Board], *Routine Duties* (1853).

The *Washington Post*, March 13, 1966.

## CHAPTER 5

Gibbs, James A., *Sentinels of the North Pacific* (Portland: Binfords & Mort, 1955).

Heap, D. P., *Ancient and Modern Lighthouses* (Boston: Ticknor & Co., 1889).

Hemmingway, William, "The Woman of the Light," *Harpers Weekly*, vol. 53 (August 4, 1909).

Holland, F. Ross, Jr., "A History of the Bodie Island Light Station," Division of History, National Park Service, February 1, 1967.

———, "Lighting the West Coast: The Story of the Building of the Pacific Coast's First Sixteen Lighthouses," Ms in possession of the author.

Kobbe, G., "Life in a Lighthouse," *Century*, vol. 47 (n.s.vol. 25) (January, 1894).

MacDonald, A. P., "Children of the Lighthouses," *Outlook*, vol. 88 (January 18, 1908).

Manning, Gordon P., *Life in the Colchester Reef Lighthouse* (Shelburne, Vt.: Shelburne Museum, c. 1958).

Munro, Kirk, "From Light to Light," *Scribner's Magazine*, vol. 20 (January, 1896).

Piper, Jean, " 'Mind the Light, Katie!'—and for 34 Years She Minded It," *American Magazine*, vol. 100 (October, 1925).

Putnam, George R., *Lighthouses and Lightships of the United States* (Boston: Houghton Mifflin Co., 1917).

Sterling, Robert Thayer, *Lighthouses of the Maine Coast and the Men Who Keep Them* (Brattleboro, Vt.: Stephen Daye Press, 1935).

Tape interview of Mrs. Beulah Coppage by Miss Paige Lawrence, April, 1967, copies at Cabrillo National Monument and Acadia National Park.

U. S. Bureau of Lighthouses, *Lighthouse Service Bulletin*, May 1, 1917; February 1, March 1, and May 1, 1918.

U. S. Commissioner of Lighthouses, *Annual Report, 1912*.

U. S. Lighthouse Board, *Annual Report, 1876; 1878; 1879; 1884; 1885* (Washington: G.P.O.).

U. S. Lighthouse Board, Letters to 5th District Inspector, 1874-1881, and 1881-1885; and Clipping Files, Medals of Honor, Cape Elizabeth Light Station, Me., and Carysfort Light Station, Fla., all in Record Group 26, National Archives.

## CHAPTER 6

Adamson, H. C., *Keepers of the Lights* (New York: Greenberg, c. 1955).

Baker, William A., "U. S. Light-Vessel No. 50, Columbia River," *The American Neptune*, vol. 9, no. 4 (October, 1949).

Chatterton, E. Keble, *The Romance of the Ship* (London: Seeley, Service & Co., Ltd., 1925).

*25th Congress, 2nd Session, Senate Doc. No. 14* (Serial #314).

*25th Congress, 3rd Session, House Doc. No. 24* (Serial #345).

*32nd Congress, 1st Session, Sen. Ex. Doc. No. 28* (Serial #617).

Cook, George Crouse, "The Evolution of the Light-

# References

ship," *Transactions, Society of Naval Architects and Marine Engineers,* vol. 21 (1913).

Gibbs, James A., *Sentinels of the North Pacific* (Portland, Ore.: Binfords and Mort, 1955).

Heap, D. P., *Ancient and Modern Lighthouses* (Boston, Ticknor & Co., 1889).

Holland, F. Ross, Jr., "A History of the Cape Hatteras Light Station," Division of History, National Park Service, September 30, 1968.

Kobbe, Gustav, "Life on the South Shoal Lightship," *Century,* vol. 20, no. 4 (August, 1891).

Putnam, George R., *Lighthouses and Lightships of the United States* (Boston: Houghton Mifflin Co., 1917).

Ridgely-Nevitt, Cedric, "A Light-vessel of 1823 built by Henry Eckford," *American Neptune,* vol. 5, no. 2 (April, 1945).

Stevenson, D. Alan, *The World's Lighthouses Before 1820* (London: 1959).

The following clipping files from Record Group 26, National Archives:

| | | |
|---|---|---|
| Lightship No. 1 | Lightship No. 18 | Lightship No. 37 |
| Lightship No. 2 | Lightship No. 21 | Lightship No. 48 |
| Lightship No. 5 | Lightship No. 23 | Lightship No. 50 |
| Lightship No. 7 | Lightship No. 24 | Lightship No. 51 |
| Lightship No. 8 | Lightship No. 25 | Lightship No. 55 |
| Lightship No. 9 | Lightship No. 29 | Lightship No. 58 |
| Lightship No. 10 | Lightship No. 30 | Lightship No. 66 |
| Lightship No. 11 | Lightship No. 31 | Lightship No. 67 |
| Lightship No. 12 | Lightship No. 32 | Lightship No. 70 |
| Lightship No. 15 | Lightship No. 34 | Lightship No. 80 |
| Lightship No. 17 | Lightship No. 35 | |

Ambrose Channel Lightvessel
*Ascension,* schooner
Brandywine Shoals Lightvessel
Eighth District Cross Rip Lightvessel
Fishing Rip Lightvessel
Martins Industry Lightvessel
Wolf Trap Lightvessel

U. S. Lighthouse Bureau, *Lighthouse Service Bulletin,* vol. 1, nos. 2, 3, 24, 26, 30, 34, 35, 46; vol. 2, nos. 16, 17; vol. 3, no. 4.

U. S. Navy Department, *Dictionary of American Naval Fighting Ships,* vol. 1 (Washington: G.P.O.: 1964).

## CHAPTER 7

Adamson, H. C., *Keepers of the Lights.*

Anonymous, "The Highland Light," *The Atlantic Monthly,* vol. 14, no. 86 (December, 1864).

Boucher, Jack E., *Atlantic City's Historic Absecon Lighthouse* (Somers Point, N. J.: Atlantic County Historical Society, c. 1964).

*25th Congress, 3rd Session, House Doc. No. 24* (Serial #345).

*32nd Congress, 1st Session, Sen. Ex. Doc. No. 28* (Serial #617).

Hugins, Walter, "Statue of Liberty National Monument: Its Origin, Development, and Administration," National Park Service, 1958.

Johnson, Arnold B., *The Modern Lighthouse Service* (Washington: G.P.O., 1890).

Leonard, Thomas H., *From Indian Trail to Electric Rail* (Atlantic Highland, N. J.: The Atlantic Highland Journal, 1923).

North Scituate Beach Improvement Assn., *A Description of the First Minot's Ledge Lighthouse, with an Account of the Great Storm of April 14-19, 1851, by Which the Lighthouse Was Destroyed* (1914).

Putnam, George R., *Lighthouses and Lightships of the United States* (Boston: Houghton Mifflin Co., 1917).

Smith, Samuel Stell, *Sandy Hook and the Land of the Navesink* (Monmouth Beach, N. J.: Philip Freneau Press, 1963).

Snow, Edward Rowe, *Famous Lighthouses of America* (New York: Dodd, Mead, and Co., 1955).

————, *Famous Lighthouses of New England* (Boston: Yankee Publishing Co., 1945).

Texaco, Inc., *Cruising Charts Nos. 1-3* (Rand McNally & Co., 1968).

U. S. Coast Guard, *Historically Famous Lighthouses* (Washington: G.P.O., 1957).

U. S. Coast Guard, *Light List, Atlantic and Gulf Coasts of the United States* (Washington: G.P.O., 1951).

Willoughby, Malcolm F., *Lighthouses of New England* (Boston: T. O. Metcalf Co., 1929).

The following light station clipping files from Record Group 26, National Archives:

| | | |
|---|---|---|
| Absecon | Cape Henlopen | Gay Head |
| Annisquam | Cape May | Ipswich |
| Baker Island | Cape Poge | Isle of Shoals |
| Barnegat | Chatham Harbor | Libby Island |
| Bass Harbor Head | Clarks Point | Little Gull Island |
| Bear Island | Cross Ledge | Long Point |
| Beavertail | Derby's Wharf | Marblehead |
| Black Rock | Dice Head | Matinicus Rock |
| Block Island | Eatons Neck | Minots Ledge |
| Boon Island | Falkners Island | Monhegan Island |
| Boston | Fire Island | Montauk Point |
| Brandywine Shoal | Fort Thompkins | Moose Peak |
| Brant Point | Fort Wadsworth | Morgan's Point |
| Cape Ann | Fourteen Foot | Mount Desert Rock |
| Cape Cod | Bank | Nantucket (Great |
| Cape Elizabeth | Franklin Island | Point) |

Nauset Beach
Navesink
Newburyport
Harbor
New Haven
Harbor
Owls Head
Pemaquid Point
Petit Manan
Point Judith

Portland Head
Race Point
Robbins Reef
Saddleback Ledge
St. Croix
Sands Point
Sandy Hook
Sankaty Head
Scituate
Seguin Island

Ship John Shoal
Statue of Liberty
Stonington
Breakwater
West Quoddy
Head
Whaleback
Whitehead Island
Wood Island

## CHAPTER 8

Bearss, Edwin C., "General Background Study and Historical Base Map, Assateague Island National Seashore," Division of History, National Park Service, December 18, 1968.

Burgess, Robert H., *The Story of Hooper's Strait Lighthouse,* pamphlet published by the Chesapeake Bay Maritime Museum.

Burgess, Robert H., ed., *Coasting Captain: Journals of Captain Leonard S. Tawes Relating His Career in Atlantic Coastwise Sailing Craft From 1869-1922* (Newport News, Va.: The Mariners Museum, 1967).

*25th Cong., 3rd Sess., House Doc. No. 24* (Serial #345).

*32nd Cong., 1st Sess., Sen. Ex. Doc. No. 28* (Serial #617.

Hatch, Charles E., Jr., "The Old Cape Henry Light: A Survey Report," February 2, 1962, National Park Service, copies in files of Colonial National Historical Park and the Division of History, Washington Office, NPS.

Holland, F. Ross, Jr., " A History of the Bodie Island Light Station," Division of History, National Park Service, February 1, 1967.

———, "A History of the Cape Hatteras Light Station," Division of History, National Park Service, September 30, 1968.

———, "A Survey History of Cape Lookout National Seashore," Division of History, National Park Service, January 30, 1968.

Leip, Hans, *The Gulf Stream Story* (London: Jarrolds, c. 1957).

Middleton, Arthur Pierce, "The Struggle for the Cape Henry Lighthouse, 1721–1791," *The American Neptune,* vol. 8, no. 1 (January, 1948).

Mills, Robert, *The American Pharos or Lighthouse Guide* (Washington: Thompson & Homans, 1832).

Smith, Milton B., "The Lighthouse on Tybee Island," *The Georgia Historical Quarterly,* vol. 49, no. 3 (September, 1965).

Stick, David, *The Outer Banks of North Carolina* (Chapel Hill: University of North Carolina Press, c. 1958).

Texaco, *Cruising Chart No. 4* (Rand McNally, 1968).

U. S. Coast Guard, *Historically Famous Lighthouses* (Washington: G.P.O., 1957).

U. S. Coast Guard, *Light List, Atlantic Coast, 1951* (Washington: G.P.O., 1951).

The following light station clipping files from Record Group 26, National Archives:

Amelia Island
Beacon Island
Cape Canaveral
Cape Fear
Cape Romain
Castle Pinckney
Charleston
Combahee Bank
Currituck Beach
Dames Point
Drum Point
Federal Point
Fenwick Island
Fort Carroll
Fort Sumter
Fort Washington
Georgetown
Harbor Island Bar
Hog Island
Hooper's Strait
Horseshoe Shoal

Hunting Island
Janes Island
Jupiter Inlet
Little Cumberland
Island
Long Point Shoal
Lower Cedar
Creek
New Point
Comfort
Northwest Point
Royal Shoal
Ocracoke
Old Point Comfort
Pamplico Point
Shoal
Point Lookout
Point of Shoals
Ponce de Leon
Inlet
Pooles Island

Pungoteague
Roanoke Marshes
Roanoke River
St. Augustine
St. Johns River
St. Simons
Sapelo Island
Sharps Island
Smiths Point
Solomon's Lump
Southwest Point
Royal Shoal
Thimble Shoal
Thomas Point
Turkey Point
Tybee
Upper Cedar
Creek
Wades Point
Windmill Point
Wolf Trap

## CHAPTER 9

*25th Congress, 3rd Session, House Doc. No. 24* (Serial #345).

*32nd Congress, 1st Session, Sen. Exec. Doc. No. 28* (Serial #617).

Holland, F. R. Jr., *The Aransas Pass Light Station: A History* (Corpus Christi: 1976).

Johnson, A. B., *The Modern Lighthouse Service* (Washington: G.P.O., 1890).

Mackenzie, George C., "Report on Application of City of Biloxi, Mississippi, For Transfer For Historic Monument Purposes of . . . Biloxi Lighthouse . . . ," Division of History, National Park Service, September, 1967.

Ormerod, Leonard, *The Curving Shore: the Gulf Coast from Brownsville to Key West* (New York: Harper & Bros., c. 1957).

Shepard, Birse, *Lore of the Wreckers* (Boston: Beacon Press, c. 1961).

Texaco, *Cruising Chart No. 6* (Rand McNally & Co., c. 1968).

U. S. Coast Guard, *Historically Famous Lighthouses* (Washington: G.P.O., 1957).

# References

U. S. Coast Guard, *Light List, Atlantic and Gulf Coasts of the United States, 1951* (Washington: G.P.O., 1951).

The following light district and light station clipping files in Record Group 26, National Archives:

| | | |
|---|---|---|
| Seventh District | Decros Point | Pointe Aux Herbes |
| Eighth District | Dog Island | Point Isabel |
| General Services, | Dry Tortugas | Port Pontchartrain |
|   Eighth District | East Pascagoula | Red Fish Bar |
| Alligator Reef |   River | Round Island |
| American Shoal | East Rigolets | Sabine Pass |
| Aransas Pass | Egmont Key | St. Joseph Point |
| Battery Gladden | Fort Point | St. Marks |
| Bayou St. John | Fowey Rocks | Sand Island |
| Barataria Bay | Franks Island | Sand Key |
| Biloxi | Key West | Sanibel Island |
| Bon Fouca | Matagorda | Shell Keys |
| Brazos Santiago | Merrill's Shell | Ship Island |
| Cape Florida |   Bank | Sombrero Key |
| Cape St. George | Mobile Point | South Pass |
| Cape San Blas | Natchez | Southwest Pass |
| Carysfort Reef | New Canal | Southwest Reef |
| Cat Island | Pass a L'Outre | Swash |
| Cedar Keys | Pass Christian | Timbalier Island |
| Chandeleur Island | Pass Manchac | Tortugas Harbor |
| Choctaw Point | Pensacola | Trinity Shoals |
| Clopper's Bar | Point au Fer | West Rigolets |

## CHAPTER 10

Bearss, Edwin C., "History Basic Data, Redwoods National Park," Division of History, National Park Service, September 1, 1969.

Gibbs, James A., *Sentinels of the North Pacific* (Portland, Ore.: Binfords & Mort, 1955).

Holland, F. Ross, Jr., "A Brief History of Cabrillo National Monument," *Journal of the West*, vol. 7, no. 2 (April, 1968).

———, "Lighting the West Coast: The Story of the Building of the Pacific Coast's First Sixteen Lighthouses," Ms in possession of the author.

———, *The Old Point Loma Lighthouse* ([San Diego]: Cabrillo Historical Association, 1968).

Hussey, John A., ed., *Early West Coast Lighthouses* (San Francisco: The Book Club of California, 1964).

Putnam, George R., *Sentinel of the Coasts* (New York: W. W. Norton & Co., c. 1937).

Schurz, William Lytle, *The Manila Galleon* (New York: E. P. Dutton & Co., 1959).

Texaco, *Cruising Charts Nos. 8 and 9* (Rand McNally, c. 1968).

U. S. Coast and Geodetic Survey, *United States Coast Pilot, Pacific Coast: California, Oregon, and Washington* (Washington: Government Printing Office, 1926).

U. S. Coast Guard, *Light List, v. III, Pacific Coast and Pacific Islands, 1970* (Washington: Government Printing Office, 1970).

The following light station clipping files from Record Group 26, National Archives:

| | | |
|---|---|---|
| Admiralty Head | Ediz Hook | Point Montara |
| Anacapa Island | Grays Harbor | Point Reyes |
| Angel Island | Heceta Head | Point Sur |
| Ano Nuevo Island | Lime Point | Port Hueneme |
| Ballast Point | Mile Rock | St. Georges Reef |
| Cape Arago | North Head, Cape | San Francisco Bay |
| Cape Foulweather |   Disappointment |   Bell Boat |
| Cape Meares | Piedras Blancas | San Pedro Harbor |
| Cape Mendocino | Pigeon Point | Santa Cruz |
| Cape Orford | Point Arena | Tillamook Rock |
| Destruction Island | Point Arguello | Trinidad Head |
| East Brothers | Point Cabrillo | Yerba Buena |
|   Island | Point Fermin | |

## CHAPTER 11

*American State Papers, Class IV, Commerce and Navigation*, V. II (Washington: Gale & Seaton, 1834).

*25th Congress, 3rd Session, House Doc. No. 24* (Serial #345).

Hatcher, Harlan and Erich A. Walter, *A Pictorial History of the Great Lakes* (New York: Bonanza Books, c. 1966).

Havighurst, Walter, *The Long Ships Passing: The Story of the Great Lakes* (New York: The Macmillan Co., 1961).

Manning, Gordon R., *Life in the Colchester Reef Lighthouse* (Shelburne, Vt.: Shelburne Museum, c. 1958).

Putnam, George R., *Lighthouses and Lightships of the United States* (Boston: Houghton Mifflin Co., 1917).

———, *Sentinels of the Coasts: The Log of a Lighthouse Engineer* (New York: W. W. Norton & Co., c. 1937).

Texaco, *Cruising Charts, Nos. 5 and 10* (Rand McNally, 1968).

U. S. Coast Guard, *Historically Famous Lighthouses* (Washington: G.P.O., 1957).

U. S. Coast Guard, *Light List, Atlantic and Gulf Coasts, 1951* (Washington: G.P.O.: 1951).

U. S. Coast Guard, *Light List, 1970, v. IV: Great Lakes* (Washington: G.P.O., 1970).

The following light station clipping files from Record Group 26, National Archives:

| | | |
|---|---|---|
| Ashtabula | Bois Blanc | Chicago Harbor |
| Au Sable | Buffalo |   of Refuge |
| Barcelona (Port- | Cedar Point | Cleveland |
|   land) | Charity Is. | Conneaut |
| Big Sodus | Cheboygan | Copper Harbor |
| Black River | Chequamegon | Crossover Is. |

## CHAPTER 12

Chevigny, Hector, *Russian-America: The Great Alaskan Venture, 1741-1867* (New York: Viking Press, c. 1965).

Gibbs, James A., Jr., *Sentinels of the North Pacific* (Portland, Ore.: Binfords & Mort, 1955).

Putnam, George R., *Lighthouses and Lightships of the United States* (Boston: Houghton Mifflin Co., 1917).

U. S. Bureau of Lighthouses, *Annual Reports* for 1910, 1911, 1913, 1916, 1919, 1921, 1936, 1937, 1938 (Washington: G.P.O.).

U. S. Coast Guard, *Historically Famous Lighthouses* (Washington: G.P.O., 1957).

U. S. Coast Guard, *Light List, Atlantic and Gulf Coasts, 1951* (Washington: G.P.O., 1951).

U. S. Coast Guard, *Light List, Pacific Coast and Pacific Islands* (Washington: G.P.O., 1970).

U. S. Coast Guard, Lighthouse Sites, Virgin Islands, V.I., Nos. 1-6; Virgin Islands Lighthouse Records, Danish, 1910-1917, both in Record Group 26, National Archives.

U. S. Lighthouse Board, *Annual Reports* for 1900-1909 (Washington: G.P.O.).

The following clipping files from Record Group 26, National Archives:

## CHAPTER 13

Gibbs, James A., Jr., *Sentinels of the North Pacific* (Portland, Ore.: Binfords and Mort, 1955).

Holland, F. Ross, Jr., "Lighting the West Coast," Ms. in possession of the author.

Johnson, A. B., *The Modern Lighthouse Service* (Washington: G.P.O.).

*Lighthouse Service Bulletin*, vol. 3, no. 3 (March 1, 1924); vol. 2, no. 12 (December, 1918); and no. 23 (November, 1919).

New York *Herald*, June 19, 1905.

Poore, Ben Purley, ed., *Message From the President of the United States to the Two Houses of Congress . . . First Session of the Forty Third Congress, with the Reports of the Heads of Departments and Selections from Accompanying Documents* (Washington: G.P.O., 1873).

Putnam, George R., *Lighthouses and Lightships of the United States* (Boston: Houghton Mifflin, 1917).

———, *Sentinel of the Coasts* (New York: W. W. Norton, c. 1937).

Texaco, *Cruising Charts*, Nos. 1-10 (Rand McNally, 1968).

U. S. Coast Guard, *Light List, Atlantic and Gulf Coasts, 1951* (Washington: G.P.O., 1951).

U. S. Coast Guard, *Light List: Pacific Coast and Pacific Islands, 1970* (Washington: G.P.O., 1970).

# Bibliography

THE RECORDS of the United States' aids to navigation from 1789 on can be found in Record Group 26 in the National Archives, and it is to these surviving papers, personnel ledgers, corespondence, journals, record books, and files that one eventually will have to go when conducting research on lighthouses and lightships. Using these records can sometimes be frustrating, since a fire in the Commerce Department in 1921 destroyed or severely damaged a segment of them. Nevertheless, a great deal of material remains, and some of the lost material has been replaced by the addition of field records of the Third through Tenth, Twelfth, and Seventeenth Lighthouse Districts. Unfortunately, the records have not been extensively used by most who have written on individual lighthouses and as a result these histories are too often of little value.

A preliminary inventory of this Record Group was prepared by Dr. Forrest R. Holdcamper in 1963, and he prepared a similar inventory to the field records in 1964. These mimeographed guides are available at the National Archives.

The various Coast Guard District Headquarters are good sources for materials on individual lighthouses, particularly for historic drawings and photographs of still active lighthouses in the specific district.

Primary material more readily accessible are government reports printed in the Congressional Serial Set, which can be found in many libraries throughout the country. Over the years, beginning with the *American State Papers,* reports about the needs for and condition of aids to navigation reached Congress and wound up being printed in the Serial Set. These reports concerned a vast variety of subjects ranging from individual lighthouses to general reports on the lighthouse systems of this and other nations. The searching and excellent report in 1852 on the country's lighthouse service, reports of inspections of segments of the coast for need of lighthouses, the 1837 inspection report on the United States' aids to navigation, verbatim testimony over the controversial letting of the contract to build the first west coast lighthouses, individual reports of examination of certain lighthouses, *Annual Reports* of the Lighthouse Board, reports and studies on proposed changes

in administration, and memoranda on recommended technological improvements indicate but a few of the types of information that can be found in the Serial Set.

In the Serial Set, information on the lighthouse service in the nineteenth century can be found in some of the annual reports of the Coast Survey, especially on lighthouse sites, and in the annual reports of the secretary of war, principally on army officers on detached duty with the lighthouse service.

A handy reference is U. S. Lighthouse Board, *Documents Relating to Lighthouses, 1789-1871* (Washington: Government Printing Office, 1871).

Bibliographies on the lighthouse service are practically nonexistent. From the beginning the Lighthouse Board compiled a library on aids to navigation and issued a printed list of its library; this list constitutes the best bibliography on aids to navigation available to that time. The U. S. Coast Guard issued in 1950 the *United States Coast Guard Bibliography,* which contains a number of citations to popular books and articles on lighthouses. Other lists of materials on aids to navigation can be found in the bibliographies of general books on the subject, such as George R. Putnam, *Lighthouses and Lightships of the United States* (Boston: Houghton Mifflin, 1917), and James A. Gibbs, Jr., *Sentinels of the North Pacific* (Portland, Oregon: Binfords & Mort, 1955).

The library of the Lighthouse Board, unfortunately, in later years was broken up. It appears that some of the items remained with the Coast Guard, but the bulk of the collection seems to have gone to the Library of Congress. Today the Library of Congress has the largest collection of printed material on aids to navigation. Its holdings range from general books on lighthouses, both domestic and foreign, to printed proposals to improve lighting systems.

The Coast Guard Headquarters in Washington, D. C., has a small, but useful, library with particularly good runs of the *Light Lists* and the *Annual Reports* of the Lighthouse Board and the Bureau of Lighthouses.

The Library of the U. S. Navy Department in Washington also contains printed materials dealing with aids to navigation, some items extremely scarce and not found in the Library of Congress or the Coast Guard Library, such as *Description of the Hydraulic Lamp, as Designed by Lieutenant George G. Meade.*

Two seldom used but very helpful sources on lighthouses and other aids to navigation are the *American Coast Pilot* and the annual *Light Lists*. The *Coast Pilot* first came out in 1796 and was revised and issued periodically, principally by the Blunts, from then until 1867. For a history of the *American Coast Pilot* see John F. Campbell, *History and Bibliography of the New American Practical Navigator and the American Coast Pilot* (Salem: Peabody Museum, 1964).

Although the country's first federal government–sponsored *Light List* came out in 1838, it wasn't until the advent of the Lighthouse Board that the *Light List* began being issued annually. The *Coast Pilots* and the *Light Lists* are especially good for basic descriptions of lighthouses and lightships as well as for changes that occur over the years in lighting and light characteristics of individual lighthouses and lightships. The best runs of the *Coast Pilot* and the *Light List* can be found in the Library of Congress.

A number of books and articles exist on aids to navigation, and a more detailed, though far from complete, listing of them can be found in the list of principal sources for individual chapters in this book. Several of the more general books should, however, be commented on. D. Alan Stevenson, *The World's Lighthouses Before 1820* (London: Oxford University Press, 1959) is without question the most reliable and comprehensive survey of lighthouses for the period covered. Stevenson is a descendant of the remarkable Stevenson family of the Scottish lighthouse service who experimented with improvements and wrote extensively on the technical aspects of lighthouses and lighting apparatuses. Alan Stevenson, *A Rudimentary Treatise on the History, Construction and Illumination of Lighthouses* (London:

John Weale, 1850), and Thomas Stevenson, *Lighthouse Construction and Illumination* (London: 1881) are but two examples of this family's production. Arnold B. Johnson, *The Modern Lighthouse Service* (Washington: Government Printing Office, 1890), is chiefly valuable as a good account of the United States' aids to navigation around 1890. Johnson was for a long time chief clerk of the Lighthouse Board and knew the lighthouse service well. The best book thus far produced on the United States' aids to navigation is George R. Putnam, *Lighthouses and Lightships of the United States*. It is a lucid, well-written summary of aids to navigation. Putnam was for about twenty-five years the commissioner of lighthouses and one can wish that in this book or in his subsequent autobiography, *Sentinel of the Coasts: The Log of a Lighthouse Engineer* (New York: W. W. Norton, c. 1937), he would have gone into some of the problems and difficulties of his administration, and that he would have discussed previous lighthouse administrators and technical developments. Everything could not have been as rosy as he indicates.

Others who have brought out books on lighthouses, such as E. R. Snow, *Famous Lighthouses of New England* (Boston: Yankee Publishing Co., 1945); James R. Gibbs, Jr., *Sentinels of the North Pacific*, and Robert T. Sterling, *Lighthouses of the Maine Coast and the Men Who Keep Them* (Brattleboro, Vt.: Stephen Daye Press, 1935), have written romantically and anecdotally about lighthouses. They did not go into the evolution of the lighthouse service nor did they put the lighthouses they discussed into the context of the development of the country's lighthouse system.

A more recent student of lighthouses is Richard W. Updike. His "Augustin Fresnel and His Lighthouse Lenses," *The Log of Mystic Seaport* 19, No. 2 (1967), and "Winslow Lewis and the Lighthouses," *The American Neptune* 28, No. 1 (January, 1968), reflect a scholarly approach to the subject, his well-researched articles being based on original sources.

# Index